Population, prosperity and poverty
RURAL KANO, 1900 AND 1970

Population, prosperity and poverty

RURAL KANO

1900 and 1970

POLLY HILL

Fellow of Clare Hall, Cambridge

CAMBRIDGE UNIVERSITY PRESS

CAMBRIDGE

LONDON · NEW YORK · MELBOURNE

Published by the Syndics of the Cambridge University Press

The Pitt Building, Trumpington Street, Cambridge CD2 IRP

Bentley House, 200 Euston Road, London NW1 2DB

32 East 57th Street, New York, NY 10022, USA

296 Beaconsfield Parade, Middle Park, Melbourne 3206, Australia

© Cambridge University Press 1977

Library of Congress Catalogue Card Number 77–23167

First published 1977

Printed in Great Britain by
Western Printing Services Limited, Bristol

TO
MY FATHER
A. V. HILL
aet. 90

Contents

List of tables		ix
List of figures		x
Preface		xi
Acknowledgements		xv
List of abbreviations and conventions		xviii

I   The economic relationship between city and
    countryside in 1900   1
    Appendices
    (*1*) *The population of Hausaland and Kano Emirate*   17
    (*1*) '*Gari*' *and the concept of settlement*   20

II Indirect rule as rural non-rule   21
    Appendix
    (*1*) *The reform of the local taxation system in Kano Emirate,*
    1903–13   49

III The Kano Close Settled Zone   55
    Appendices
    (*1*) *Variable conditions in the Kano Close Settled Zone*   69
    (*2*) *The size of towns*   71

IV A brief introduction to Dorayi   74
    Appendices
    (*1*) *Historical notes on Kumbotso District*   87
    (*2*) *The Dorayi population*   88
    (*3*) *Estimated population growth in Kumbotso District*
    and Dorayi, 1932–72   91
    (*4*) *Henna*   92
    (*5*) *Kirimbo*   93

V   The consequences of persistent population pressure:
    a summary   95
    Appendix
    (*1*) *Notes on Batagarawa*   104

vii

VI   The evidence for economic inequality   106
      Appendices
      (*1*) *The size-distribution of farm-holdings in Dorayi*
            and Batagarawa   121
      (*2*) *Grain yields per acre*   122

VII   The attitude to farmland   124
      Appendix
      (*1*) *The farm-mapping*   136

VIII The married son   138

IX   The failure to migrate   146
      Appendix
      (*1*) *Migration from rural Fanteland*   151

X   The rich men   152
      Appendix
      (*1*) *Notes on seventeen rich men*   159

XI   Extreme poverty   164
      Appendices
      (*1*) *The 'labourers' in the city*   176
      (*2*) *Notes on various occupations*   177
      (*3*) *Women's house trade*   178
      (*4*) *Landlessness*   179

XII   The big house   180
      Appendices
      (*1*) *Genealogies for three big houses*   194
      (*2*) *The geographical distribution of big houses*   198

XIII From slavery to freedom: farm-slavery in Dorayi   200
      Appendices
      (*1*) *Lugard's* Memorandum *No. 22 of 1906*   221
      (*2*) *Clapperton's observations on farm-slavery*   222

      List of references   223
      Index   229

Tables

		page
IV.1	The Dorayi population	89
IV.2	The population of Kumbotso District	91
VI.1	Wealth and age	114
VI.2(A)	Wealth, age and number of wives	114
VI.2(B)	Wealth, age and number of wives	115
VI.3	Wealth, age and numbers of dependants	116
VI.4(A)	Wealth and the size of farm-holdings	117
VI.4(B)	Wealth and the size of farm-holdings	117
VI.4(C)	Acreages per head of weighted population	118
VI.5	Wealth and principal non-farming occupations	119
VI.6	Estimated proportion of manured farmland in holdings of largest farmers	122
VI.7	The sizes of farm-holdings in Dorayi and Batagarawa	122
VII.1	Areas of farm-plots	130
VII.2	Number of plots per farm-holding	130
VIII.1	The position of married sons	140
VIII.2	The married sons of rich and poor fathers	141
VIII.3	The relative wealth of fathers and sons	142
IX.1	The destinations of migrants	148
X.1	Inheritance and wealth	153
X.2	Principal non-farming occupations of rich (fatherless) men	154
XI.1	The causes of landlessness	179
XII.1	The 'size' of houses	181
XII.2	Big houses: relationship to *mai gida*	184
XII.3	Big houses: number of married men per *mai gida*	185
XII.4	Wealth and poverty in big houses	189
XII.5	Generation of founder of big houses in relation to the *mai gida*	192

Figures

		page
1	Fourteen Kano Districts 1907–8	38
2	Kano Emirate and the Close Settled Zone	56
3	Twenty-five present-day Kano Districts	58
4	Principal caravan routes and paths centering on Kano city, 1904	68
5	The distribution of houses on the Dorayi farmland	74
6	A map of the Dorayi farmland	78
7	Gidan Sambo	186

Preface

In my book *Rural Hausa: A Village and a Setting* (1972) I examined the socio-economic affairs of Batagarawa, a small village near Katsina city in the extreme north of Nigeria, and I also provided a long alphabetical Commentary (and glossary), of some 130 pages, which set that village within the general framework of present-day rural Hausaland and was partly intended as a separate browsing ground. In writing this companion volume I have again adopted a dual approach. On the one hand I have sought to compare and contrast 'Dorayi' (an extremely densely populated farming area of dispersed settlement near Kano city) with Batagarawa, with special reference to the consequences of high population density; on the other hand I have endeavoured to place Dorayi in historical perspective by examining socio-economic conditions in rural Kano generally in immediately pre-colonial and early colonial times. Although the latter task has led me into far deeper waters than I had originally intended, it proved inescapable mainly because I was unable to comprehend the present-day stability of stagnating, impoverished, overcrowded Dorayi without grasping the basis of the earlier prosperity of the densely populated farming zone in which it is situated; also, the golden opportunity of consulting the memories of elderly informants who were born before the brief colonial interlude of less than sixty years was irresistible, for it will soon be too late.

Two main difficulties have dogged me in writing this book. First, I have found it most painful and depressing to examine, albeit 'clinically', the miserable circumstances in which so many Dorayi people find themselves: to my mind, it is no wonder that the study of individual poverty has been so greatly neglected in rural Africa. Second, has been the problem of avoiding repetitiveness while producing a volume which may be conveniently read without necessary reference to *Rural Hausa* (though many page-references to that book are given for the sake of those who are interested): fortunately the time has long since passed when it is necessary to preface every book on Hausaland with a potted history going back to the *jihad* of 1804.

Within the vast expanse of rural Hausaland, which may have a population of the order of twenty million, farmland is not generally scarce and there are many sparsely populated regions and districts. When writing about Batagarawa, where farmers are free to clear and cultivate as much bush land as they require, I came to the conclusion that it was a not unrepresentative kind of place – which is not to say that I hold with any concept of a 'typical village'. Dorayi, on the other hand, is most atypical: with its (increasing) population density of some 1500 per square mile, and its low rate of outward migration, it is an extreme, even a bizarre, case, which shows what *can* happen but not what *will* happen generally elsewhere in rural Hausaland – for it is safe to assume that in most localities high rates of outward migration, particularly for farming, would start to relieve population pressure when (as in Batagarawa) densities were but a small fraction of that in Dorayi. But since the condition I denote as *individual impasse* may occur at population densities far lower than 1500 per square mile, Dorayi is nevertheless a very interesting case.

With the exception of Chapter XIII (which is concerned with the conversion of a slave-owning economy into one based on free labour), the historical chapters do not represent an attempt to follow through the processes of socio-economic change between '1900' (a shorthand expression for 'immediately pre-colonial') and today. As during the early colonial period large and small Emirates had equal numbers of British political officers, the archival material relating to large Emirates, such as Kano, is exceptionally deficient and their recent socio-economic history cannot be written until far more fieldwork has been undertaken. Consequently, my historical chapters are separate essays on certain selected themes relevant to an understanding of present-day rural stagnation or impasse – 'under-development' is far too weak a word. The crude notion that rural communities are merely exploited by city dwellers needs to be reinforced, in the case of Kano, by an insistence that they stand deprived of their old-established functions as long-distance traders and manufacturers: that they have become economically disenfranchised, as a simple comparison of 1900 with 1970 immediately reveals. In 1900 when rural Kano was the matrix within which most economic activity was set and when farmers with their donkeys carried nearly all the heavy loads, it was positively advantageous for agricultural communities to live dispersedly on their farmland; nowadays all is reversed, and the perversities of dispersed settlement are to be equated with isolation and backwardness.

I left Dorayi in July 1972 since when its people have endured the effects of the great droughts of 1972 and 1973 and the near-failure of the 1975 groundnut crop. But even more serious than this succession of calamities are the dire and lasting consequences of the continuing Great

Inflation which (unknown to most 'Westerners') claims its chief victims in rural communities of the Third World where earnings lag further and further behind the advancing price indices for essential manufactures and services such as lorry transport.

In the first of my thirteen chapters, which is on the economic relationship between Kano city and the countryside in 1900, I justify my provocative thesis that most trade and industry in Kano Emirate was rurally based; in a general attempt to 'reinstate the countryside', I criticise the common practice of employing terms derived from European feudalism, since the use of such jargon obscures the inherent vitality and autonomy of pre-colonial rural economic enterprise. In Chapter ii, which demonstrates with the aid of archival material that the colonial policy of indirect rule amounted (except for the slavery proclamations) to 'rural non-rule', I attempt to examine the politico-economic roots of present-day rural neglect; Part 1 of that chapter deals with colonial policy in 1903–12 in rural Northern Nigeria generally and Part 2 with the remarkably unsuccessful endeavour to reform indigenous rural administration in Kano Emirate. For all that the very densely populated farming area around Kano city (the Kano Close Settled Zone) is very much larger and more populous than any comparable region in savannah West Africa, its existence has somehow been taken for granted: Chapter iii is an attempt to pose certain questions about the recent history of the Zone which cannot yet be answered.

In the next nine chapters I examine socio-economic conditions in present-day Dorayi with special reference to demographic factors. Those readers who are interested in the general implications of my findings on the consequences of persistent and severe pressure of population on the land, rather than in the details of the Dorayi case, may find that the summary of those findings in Chapter v together with the brief introduction to Dorayi in Chapter iv provide adequately for their needs. For Dorayi, as for Batagarawa, the implications of pronounced economic inequality are a dominant theme: the subject is introduced in Chapter vi and further pursued in Chapters x and xi relating, respectively, to 'rich' and 'poor' men. In Dorayi the fortunes of married sons are closely linked to those of their fathers, as Chapter viii relates. Inheritance, land-selling and other aspects of 'the attitude to farmland' are dealt with in Chapter vii; Chapter ix is concerned with the very low rate of outward migration from overcrowded Dorayi; and Chapter xii with the very big houses, inhabited by up to 106 people, which (it is argued) have come into existence owing to the high population density.

Finally, the manner in which the details relating to particular cases, such as Dorayi, may provide the raw material illustrating broad basic themes is illustrated by Chapter XIII on the transition from farm-slavery to freedom in rural Kano. In Muslim communities where land-holding lineages and tenancy systems were lacking, ex-slaves and their descendants neither suffered assimilation as pseudo-kin nor rejection as tenants but rather asserted their absolute freedom as farmers. The study of an earlier, inegalitarian, agrarian system based on the ownership of farm-slaves by ordinary, richer, farmers, who were not members of a ruling class, gives perspective to contemporary studies and helps one to avoid the most dangerous of all misbeliefs, that present trends, such as developing economic inequality, are necessarily something new in kind.

Acknowledgements

Full financial support for my work in rural Hausaland, which lasted for fourteen months between April 1971 and June 1972, was provided by the Social Science Research Council. Owing to the extreme scarcity of skilled manpower in Northern Nigeria, I was unable to recruit a Hausa assistant with higher educational qualifications or more than two other suitable men, so that it was shortage of labour rather than finance which limited my activities.

However, after much delay, I was so fortunate as to obtain the services of M. Husaini Yahaya, who had had much previous experience as a field assistant; as my constant companion during the ten months when I mainly worked in Dorayi, I greatly appreciated his work as a skilled interpreter, who had a kindly, humorous and genuine interest in rural life. I am also most grateful to M. Musa Ibrahim Bagudu who despite his total lack of the appropriate training (and my own inexperience) successfully mapped all the farms in about three square miles of farmland in, and around, Dorayi, with the aid of an aerial photograph. Despite the great heat at certain seasons, Malam Musa undertook this arduous work uncomplainingly and was very reliable and painstaking; he was also responsible for our house-to-house enumeration of the population which, through no fault of his own, had to be repeated several times.

Perhaps my inability to recruit any other full-time assistants for my work in Dorayi was ultimately a blessing, as it forced me to lean very heavily on the part-time services of five Dorayi men who proved far more helpful, frank, reflective and at times inspired than I had any reason to expect. Had it not been for the initial welcome and later assistance I received from Mahamman Lawal, the Mai Unguwa (Hamlet Head) of Cikin Gari, Ciranci, who unfortunately died at the age of about eighty in 1974, I doubt whether I would have had the strength to have worked in a place where most people were (understandably) entirely baffled by my continued presence. (Never before have I felt the anthropologist's central conflict so keenly: that the ordinary victims of one's intrusive inquisitiveness are right to complain that they have nothing to gain from it.) Such respectability as I had in Dorayi derived directly from Mahamman Lawal; and it was his wonderful memory and accuracy which formed the essential basis of my work on farm-slavery. The excellent help I received from my other four Dorayi assistants, who treated me with great kindness and patience, is gratefully acknowledged on p. 109 below. I also owe particular thanks to the Village Head of Kirimbo whom I visited on many occasions.

During my stay in Nigeria I received much general help and encouragement from my friends Professor Lalage Bown, Professor Michael Crowder, Dr Adamu Fika (whose unpublished thesis I have cited), Mrs Lindsay Friedman, Mr John Grey-Theriot, Mr John Lavers and Alhaji Sabi'u Nuhu; and I am especially grateful to Miss Renée Pittin for the numerous occasions on which we discussed her research work on secluded women in Katsina city – and much else besides.

The last stages of writing this book were immensely assisted by a visit I made to Kano in January 1976 to attend an international seminar organised by Ahmadu Bello University on the economic history of the central savannah of West Africa. Many people were there and I must content myself by thanking Dr Mahdi Adamu, chairman of the seminar organisers, for arranging the most enjoyable and stimulating conference I have ever attended in my life. Following this event I was able to consult Dr Yusufu Bala Usman's valuable thesis on the history of Katsina Emirate at Ahmadu Bello University, and I am most grateful to him for his permission to cite his unpublished work. My re-meeting with Dr P. J. Shea at the seminar was really opportune, for I know very well that the opportunity of citing his unpublished thesis on the development of the cloth industry in Kano Emirate in the nineteenth century has enormously increased my credibility in the first chapter. I also benefited from renewed discussions with Mr M. J. Mortimore, the pioneer worker on the Kano Close Settled Zone.

Here in England I wish to thank Professor Sir Edmund Leach for encouraging me in a practical way to return to Hausaland, Professor M. I. Finley for advice on the history of farm-slavery, Dr Barbara Ward and Mr A. H. M. Kirk-Greene for reading parts of the typescript, Dr Basil Davidson for finding the time to engage in a long correspondence about Hausaland from which I, alone, derived benefit and, in particular, Dr Murray Last who has wasted much time reading earlier drafts and who has been a constant support in this enterprise, though far better qualified to undertake something similar himself. None of these people should be held responsible for any of the views I express. I would not have sustained the ordeal of writing this book without the intellectual and moral support I have received from Dr Susan Drucker-Brown, Mr John Dunn, Professor

Meyer Fortes, Mr Thomas Hodgkin, Dr J. R. Hood, Dr Patricia Vinnicombe, Mr David Williams (who was originally responsible for my visiting West Africa in 1952), my daughter Susannah Humphreys, the fellows and members of Clare Hall, Cambridge and (yet again) the Cambridge University Press. Also, my thanks are due to Mr Michael Young for his excellent draughtsmanship and to Mrs Lisa Woodburn for her stylish and accurate typing. Since the exigencies of the economic situation have precluded the use of footnotes, I am grateful to the Cambridge University Press for permitting me to place all reference material in parentheses in the text, thus avoiding the use of endnotes.

Finally I have to thank the managers of the Smuts Memorial Fund for general support given during my tenure of the Smuts Readership in Commonwealth Studies at Cambridge.

Clare Hall Polly Hill
August 1976

Abbreviations and conventions

KCSZ   The acronym of the Kano Close Settled Zone, the densely populated farming area around Kano city in which Dorayi is situated.

NAK   (Nigerian) National Archives, Kaduna.

PRO   Public Record Office, London.

R.H.   These initials refer to my book *Rural Hausa: A Village and a Setting* (1972).

Currency   Although the old Nigerian currency of £s, shillings and pence was replaced by the Naira and Kobo immediately after I left Dorayi, I have found it necessary to follow my notes by retaining the old currency: this is partly for the sake of historical continuity, partly because a change of currency itself tends to affect rates of payment (such as wages), partly because of fluctuating rates of exchange and partly for the benefit of British readers.

Decimilisation   Comparisons with Batagarawa would have been intolerably confused had I here employed hectares rather than acres.

Parenthetical references   References such as (Last, 1967, p. 135) relate to entries in the list of references on pp. 223 *et seq.* – in this case M. Last's book of 1967.

Rounding   As the use of decimal points in my statistical tables would have given a spurious sense of accuracy, I have rounded all percentages to the nearest integer with the result that they do not always total 100.

I

The economic relationship between city and countryside in 1900

The economic relationship between Kano city and the countryside in '1900' (a date which implies 'immediately pre-colonial') will remain basically incomprehensible until intensive historical fieldwork has been undertaken in the countryside along the lines of that recently achieved in Katsina Emirate by Dr Yusufu Bala Usman (Usman, 1974). It is not merely that so little is known about the earlier development of settlement patterns, urban and village administration, the organisation of rural craftwork, trade and markets, the role of farm-slavery, land tenure and so forth, but also that such smattering of knowledge as we do possess lacks all coherence.

According to Usman the settlement pattern of Katsina in the late eighteenth century 'was made up of a series of *birane* [large towns] and *garuruwa* [smaller towns] surrounded by areas of permanent cultivation in which were located the *kauyuka* [villages] and *unguwoyi* [hamlets] dependent on these towns'. Beyond this belt of permanent settlement, where the main commercial, industrial and agricultural activities were carried on, were the less permanent and smaller settlements inhabited largely by hunters, woodcutters, pastoralists, miners (of iron ore) and by some farmers. Some of the larger towns developed sufficient hegemony over an area to become the centre of what Usman denotes 'regional clusters', within which 'close relations of economic and cultural interdependence were developed, which were often reflected at the political level'. Other towns maintained greater self-sufficiency or developed relations with more distant places.

In Katsina the pre-Jihad political system was based, according to Usman, on a hierarchy of chiefs ruling over the larger and smaller towns, who regulated the major forms of economic activity and who had other functions including organising the army. By the late eighteenth century hundreds of towns and immigrant groups of diverse origin were integrated into a political community under Sarkin Katsina. Even from an early period the principal bonds of the political community had been occupation, location and religion, rather than kinship; and the basic and most cohesive entities were the permanent settlements. It was from the Sarkin Katsina that the town chiefs derived their authority; and there was a hierarchy of chiefs through whom authority was exercised. 'Although they represented an older form of political authority, older than the kingship', it was the chiefs of the ordinary smaller towns who came to form 'the local organs of administration'. As for the central administration, there were five divisions: one comprised the *sarakunan sana'a* (the heads of the various crafts and other economic activities) who were responsible for specialised economic activity and who went on tour; another was concerned with the supervision of the ordinary town heads (*masu gari*).

The Hausa word for a high official position to which a person is appointed is *sarauta*, and Usman terms the pre-Jihad politico-economic system 'the *sarauta* system'. In Katsina this type of rule was overthrown by the Jihad (and by events immediately preceding it) after which new systems of central and local administration evolved – systems which would be incomprehensible were knowledge of the pre-Jihad situation lacking. By the time of the reign of Emir Ibrahim (1871–83) 'the major responsibility of the central administration' was the supervision of the territorial rulers (the *hakimai* or *sarakunan kasa*) – the predecessors of those whose alternative title is now District Head. Each *hakimi* had several subordinate rulers under him (*masu gari* or *dagatai*) and, as it had been before the Jihad, each *mai gari* had his own officials and agents whom he appointed, the towns forming 'distinct administrative units'.

Very little is known about systems of local administration in Kano Emirate at the end of the nineteenth century. Dr Adamu Fika, in his important thesis relating to the political and economic re-orientation of Kano Emirate in 1882–1940 (Fika, 1973), is concerned largely with central administration and his discussion of pre-colonial local administration leans very heavily on a single source, namely the 1937 Assessment Report on Dawakin Kudu District by D. F. H. MacBride (see p. 47 below) which includes far more historical material on District and Village organisation than any other Kano Assessment Report available in the National Archives at Kaduna. On the basis of oral evidence Fika placed twelve Kano towns in rank order. He notes that the Fulani clan leaders in the city had some kinsmen in the Districts who held official positions as chiefs of major towns although members of the royal family relied almost entirely on agents (*jakadu*); and he draws attention to the chaos which resulted from the Kano civil war (Basasa) of 1893–4. From his interesting discussion of the functions of the territorial officials (*hakimai*), most of whom lived in Kano city, the impresson is gained that pre-colonial local administration, outside a few large towns, was very weak;

this impression hardens into a certainty when one considers the extra-ordinary difficulties which the colonial administration encountered in establishing any coherent system of village administration based on the old pattern (this being a matter which is discussed at length in Chapter 11 below), as well as the implications of the remarkable lack of populous towns. Usman's work is of relevance in suggesting that both the weakness of Kano local administration, and the poor economic linkage between city and countryside in the immediate pre-colonial period, should be under-stood in terms of a major upheaval in earlier times.

There has recently been a general quickening of interest in politico-economic conditions in Hausaland in early colonial times, so that despite the lack of basic historical groundwork we are less ignorant than our forebears and may start clearing the air by critically examining some of the generally accepted ideas regarding the relationship between city and countryside which appear to obstruct our thought. I shall show that some of these fallacies derive directly from ideas disseminated by Lugard in his early days which have never received the critical examination that they deserved; and that others stem from various stereotyped notions about economic control in centralised states which are peculiarly inapposite in the case of Kano.

THE POPULATION OF KANO CITY

Because the ancient cities (*birane*) were so impressive, and attracted so many strangers who reported on them, their size has been unconsciously exaggerated, whereas the immensity of rural Hausaland, and of such huge Emirates as Kano and Katsina, has been little appreciated. If in 1900 the total population of Kano Emirate was of the order of three million – see Appendix 1(1) – and if the population of Kano city was then as high as 60 000 to 90 000 (against the first officially recorded figure of 39 000 in 1911), then no more than some 2% to 3% of the Kano popu-lation was resident in the metropolis.

Trading strangers composed a large part of the city population, their numbers ebbing and flowing seasonally; in 1851 the traveller Heinrich Barth (Barth, 1857), who had been deeply impressed by the splendid cosmopolitan city (the largest by far in the central Sudan), supposed that during the most populous season about half of the estimated population of 60 000 consisted of trading strangers, the chief elements of the com-mercial population having been Kanuri, Hausa, Fulani and Nupe people, together with some Arabs. As for the permanent population of the city, this was presumably composed, as it had been in ancient times, of 'many groups of diverse origins lacking kinship relations one with the other'

(H. F. C. Smith, 1971, p. 187 – see also, p. 65 below). Considering that the number of high-ranking officials was relatively very small, the city population basically consisted of (permanent) immigrants (who maintained themselves by trading, craftwork and farming) and (temporary) stranger-traders, together with many slaves. As an entrepôt it was encapsulated in the countryside, as will be seen.

The great proportion of all the farmland in the Emirate, with its area of some 13 000 square miles, was cultivated and effectively owned by local farmers. While some prominent city residents, both administrative officials and members of the commercial classes, owned farmland culti-vated by slaves, their estates represented a trivial proportion of Kano lands. Then, as now, farm-renting and share-cropping systems involving absentee land-owners were unknown; and many Hausa city-dwellers must have retained few links with the countryside outside the city walls. Far from dominating the commercial activities and agriculture of the country-side, the top layers of the population in the city exerted little economic control and, as we shall see, most long-distance trade and industry was rurally based.

The most densely populated large area of dispersed settlement in the central Sudan was the so-called Kano Close Settled Zone around Kano city, where between one and two million farmers and pastoralists together with their dependants and slaves probably lived in 1900 – see Appendix 1 (1). I shall offer some speculations about the origins of this Zone, and its relationship to Kano city, in Chapter III.

TOWNS

It is commonly believed (see, for example, Hopkins, 1973, p. 19) that a high proportion of the population of Hausaland in 1900 lived in towns or villages. Perhaps this was true of certain sections of Hausaland, such as northern Zaria and parts of Sokoto, but there is no doubt that in many districts of Kano Emirate most people lived dispersedly either in home-steads entirely surrounded by farmland or in small house-clusters. In Kano Emirate most towns, whether walled or not, were small on any standard – judging from later demographic material (see Chapter III), it would seem that their modal population might have been of the order of 1000–1500; and there must have been very few places (if any) with populations exceeding, say, 5000 – they are unlikely to have numbered more than three in 1920. As in many other regions of the West African savannah where towns are anomalous, there were large tracts of inhabited countryside devoid of any compact settlement which might be regarded as even a minor central place.

The Hausa terminology for residential settlements of different functions and sizes presents much difficulty. Nowadays *birni* (pl. *birane*) always denotes a capital city (which had formerly been walled) – the seat of an Emir; formerly, as Usman's usage makes clear, *birni* might have denoted any large walled town which was a central place. All other compact settlements of any size, whether walled or not, are denoted *gari* (pl. *garuruwa*); this word may also mean 'any collection of compounds with or without an enclosing wall' (Bargery's Dictionary) and some large *garuruwa*, for example Dutse in eastern Kano Emirate, lack all compactness, the habitations being dotted about over a large area which is essentially farmland – see Appendix 1(2). As *gari* applies both to important market-towns or trading centres – like Bebeji on the old Kano to Zaria road – and to insignificant settlements which might even have populations of less than 750, there is no linguistic means of distinguishing between compact settlements, other than *birane*, in terms of function or size. As for the word *ḳauye* (pl. *ḳauyuḳa*), which is usually (and misleadingly) rendered 'village', its meaning varies with context: it is seldom applied to a compact settlement of any size; it is often used in a negative way to indicate groups of isolated homesteads and small clusters of habitations which are situated outside a particular *birni* or *gari*; and townsmen are apt to employ it in a derogatory way to imply inhabited 'bush'. Finally, there is the word *unguwa* (pl. *unguwoyi*), which in the countryside is always rendered 'hamlet'; it is more meaningful than *ḳauye* for it more often represents a group of habitations with considerable sociological coherence – see Appendix 1(2).

The ruler of a city or important town is known as *sarḳi*. Although this title is commonly used to denote the appointed head of numerous types of polity, group or organisation, however high or humble – thus Sarkin Kano (the Emir of Kano), Sarkin Bebeji (chief of Bebeji), Sarkin Makera (chief blacksmith), Sarkin Bariki (the man in charge of a Rest House) – it is significant that the 'chiefs' of smaller towns are not *sarakuna* (sing. *sarḳi*), but rather *masu gari* (sing. *mai gari*), meaning the town head or representative, metaphorically the 'owner' of the town, a position analogous to the head of a hamlet or household – *mai unguwa* or *mai gida*. (Significantly, there is no such title as *mai ḳauye*.) Nowadays, unless a town is the seat of a District Head (and there are only twenty-five Districts in Kano) its ruler, whether his title be *sarḳi* or *mai gari*, holds the office of Village Head, commonly, though not invariably, being known as a *dagaci* (pl. *dagatai*). In areas of dispersed settlement those 'village authorities' who are superior to *masu unguwoyi* are also known as *dagatai*.

In Kano in 1900 there were many *garuruwa* which were moderately important market or trade centres, but few (if any) of them were worthy

of being denoted metropolises or centres of regional clusters, such as existed in Katsina in the eighteenth century. Rano, Birnin Kudu, Dutse and
Gaya were the 'capitals' of semi-autonomous Kano Districts (Paden, 1973,
p. 242) with Fulani rulers of local origin who resided in them; but with
the possible exception of Sarkin Gaya (see p. 45), there is no evidence that
these rulers resembled those of certain large towns in Katsina in the
eighteenth century in having had, like Maska for instance, their own
hierarchy of *sarakuna* supervising the numerous *masu gari* which were
subordinated to them. The towns were important in their own right but
they were not properly constituted administrative apices: they were most
certainly not the capitals of small city states whose rulers were capable
of dominating the administration, or the commercial or agricultural
activities, of their territories.

As will be related in Chapter II, the early colonial administrators in
Kano assumed that the ordinary small *gari* was surrounded by satellite or
subordinate settlements: they were greatly disconcerted when they discovered that the control exerted by most *masu gari* did not extend into
the countryside. Apart from the *masu unguwoyi*, who were 'natural'
though unimportant representatives of localised groupings which tended
to be strongly linked by ties of kinship, what political authorities existed
in the countryside? With whom did the non-resident tax collectors deal
when extracting tax from the rural population?

After a very prolonged struggle (see Chapter II), the British imposed
an hierarchical, though rickety, administrative structure (which had few
functions apart from tax collection), with Hamlet Heads (*masu unguwoyi*) subordinate to Village Heads (*dagatai*) who were in turn subordinate to District Heads (*hakimai*). Their main difficulty involved the
Village Heads, or rather those of them (and they were the majority) who
were not heads of compact settlements but rural authorities in areas of
dispersed settlement who have already been defined, in a negative way,
as superior to Hamlet Heads. In Kano Emirate in 1900 there must have
been many hundreds of rural *dagatai* – they were also apt to be known
by numerous other titles of which the most common may have been
magaji and Sarkin Fulani. Since the functions, degree of autonomy,
efficiency and importance of these *dagatai* varied greatly, they did not
constitute a governing stratum which conformed to any generalisations;
moreover the various communities in Hausaland (Hausawa, Fulani, pagan
Maguzawa) were apt to have different types of representative, many being
prominent men who had achieved their leadership spontaneously or
through local competition, some being lineage elders of Fulani or Maguzawa communities, and others having been chosen from outside the
community. The British were baffled by these representatives and as most

present-day *dagatai* are heads of Village Areas (or Units) which were arbitrarily created by the colonial administration, the traditional office has gone largely unstudied.

In many regions of the world the relative dearth, in relation to the size of the population, of significant administrative centres might be thought to imply the economic isolation of the countryside. But this was not so in Kano where, on the contrary, most commercial activity, including the long-distance caravan trade, was rurally-based. I shall be presenting the idea (see Chapter III) that in the nineteenth century the very high population density was positively advantageous to the people of the Kano Close Settled Zone and of similar, though smaller, areas – that the Zone was a special category of rural area where agriculture, stock rearing, industrial production (notably weaving and dyeing) and medium- and long-distance trading flourished integratedly within the matrix of the countryside where most people lived dispersedly in houses surrounded by farmland. Owing to the existence of a detailed nexus of paths, cattle routes and minor and major trade routes, dispersal there did not imply isolation. As pointed out by Usman, trade routes 'did not simply spread out over an open terrain, as is widely assumed about routes in the savannah areas of West Africa': it was rather that the creation of vast areas of permanent cultivation (*karakara*), through the activity of man and livestock, was a pre-condition for the establishment of these regular routes. Bargery defines *karakara* (or *karkara*) as 'land, near a city, which is covered with hamlets and farms'; but in Katsina and Kano Emirates a large proportion of all the farmland in densely populated areas has long been *karakara*, being manured and cultivated every year, whether it is near to a city or not (see *R. H.*, pp. 303–6).

ECONOMIC FEUDALISM?

In Kano, as in Katsina, the territorial rulers – the *hakimai* – were empowered to organise the collection of tax, on behalf of the Emir, in the territories assigned to them. It is doubtful whether they had any other economic functions, and the non-resident *hakimai* certainly had no judicial functions. Whereas in Katsina in the nineteenth century each *hakimi* lived mainly in his own District capital (though most of them also kept houses in Katsina city), most of the Kano *hakimai* (as we know) resided solely in Kano city. According to Adamu Fika (1973), members of the Sullubawa, the Yolawa, the Dambazawa and Jobawa clans filled the major state offices open to free men and their titled leaders (including members of the royal family) had a 'multiplicity of fiefs' which could be located anywhere in the Emirate, according to which Fulani clan had conquered which general area; in 1882 there were also ten major slave *ḥakimai*. On the basis of oral evidence, Fika put the total number of 'fiefs' at more than 400. Some of these territories constituted solid blocks of land; others comprised numerous non-contiguous areas, which might have been widely scattered. Lugard denoted the territories as fiefs, the officials as fief-holders – feudal terminology which has been uncritically adopted by most subsequent writers.

After the eighteenth century, 'feudalism' 'came to denote, through abuse of language, such social realities as the political predominance of a landholding aristocracy and the exploitation of the small and weak by the powerful' (*International Encyclopaedia of the Social Sciences*). However, the term can scarcely be stretched to cover the Kano case. The *ḥakimai* did not constitute a 'landholding aristocracy' – while as for the exploitation of the small and weak by the powerful, this is a universal principle in many societies which are never classified as feudal. I insist that from the angle of the economic organisation of rural life, it is entirely misleading to employ terms derived, without modification or redefinition, from European feudalism, and that the use of such jargon (it is nothing better) obscures the inherent vitality and autonomy of pre-colonial economic enterprise in the Kano countryside. I shall now summarise some of my main justifications for an assertion which is still curiously provocative despite the widespread influence of the general views expressed on African feudalism by J. R. Goody (1971) and the lack of a 'feudal technology'.

First, there was no sense in which a *ḥakimi* owned (or even thought he owned) the land in his territory, which, for convenience, I shall henceforth term his 'District'. While the British were anxious to foster the idea that ultimate rights in land resided 'in the Fulani dynasty as conquerors' (Lugard's expression), for they would then have been conveniently transferable to the British Crown, the nature of these rights was not such as would have enabled *ḥakimai* (or, indeed, Emirs) to have demanded labour-services of farmers in return for the right to cultivate certain portions of land. The fact is (as will be seen in Chapter XIII) that local land tenure systems were incomprehensible to the British who did not realise that portions of land were never formally allocated to individual farmers by any authority; that resident farmers were always free to clear and cultivate unoccupied land (provided that no communal rights, such as grazing, were exercised there); and that the rights thus established so nearly approximated to outright ownership that farmers were free to sell their farmland for cash – a right which they often exercised in pre-colonial times (see *R. H.*).

Second, most of the *ḥakimai* were not landed gentry living on their estates in their Districts, but city aristocrats (including high-ranking slaves) who resided in the capital. Being non-resident, often unfamiliar with their territories and reluctant to travel, most of the *hakimai* delegated the task of tax collection directly to their agents, who were usually known as *jakadu* (sing. *jakada*), who descended on the territories in shoals, for they too were non-resident. As executive or political officers (for the Emir as well as the *hakimai*) these *jakadu* – who were often misleadingly termed 'messengers' by the British – must have dealt with many matters besides tax collection; but as an unstructured group of individuals they were scarcely capable of exercising much constructive authority on behalf of their overlords who were ignorant of local conditions and in this connection they must have been gravely inconvenienced (see Chapter II) by the powerlessness and insignificance of many of the rural authorities (*dagatai*) with whom they were obliged to deal. Such a political system contrasts very markedly with that in the small border Emirate of Katagum where *resident* chieftaincies were allocated to members of the royal family and their descendants; although each of these chiefs was accountable to a court official, known as an *uban daki*, it is significant and appropriate that V. Low (Low, 1972, pp. 126–31) should refer to the chiefs, not the *uban daki*, as having been the fief-holders, even though the latter derived most of their income from the territories 'in shares of taxes, fines, and indemnities levied, and in portions of the estates of deceased men of wealth' (*ibid.*, p. 129).

Third, while individual *hakimai* commonly owned farmland on which basic crops were cultivated, their estates were usually diminutive in size relative to that of their District; were sometimes situated outside the District (for instance near the capital city); did not necessarily pertain to their offices – unless they belonged to the small class of resident *hakimai*; and were farmed, like the Emir's estates, by slaves, not by free farmers.

Fourth, not only were ordinary farmers of free-descent not bound by conditions of servitude, but they themselves owned most of the farm-slaves (see Chapter XIII); even in Dorayi, which is very close to Kano city, most farm-slaves were owned by private farmers.

Fifth, many of the territorial portions which made up the non-conglomerate Districts were apt to be small, interlaced with other Districts, and devoid of economic coherence. There was a sense in which 'Districts' were not territorial units at all, but arbitrarily demarcated groups of householders from whom the *hakimi* was entitled to extract tax on behalf of the Emir. When he came to revise his *Political Memoranda* in 1906 (see p. 201, below) Lugard had seen this clearly:

The lands. . .arbitrarily assigned to the rapacious rule of the Emir's nominees were frequently not homologous. A district which happened to be available owing to the death or removal of its feudal Chief would be granted to a favourite, irrespective of whether it lay near his territory or not. . .It came about that a territorial Chief might hold jurisdiction over and claim taxes from, a number of detached areas situated like islands in the heart of another jurisdiction. (*Political Memoranda*, 1919 in Kirk-Greene, 1970, p. 181.)

Sixth, as tax-collectors the *hakimai* had limited powers, for it seems that, at the end of the nineteenth century, the sophisticated and elaborate Kano taxation system tended to involve uniform tax rates – see Appendix II(1). Lugard held the view that 'extortion by local Chiefs and embezzlement of tribute exacted seems to have been a more marked feature than extortion by the Jakada. . .' (*Memorandum on the Taxation of Natives*, 1906). However that may have been in Kano, there would have been many besides the *hakimai* who appropriated shares of the revenue before it reached the Emir – who, in any case, employed his own *jakadu* for direct tax collection in the Districts.

Seventh, the non-resident *hakimai* lacked judicial powers. Information about the number of district courts headed by Muslim judges (*alkalai*) in 1900 is remarkably scanty – and it may be that most cases of importance that came before them were referred upwards to Kano.

MARKET-PLACES

Most of the Kano *hakimai* were not, therefore, in the usual sense of the word 'rulers'; nor did the Emir delegate many functions directly to them for he (unlike the British) tended to pursue a policy of *direct* rule (see Chapter II). The weakness of the hierarchical structure of authority – or the existence, if I may put it this way, of an 'apex' with no proper substructure – was associated with the lack of an hierarchical ordering of settlements and market-places. In an important article on rural periodic markets in pre-1949 China, G. W. Skinner concluded (Skinner, 1964) that the hierarchy of higher administrative centres in that country corresponded with the hierarchy of markets and that the economic function of a settlement 'was consistently associated with its position in marketing systems which are themselves arranged in a regular hierarchy' (*ibid.*, p. 5) – i.e. goods tended to pass upwards and downwards through a chain of markets, more and more bulked wares being handled the higher the position of the market in the chain. His conclusion that an hierarchical structure of market-places was 'characteristic of the whole class of civilisations known as "peasant" or "traditional agrarian" societies' (*ibid.*) has to be called in question in the light of the Kano case.

Little is known of the history of rural periodic market-places in Hausaland, which presumably existed many centuries ago, especially in some localities. Y. B. Usman suggests that the earliest Katsina markets were formed around the activities of the retail grain measurers (*ma'auna*) and the butchers; while M. G. Smith believes that 'markets emerged with the large-scale caravan traffic before the development of a uniform currency such as the cowrie' (Smith, 1962, p. 304). The nineteenth-century explorers and travellers unfortunately described very few rural markets in Hausaland and archival material relating to early colonial days does little to fill this gap. In the cases of Kano and Katsina Emirates it is likely that this dearth of information is due to the fact that the number of very large markets which attracted many long-distance traders was very small. The fact, which is well documented (see Hill, 1971, p. 307), that rural periodic markets met only in the afternoon or evening suggests that they were mainly attended by local farmers, who were both buyers and sellers, after their main day's work was done. The chief function of all but the largest markets was probably to provide a local outlet for livestock, for meat, for locally manufactured craft goods and for non-basic farm produce – most buyers being local people (see also Chapter III, p. 68). Although, of course, some markets were much larger than others, the likelihood is that in 1900, as today, most goods did not pass through a chain of markets before reaching the final consumer.

While most compact settlements with populations exceeding, say, two thousand people presumably had market-places, as they do today, markets were not necessary institutions so far as any particular locality was concerned, and their geographical distribution was not closely related to that of the rural population (see Hill, *ibid.*). Nor were markets necessarily situated in compact settlements, for they might have lain, for example, on cattle routes, where Fulani pastoralists bought grain in exchange for milk and butter (see p. 68, below). The fact is that much trade, of various types, was conducted outside market-places.

There were many different types of extra-market trade. First, was the ancient 'landlord system of long-distance trade' under which stranger-traders lodged with a landlord (usually known as a *mai gida* or a *fatoma*) who stored their goods and commonly sold them from his house: this system has been described elsewhere (Hill, *ibid.*) so that it is only necessary to add that certain of the most important items of long-distance trade, including kola-nuts, were never sold in bulk in market-places outside cities, and that only the very largest markets had slave-sections. Second, was the flourishing trade conducted by women from their houses which were linked by children: prevented by Muslim notions of propriety (and more recently by total seclusion) from appearing in open market-places, women by-passed the markets, selling a great range of wares, and it is likely that the bulk of threshed grain (most of it produced or bought by their husbands) was *retailed* by them (see Hill, *ibid*. and 1969). Third, was the inclination of men to buy many items for their own use directly from their neighbours: farm-slaves, small livestock, unthreshed grain and other produce (often for resale by women), cornstalk and fodder, certain craft goods (notably blacksmiths' tools), were among the numerous wares which men were apt to buy from one another. (I am grateful to Dr Mahdi Adamu for the information that in the Central Sudan up to the end of the eighteenth century, expensive wares – including slaves – were rarely taken to market, for those who could afford them considered it beneath their dignity to conduct business in an open arena.) Fourth, was the prevalence of small-scale itinerant trading by men who walked from house to house, penetrating deeply into the countryside. Fifth, were the donkey-traders (*'yan kwarami*) who travelled widely within the Hausa countryside and beyond either in small groups or individually, for the purpose of buying produce such as grain directly from houses in more remote areas, where it was cheaper than elsewhere. Sixth, were the country-based long-distance traders (*fatake*) who were far more numerous than their Hausa counterparts in the city; they often had little occasion to buy their wares, such as cotton cloth, tobacco, or small livestock, in a market-place. Before this discussion proceeds any further it is necessary to consider the geographical distribution of cloth production in Kano Emirate.

WEAVING AND DYEING

Considering the small size and peculiar composition of the permanent population of Kano city, it is at once obvious that few of the huge number of Hausa caravan-traders could have lived there and that most 'Kano cloth' must have been woven and dyed in the countryside. But so strong is the belief that the famous cloth which entered into international trade (being carried all over the Western Sudan and into the Sahara and North Africa) had necessarily been produced in the city, that I have always found that any statement to the contrary based on demographic principle was greeted with entire scepticism. It is, therefore, fortunate that Dr P. J. Shea's thesis (1975) which is concerned with the development of an export-oriented dyed cloth industry in Kano Emirate in the nineteenth century, should abundantly confirm a common sense conclusion. It is not merely that at the end of the nineteenth century the number of dye-pits in Kano city (between 1300 and 2000) was so small as to amount to only one quarter of that reported for the single Kano District of Wudil, but that the highest quality cloth for export was nearly all woven and dyed in the countryside.

What accounts for the persistent belief that Kano city was 'the Manchester of West Africa' (Hopkins, 1973, pp. 48, 50), in which production for export was concentrated? Certainly the very ambiguity of the term 'Kano cloth' was likely to lead to confusion – imagine the ambiguities that would have arisen had the Ghanaian city of Kumasi been called Ashanti! But much more important is the implicit belief that goods of high quality, on international standards, must necessarily have been produced by (sophisticated) townsmen rather than by (mere) rustics. This has sometimes led to a misreading of Barth, who referred (1857, II, p. 125) to the 'principal commerce' of Kano as having consisted of cotton cloth woven and dyed in the city *or in the neighbouring towns*. And his famous statement (*ibid.*, p. 126) that the great advantage of Kano was that 'commerce and manufactures go hand in hand' does not necessarily relate only to the city.

Again, Barth's statement that there were more than 2000 dye-pits 'in the town alone' (*ibid.*, p. 144) suggests that he was aware that some export cloth was dyed elsewhere. Considering that some of the city dye-pits would have been utilised for dyeing cloth for local wear, their total number would have been quite insufficient for the dyeing of exports which Barth estimates (*ibid.*, p. 127) were worth 300 million cowries, say £30 000 at the exchange rates he provides. And if Barth studied cloth exporting from the city only, his estimates of the value of exports are likely to have been far too low.

In considering the location of dyeing, Shea emphasises the need for plentiful supplies of water, cotton and indigo – particularly the latter since 150 lbs. or more of indigo was required for the solution of one dye-pit, which required constant replenishment. The areas which produced the highest quality indigo all developed as centres of large-scale dyeing for export in the nineteenth century. Shea identifies eight Kano Districts where there were centres specialising in the production of high quality shiny black cloth for export and emphasises the general tendency for areas to specialise in producing dyed cloth for particular markets, there having been permanent resident distributors at either end of the linking trade routes – thus Kura provided cloth for Tuareg in the north and Dal (in southern Wudil) for Kanuri in Borno. Raw cotton for weaving (unlike indigo) was readily transportable and as Kano Emirate was far from self-sufficient in cotton, large quantities were obtained from Zaria Emirate. Partly for this reason and also because the best quality indigo was cultivated in southern Kano Emirate, most of the important cloth production centres were situated south of the latitude of Kano city, where the water table was conveniently high.

Kano city was not well-favoured in terms of supplies of indigo, water or

cotton; and the number of cloth beaters, who were involved in the production of the highest quality black glazed cloth at the end of the nineteenth century, was relatively small. Shea concludes that most of the cloth
production of the city at that time was for the local market. One of the
most important and oldest dyeing centres of Kano city was Karofin
Wanka da Shuni, located near to the central market. The dyers there
lacked the facilities necessary for beating high quality black cloth and employed a stone for beating rather than a log from a shea nut tree; although
they had had long and intimate contact with long distance traders, by the
end of the nineteenth century they obtained most of their merchandise
from rural centres of production.

LONG-DISTANCE TRADE (*fatauci*)

When considering long-distance trade, it is necessary to distinguish between the type known as *fatauci* (which involved Hausa-traders who often
travelled in caravans with their donkeys) and 'international trade' which
was largely based on Kano city and mainly involved non-Hausa traders
from distant places. There were two good reasons why the former type of
trade was generally country-based (see also, *R. H.*, pp. 243 *et seq.*). First,
the main wares were of country origin: cotton cloth and garments, leather
goods, tobacco, locust bean cakes (*daddawa*), natron (*kanwa*) and small
livestock were among the most important items in a surprisingly short
list. Second, the relatively small number of Hausa traders who resided in
the city were less favourably situated than farmer-traders in the countryside
who were free to journey in the dry season, who owned the donkeys and
who could conveniently purchase all their wares, save natron, in rural
Kano – much of the natron was bought in mining areas in the present-day
Niger Republic. Even if the leader (*madugu*) of a large caravan happened
to be city-based, most of the traders who accompanied him would be likely
to be members of subsidiary, country-based caravans, which had attached
themselves *en route*. Such caravans tended not to link rural periodic
market-places: indeed they aimed at avoiding towns as stopping places,
maybe resting at recognised way-side camping places or caravanserai
(*zango*), where their trade-animals could graze and where their donkeys,
which suffered high mortality *en route*, could recuperate. They tried to
avoid selling their wares before their final destinations were reached, and
presumably often evaded the urban toll-collectors by vanishing into the
countryside. Little is known about the means by which the caravan traders
(*fatake*, sing. *farke*) acquired their supplies of cloth and apparel. P. J.
Shea refers to immigrant cloth dealers (*fatoma*) who lived in the production areas and who were apt to specialise in supplying certain types of

cloth; and he claims that many dyers, beaters and ordinary villagers (as well as the *fatake* themselves) invested in small quantities of cloth which they might hold for a price-rise. It is quite probable that the *fatake* obtained nearly all of their cloth supplies outside market-places.

At the end of the nineteenth century many of the *fatake* who journeyed to Yorubaland and Lagos invested most of their proceeds in the purchase of kola-nuts for sale in Kano Emirate. But the famous kola caravans which went to Gonja, north of Ashanti, were an altogether peculiar case, partly because their leaders tended to be specialist traders based on Kano city, but also because, as P. E. Lovejoy claims, many of their members belonged to three immigrant groups, the Agalawa, Tokarawa and Kambarin Beriberi, which had retained their ethnic identity after settling in Hausaland. However, Lovejoy's recent research (1973) reveals that most Agalawa and Tokarawa traders lived mainly in the countryside around Kano city, possibly on trade routes.

THE MARKET IN KANO CITY

The great market in Kano city (Kurmi) had two main functions. It served as an entrepôt and trading centre for long-distance traders from distant places who were both buyers and sellers, and it was a retail institution where city-residents and strangers alike could buy their everyday requirements. (In 1910 E. D. Morel noted (1911, 1968 edition, p. 127) that the market was essentially a retail one: 'the more valuable clothes are seldom seen...transactions in objects of more costly worth taking place within the shelter of private houses'.) The long-distance traders sold manufactured merchandise (much of it of European, Arabic or North African origin, one of the chief wares being low value calico from Manchester – Johnson, 1976), slaves, natron, salt, horses, cattle, camels, sheep, ostrich feathers, ivory and a great range of other exotic wares; their purchases presumably included many of the same foreign goods, with the addition of some locally manufactured items, of which far and away the most important was Kano cloth and apparel – followed, perhaps, by leather goods and hides and skins. The likelihood is that most of the textiles and clothing were brought in from the countryside by agents and traders who had dealt directly with the producers, for had these goods been sold (for export) in rural periodic market-places the famous regions of cloth production would all have been studded with market-places as appears not to have been the case (see Chapter III).

We are entirely ignorant regarding the means by which foreign merchandise penetrated the Kano countryside. Was it apt to be handled, like slaves, by specialist traders who conducted much of their selling outside market-places? Were certain rural periodic market-places renowned for particular exotic goods? What was the role of pedlars and other itinerant traders? (Even today, traders who travel on camel-back from the Niger Republic sell palm fronds (*ƙaba*) directly to rural mat-makers at their houses.) Did the traders and agents tend to be based on the countryside? We can answer none of these questions. As for the means by which Kano city was provisioned with grains and other agricultural produce, here again we can do no more than presume that country-based traders brought in most of the supplies.

A CITY STATE?

Centralised kingdom though it was, it is now clear that Kano Emirate in 1900 bore no resemblance to a city state. M. M. Postan has defined the typical Roman *civitas* as 'a near-city state gathering to itself the top layers of the population and dominating the administration, the commercial activities and even the agriculture of the countryside' (Postan, 1972, p. 8). Like most Romano-British towns, Kano was a mere 'part-city', claiming only 'one or some of the urban functions'; and its hold over the country and its influence over the people's lives in it was correspondingly partial (*ibid.*, p. 9).

Y. B. Usman considers that the city states of medieval Europe differed from the great pre-Jihad Hausa kingdoms in some fundamental respects and that the analogy with such states 'has obscured rather than clarified some significant features of the [Hausa] settlement pattern'. In his opinion the significance of the pre-Jihad Hausa pattern did not lie in the dominance of one urban centre, as the term 'city state' implies, but 'in the existence of numerous urban centres which constituted the cells of the political community...but which maintained a corporate existence and *some measure of autonomy from the capital and from each other*' (my italics). Although in 1900 there were relatively so few urban centres in Kano Emirate, yet rural communities (however defined) had far more economic autonomy than the European analogies would suggest.

But such negative conclusions do little more than enhance our bewilderment. How was the socio-political structure of Kano Emirate maintained in the absence of both a properly organised, institutionalised, hierarchy of authority, and of segmentary lineage systems which might form the framework of the political system? Insofar as these two systems should be regarded as alternatives – as *African Political Systems* (Fortes *et al.*, 1940) would imply – must Kano be regarded as a special case? It is clear that this question cannot be answered until intensive historical fieldwork has been undertaken, with special reference to the functions of the *jaƙadu* –

those mysterious tax collectors and 'political officers' who linked rural communities with the centre of power and the rural *dagatai*.

In their introduction to *West African Kingdoms in the Nineteenth Century* (1967), D. Forde and P. M. Kaberry emphasise (p. xiv) that a central theme was the relationship between 'the territorial structure of the state and its economic basis in the control and exploitation of resources, and their distribution through tribute and trade' and such matters as 'the analysis of politically significant social groups and categories' and 'the prerogative of politically dominant elements'. They asked their various contributors to provide material on territorial administration, but attempted no summary of their presentations. I suggest that the situation in the pre-colonial Kingdom of Benin, as described in that book by R. E. Bradbury, is reasonably representative of the kind of administrative hierarchy which centralisation might be thought to imply in a state where, as in Kano, rights over land were effectively vested in village communities. In the Benin village 'the predominance of community over kin-group interests was maintained through a three-tier age-grade organization' (*ibid.*, p. 9) – such as is lacking in Kano. Although in most villages the oldest man was 'the sole village head', his authority was apt to be shared with, and limited by, an hereditary chief who was commonly descended from 'the immediately junior brothers of past kings'. Finally, there were territorial officials (whom, for convenience, Bradbury denotes 'fief-holders'), who used their own servants and kin to carry instructions to the local chiefs, and who had a right to receive a share of the king's tribute and to demand labour services, but who had no control over land or resources. Such a system appears to be orderly, comprehensive and coherent compared with that in Kano.

APPENDIX I(1)
The population of Hausaland and Kano Emirate

The Colonial Government was, throughout, much too sanguine about the possibilities of estimating the population of Northern Nigeria with any degree of accuracy and official figures relating to the colonial period continue to meet with far too ready an acceptance today. In the *Annual Report* on Northern Nigeria for 1906–7 (Cd 3729, 1907) it was blandly asserted that the estimated population had been reduced to 7 164 751 compared with earlier estimates of 20 million – or even higher. Official estimates stood around 10 million for several decades thereafter, for few were prepared to listen to C. L. Temple in 1909 when he hazarded the prediction that 'the population of the Protectorate will be found eventually to be nearer fifteen than seven millions'. (From a despatch of 17 November 1909 from Governor Girouard, PRO, CO 446, 82.)

As late as 1919 Lugard claimed (see Kirk-Greene, 1968, p. 61) that the population of the whole of Nigeria was only 16 to 17 million (probably including
some 10 million in the North) and the 1931 census yielded a figure for the
North of only 11.4 million. Perhaps in the early years there were many who
agreed with Lugard that the population of the North had been dwindling
rapidly prior to 1900 – though, in 1919, he expressed this view with un-
accustomed vehemence and venom.

> The population of the North – described 60 years ago by Barth as the densest
> in all Africa – had by 1900 dwindled to some 9 million, owing to inter-tribal
> war, and, above all, to the slave raids of the Fulani. . .
> In 1900 the Fulani Emirates formed a series of separate despotisms, marked
> by the worst forms of wholesale slave-raiding, spoilation of the peasantry,
> inhuman cruelty and debased justice. (*ibid.*, p. 56.)

However, as R. R. Kuczynski noted (1948, p. 760), most of the slaves captured
by the Hausa-Fulani population had remained in the North.

All official statistics issued before the 1952 population census were largely
based on figures collected in connection with local taxation and we can be quite
certain that such returns were necessarily gross under-estimates – as they still
tend to be today, see Appendices IV(2) and IV(3). This is partly because of the
pronounced under-enumeration of children and youths (which may be noted
in many Assessment Reports in the National Archives) together with the
customary omission from the tax records of all old and ill people (and their
dependants) who were excused tax as well as husbandless women (most of them
elderly); but it is also because all other types of error would tend to have been
those of omission. My own experience in Batagarawa and (especially) in
Dorayi has shown that successive counts of the same population always tend to
yield higher figures until the series stabilises, and the difficulties of enumerating the populations of big houses, with the assistance of the *mai gida* only (as
census instructions until 1973 demanded), have to be experienced to be believed.

As was noted in the official *Report* of the 1931 Census of the Northern
Provinces (published in 1933), most of the figures were necessarily assembled
from available data, for funds had been reduced to a minimum owing to the
trade depression, and a widespread locust invasion was the prime concern of
most of the small number of supervisors. It is therefore not surprising that (as
the Government Statistician himself admitted) the ratio of children (of both
sexes) to adult males was most suspiciously low at 1.154 for the Northern
Provinces in 1931. Since the corresponding ratio for Katsina Province was
1.928 (a figure which was unlikely to have been inflated), I suggest that the
correct ratio for the Northern Provinces should have been of the order of 2.0
– see also, Appendix IV(3). If adults had been undercounted to the tune of about
one-quarter (a thoroughly realistic figure) the total number of adults was of the
order of 10 million (7.2 million in the census) corresponding to a total population of around 20 million – an increase of about 75% on the recorded figure
of 11.4 million (see also, *R. H.*, p. 309).

The 1911 census had been a mere 'informed guess' and the 1921 census was hardly an improvement: applying the upward adjustment of 75% to the recorded figures of 9 and 10 million for those two years, the totals are raised to some 17 and 18 million. As in recent years about a half of the population of Northern Nigeria has been recorded as resident in the North-Central, North-Western and Kano States where most Hausa people live, it is well within the bounds of possibility that the population of Hausaland in early colonial times was of the order of 8 to 10 million.

In 1952 the recorded population of Kano Emirate was about a third of that of Hausaland. On that basis, the population of Kano Emirate in early colonial times (when many farm-slaves and their dependants went unenumerated) might have been 3 to 4 million. As the above mentioned ratio of children to adult males was as low as 0.84 for Kano Province in 1931, it seems that the recorded population of 2 million for that year should be raised by more than 75% – say to 4 million. (In rural Kano tax records only were used.)

According to the *Kano Gazetteer* of 1920 (Kirk-Greene, ed., 1972, p. 41), the population of Kano Emirate was only 1.7 million at that time and it was estimated that only a million people lived within thirty miles of Kano city, where the average density was reckoned to be only 350 per square mile. Considering that a population density map for 1917 in that publication indicated that only two Districts (Mundu Bawa and Dan Ya, both east of the city) had densities of over 400 per square mile and that Dan Isa District (later named Kumbotso) had a recorded density of only 300 to 400 per square mile (see Chapter IV for evidence that this was much too low), it would seem quite probable that the population resident within thirty miles of the city was nearer 2 than 1 million, and that the population of the Emirate was nearer 3 than 1.7 million.

The 1952 census, which is generally recognised as an undercount, yielded a total of 3.0 million for Kano Emirate: on the basis of the foregoing arguments it would seem that a figure of say 4½ million would be a better estimate. The recorded figure in the 1963 census (which is usually considered superior to that of 1962) was about 5 million; perhaps this census, which remains suspect owing to the possible inflation of figures for political reasons (see *R. H.*, p. 309), was the first count to yield figures of a reasonable order of magnitude – the high level 'cooking' having compensated for the inherent tendency towards undercounting at the local level. (This view would accord with the conclusion of J. C. Caldwell *et al.* (1971) that it was doubtful whether the 1963 census was a substantial over-count.)

The Nigerian Government has now discarded the results of the 1973 census and the 1963 figures are now 'official'. Provisional totals for States (see *West Africa*, 20 May 1974) had earlier shown the population of Kano State in 1973 as 10.9 million, corresponding to perhaps 10 million for Kano Emirate – a figure which would appear to be impossibly high, despite the great expansion of Kano city. See also Appendix III(3).

APPENDIX I(2)
'Gari' and the concept of settlement

Since completing this book my attention has been drawn to 'The concept of settlement in the West African savannah' by D. Dalby (see Oliver, 1975), – and to an earlier semantic study of the Hausa word *garii* (which throughout this book is rendered in its more usual form *gari*) by the same author (Dalby, 1964). In the latter study which is of great general interest, Dalby provides 203 examples of the usage of *gari* ranging from its basic meaning of village or town with its surrounding lands (see p. 5, above), to any part or aspect of a settlement and its community, including centre of habitation, human population, local weather or sky. He argues that rather than treating the term as having a wide range of associated but variant 'meanings', it is more satisfactory to consider it as retaining 'the basic sense of human settlement throughout' (1964, p. 298). He concludes (1975, p. 205) that the study of *gari* 'demonstrates the importance of language in providing an understanding of vernacular settlement-types, of their relationship to the environment and of the way they are regarded by their occupants'. However, he makes no reference to problems of terminology associated with the kind of dispersed settlement devoid of nucleated central places, which is so typical of the KCSZ.

With regard to my discussion, on p. 5 above, of the various terms for ruler or chief, this matter, also, is most interestingly discussed by Dalby (1964, pp. 299–300). Apropos of the word *ḳauye* ('village') (see p. 5 above), he makes the point (*ibid.*) that it denotes a 'rural settlement' from the point of view of a speaker who is seldom a member of it.

II

Indirect rule as rural non-rule

INTRODUCTION

Many writers, most notably Margery Perham in her biography of Lugard (Perham, 1960), have emphasised that there was no practicable alternative to the adoption of a policy of indirect rule in the Protectorate of Northern Nigeria – that a system of ruling through 'native chiefs' was a matter of expediency rather than of high moral, political or philosophical principles. Lugard was, as Perham puts it, 'shackled by the poverty of his revenue' (*ibid.*, p. 139): he was obliged to open up and to attempt to control (if not to administer) a vast territory, 'much of which had never even been viewed by himself or any other European' (*ibid.*, p. 27), with the aid of a small and reluctant Imperial grant-in-aid, sufficient only for the employment of a tiny cadre of 'political' (i.e. administrative) officers. A policy of 'direct rule', whatever that could conceivably have meant at the time, was impossible to contemplate – even though the Proclamations on Slavery (see Chapter XIII) constituted direct commands. Accordingly, as Lugard put it in one of his *Political Memoranda* of 1906, 'we must utilise the existing machinery and endeavour only to improve it' (*ibid.*, p. 151).

Because Lugard was so eccentric, ambitious, wilful and outspoken, and so impressed with his own indispensability, it would be easy to suppose that his constant quarrels with the Colonial Office, before his temporary withdrawal from the Nigerian scene in 1906, were of his own making. However, the parsimony of the Colonial Office (and of its master the Treasury) was the real cause of most of the trouble, for it prevented the British from ruling, in any positive sense, at all. Certainly in the years up to 1906 the British achievement in pacifying the Protectorate, and reducing slave-raiding, had been considerable; but except for the decline in trade resulting from the imposition, in 1902, of the iniquitous caravan tax, life in the countryside remained entirely unchanged, and some years were to elapse before Lugard's Native Revenue Proclamation of 1906 could be implemented.

But even had the Colonial Office been less parsimonious and had allotted Lugard all the administrative staff he had thought was necessary, little progress would have been made, for the policy of indirect rule, in its application to Northern Nigeria, was based on fundamental misconceptions regarding the powers exercised by the Fulani Emirs, who were not 'native chiefs' in any normal understanding of that term – though constantly referred to as such by both Lugard and the Colonial Office. While Lugard was much troubled by the knowledge that the Emirs, like the British, were alien conquerors and had gone so far as to contemplate 'the alternative policy of discovering and reinstating the former Hausa dynasties' (*ibid.*, p. 146), yet having endorsed the Emirs as rulers he found it entirely consonant with the policy of indirect rule to act as though they were indigenous chiefs whose instructions could be readily transmitted to their people down an unbroken chain of authority. He was critical of the Emirs for over-centralising their rule; but he did not realise that, as they had imposed themselves on peoples who generally lacked hierarchical systems of chieftaincy and village administration, this centralised rule was necessarily a peculiar species of direct rule, with the *jakadu* (or 'messengers') serving as 'political officers', but yet exerting no direct control over the commercial and farming activities of the countryside. He did not see that by operating exclusively through the Emirs his administration was necessarily cutting itself off from the people. He did not realise the irony of pursuing a policy of indirect rule through the medium of those with a contrary policy. As the system was dislocated, so the logic was lacking.

In order to counteract over-centralisation, Lugard's policy was that of consolidating the Districts (the so-called 'fiefs') and then persuading certain of the territorial magnates (the officials known as *hakimai*, whom he denoted fief-holders) to leave the Emirate capitals, where most of them resided, taking some of the *jakadu* with them. While, to do him justice, he had entertained the false hope that the newly appointed District Heads would, so far as possible, be local men of influence, he did little to emphasise the necessity for this policy if rule were to be other than direct and did not appreciate the almost entire lack in Kano Emirate of influential chiefs holding sway over populations of more than 5000 or so (the size of a substantial walled town) or the implications of dispersed settlement. Thus it was no accident that in Kano Emirate the new District Heads were nearly all strangers to their Districts – bureaucrats who had been appointed (without consultation) by outside authority, not chiefs who had risen from the people. Such *hakimai* were as much direct rulers as the Emir himself had been: they remained aloof from their people (who were indifferent as to whom was appointed), were subject to constant transfer or dismissal, and were altogether uninterested in building up village administration, which remained extremely weak. Their civil servants, the *jakadu*, necessarily remained, in huge numbers, in their posts.

In retrospect – in his *Political Memorandum IX* in Kirk-Greene (1970) – Lugard justified his policy of indirect rule on three grounds: First, because the 'political staff' available for the administration of so vast a country, inhabited by many millions, was necessarily inadequate for 'complete British administration in the proper sense of the word'; second, by reference to 'the loyalty and progress' achieved in the Protected States of India 'under the sympathetic guidance and control of Residents'; and, third, by the obvious folly of attempting drastic reforms until 'an increased knowledge both of Moslem methods of rule and of Native law and custom' had been acquired. But, as he sadly remarked under the second head, 'the status of the Chiefs in Nigeria differs fundamentally from the Independent Native States in India'.

'So long as the revenue and expenditure of Northern Nigeria were under the paralysing control of their Lordships of the Treasury' wrote Lugard, in 1913, after his return to Nigeria, 'no progress was possible.' (PRO, CO 446, 111.) Although the main theme of this chapter, as developed in its second section, is the contention that indirect rule in Northern Nigerian circumstances was *necessarily* rural non-rule – that Their Lordships of the Treasury were unavoidably helpless – I start by examining some of the direct consequences of the lack of funds in the period up to 1912.

PART I: COLONIAL OFFICE POLICY, 1903–12

Indifferent as it was to the factor of population, the Colonial Office considered it to be 'unnecessary and undesirable and contrary to the policy decided upon, to interfere in N. Nigeria to the same extent in the details of administration as in the Colonies and S. Nigeria' (PRO, CO 446, 39, minute by R. L. Antrobus of 22 August 1904), so that a much smaller staff in proportion to area should be sufficient. Northern Nigeria, with its population much exceeding ten million, was not even to be compared with Lagos or Southern Nigeria but rather with the Northern Territories of the Gold Coast, with its population of perhaps one to two million, where 'as in N. Nigeria, the action of foreign powers has compelled the extension of administrative control before it could be justified upon economic and commercial grounds, and where as the country produces very little revenue...the action of the government should be limited to what is absolutely necessary' (*ibid.*). R. L. Antrobus went on to argue that there were no political officers in Northern Nigeria (other, of course, than the High Commissioner himself) who were comparable in importance to the Chief Commissioners of Ashanti and the Northern Territories of the Gold Coast – each of whom administered a territory far less populous than a single large Emirate such as Kano.

When Lugard sought to justify an increased staff in terms of the additional revenue that would result, the Colonial Office said it was very reluctant to use an argument 'which would seem to commit us here to the view that the main function of a political officer is *to collect revenue*'. 'My belief is that if the present staff were occupied with the proper duties of political officers, in an undeveloped country – i.e. travelling about their districts, keeping the peace, making roads and supervising the administration of justice – they would not be overworked' (PRO, CO 446, 45, minute by C. S. Strachey of 5 July 1905). Following up this line of argument, Antrobus pointed out that in 1899 Joseph Chamberlain had thought that the sum of £70 000 for ordinary annual expenditure for civil (as distinct from military) purposes was too high and he called attention, in this connection, to British New Guinea, whose annual expenditure, over a ten-year period, had been limited to £15 000! Overlooking the allegation that political officers were mere revenue collectors, with no time to spare, Antrobus concluded by referring to Lugard's tendency 'to destroy the influence of the native rulers and to govern the country by white officials' (22 July, *ibid.*).

In a famous minute of 24 February 1906 on the Munshi (i.e. Tiv) disorders, Winston Churchill, as Parliamentary Under-Secretary for the Colonies, has usually been considered ill-informed when expressing the opinion that the British should withdraw from a large portion of the 'Lagos Hinterland' which 'we now occupy nominally, but really disturb without governing' (PRO, CO 446, 52). But surely Churchill was being perceptively realistic about non-government? However, Lord Elgin, the Colonial Secretary, as usual had the last word: 'It is sometimes, but not often, possible to decline responsibilities in a Hinterland – but I much doubt if this is really a Hinterland' (*ibid.*).

The political officers

In 1903, when the conquest of Northern Nigeria had been completed, the Protectorate was 'administered' by fifty-two so-called 'political officers' of various grades (including eleven revenue officers – a grade which was soon abolished) all of whom, under the policy of indirect rule, resided in the Emirate capitals, where such existed. If, as is quite possible – see Appendix 1(1) –, the population of the Protectorate was between fifteen and twenty million, there were about three political officers for every million inhabitants – in practice fewer, for it was usually reckoned that officers were on leave, or were otherwise absent, for about one-third of their time. In the large populous Provinces the ratio was much lower for, amazingly, all Provinces were treated alike; thus there were only three political officers in Kano Province (which included Katsina) in 1903.

At the end of 1903 the Colonial Office considered that each of the sixteen Provinces should be administered by a minimum of four officers: 'as these officers are responsible for the collection of taxes and the maintenance of order over so large an area, it is not possible to carry on with a smaller establishment'. (PRO, CO 446, 33) As we have seen, it was when Lugard sought to raise the establishment, or to improve conditions of work, that he found himself colliding head-on with the Colonial Office, which regarded 'detailed administration', i.e. any degree of rural administration, as amounting to 'interference'.

However, the establishment rose slowly, reaching eighty-seven officers in 1905. But when, at the end of that year, Lugard sought authority for the appointment of twenty-four additional Assistant Residents (the lowest grade in the service), which would have allowed for an average of nearly six officers for each of the seventeen Provinces, the number was cut to eight only (PRO, CO 446, 47).

Although after Lugard's departure the Colonial Office was gradually won over to the view that an increased establishment would pay for itself in terms of the tax revenue collected (everyone was astonished by the rise in the revenue from £61 000 in 1907, to £124 000 in 1909, to £180 000 in 1911 and to £215 000 in 1913, for actual receipts constantly exceeded estimates), the number of political officers in 1911, namely 149, was only three times as great as in 1903.

Kano Province, in particular, remained grossly understaffed. In 1907 it had twelve political officers (usually only six or seven on the job); in 1909 it had only seventeen. In a report on his tour of inspection of Kano and other provinces in 1908-9, Lugard's successor, Sir Percy Girouard, pointed out (PRO, CO 446, 82) that if Kano had had a staff in proportion to its population it would have required at least forty political officers; with existent staff there was no possibility of reviewing the native assessment of taxation, although, in his view, the land revenues of Kano, if applied on the same incidence as in India, would have produced £200 000 per annum. (At that time H. R. Palmer had long been the sole political officer in populous Katsina Emirate, being assisted only by two 'Coast clerks'.) Girouard attempted to exonerate his predecessors by remarking that the populous Emirates, being homogeneous in population, were 'more easily handled' and noted that it was the 'natural anxiety to bring the entire Protectorate under administrative control, with a very small staff' (*ibid.*) which had led to their neglect. Also Kano Province, in particular, had suffered from lack of continuity so far as the Resident-in-Charge was concerned: five different men (one of them 'Acting') had held the post between October 1906 and January 1909.

As, contrary to Lugard's intentions, Kano Province remained under native assessment of taxation until 1910–11 – see Appendix II(1) – there are no early Assessment Reports, such as had been recommended in Lugard's *Memorandum on Taxation* (1906) and no possibility of judging how the tiny staffs in the several Emirates were principally occupied. However, in 1908 the ten political officers who were then on duty in Kano Province spent nearly a third of their time on tour (an average of twenty-five days a quarter) (PRO, CO 446, 82), which is to say that the rural population of, say, six to seven million was 'administered' to the extent of one thousand man-days annually, most of the time being spent on horseback. When Resident Cargill was officially reprimanded in 1907 for spending too much time on tour, he said that this was due to his anxiety 'to observe the attitude of the people outside Kano [city] with a view to gauging what, if any, truth there was in [official] annual reports' (PRO, CO 446, 61).

As time went by, political officers of rank lower than Resident-in-Charge of a Province or Emirate were referred to, increasingly, as District Officers, or Assistant District Officers, rather than as Assistant Residents – in 1911 the former Political Department was termed the Provincial Administration. But as no political officers were stationed in the Districts this was, and remained, an entire misnomer.

The administrative system established during the period up to 1912 persisted throughout the colonial period. Commenting on the Annual Report on Kano Province for 1921 (NAK, SNP 548/1922), the Lieutenant Governor asked the Resident about the advisability of having three or four political officers permanently stationed outside Kano, for this would be better than having officers 'going on tour, sleeping in towns for one night only and visiting a large number of Districts'. But the Resident did not see how it would be possible 'to post political officers to permanent stations in the Districts without destroying the Emirate'.

Very much later on, a few young touring officers were appointed. One of them was John Smith who, in 1951, was instructed to investigate rural population movements in Kano Emirate. Starting in Ungogo and Kumbotso Districts (Dorayi is situated in the latter), he wished to find out 'just how far land pressure was driving farmers away from the densely populated and intensively cultivated environs of the city to seek land elsewhere' (Smith, 1968, p. 30). The task proved quite beyond him: this was doubtless partly due to lack of basic data for he reported that these two Districts 'were not included in any touring area and seldom visited except on evening drives by the S.D.O. [Senior District Officer]' (*ibid.*). He visited Kauru District, south-east of Zaria, in 1954; it had not been thoroughly toured by an administrative officer since 1938, and the welcome he received was everywhere 'pathetic in its magnitude'. Flippant though Smith's tone is apt to be, one is grateful to him for recording the following comment made on a boat by a Resident from the Western Provinces: 'The trouble with the North is that you not only put the women in purdah but the Residents go into it with them.' (*Ibid.*, p. 47.)

Improvements and developments in rural areas

It must never be forgotten that we are 'protecting' a people in spite of themselves, and that almost every improvement and development initiated by us is absolutely opposed to all their instincts and traditions. (Despatch from Sir Hesketh Bell, 14 November 1910, PRO, CO 446, 96.)

Given the shortage of administrative officers and the policy regarding touring, few 'improvements and developments' affecting rural areas could possibly have been implemented in the period up to 1912; even so, it is remarkable how little was contemplated, let alone 'initiated'. It was not until December 1911 that the Colonial Office, after many hesitations, agreed to the appointment of a Director of Agriculture, and the various centralised Departments which had existed since the early years continued to have no direct concern with the socio-economic welfare of the mass of the people. In 1903 'the average number of Europeans actually in the country' was put at 309 (a figure which rose to 641 in 1911), of whom the very great majority were in the Northern administration at Zungeru (in the Secretariat, Treasury and so forth), in the West African Frontier Force (WAFF), the Political Department, or the Medical Department – which employed thirty doctors, whose concern with the non-European population was minimal. Nor, with the exception of the WAFF, was this tiny body of men backed up by significant numbers of 'native clerks' and other indigenous functionaries, as they would have been in India.

At all stages, but especially from 1905–6 onwards, a large proportion of the Imperial-Grant-in-Aid, which was so reluctantly issued by the Treasury, was absorbed by the WAFF. As Nigerian revenue increased, this Grant fell from £405 000 in 1904–5 to £200 000 in 1911; in that latter year total expenditure by the Northern Nigerian administration was £620 000, of which £148 000 was spent by the WAFF, which had been reduced in size. (By 1918, the last year of the Grant, a total sum of £4 872 000 had been disbursed.) The three principal spending Departments – Political, Medical and Transport – accounted for only £77 000,

£33 000 and £27 000 respectively. Few other Departments spent significant sums for half the total revenue was paid to the recently established
native administrations (N.A.s).

As the expenditure of the N.A.s was rigidly controlled by the Residents
– 'the Resident in point of fact controls and indeed originates every item'
(Lugard, 1913, PRO, CO 446, 111) – total expenditure was no whit less
centralised than formerly. Rather than devote funds to rural economic
development the Residents of large Emirates permitted (and continued to
permit) large unutilised balances to accumulate. In 1910–11 when the
Kano N.A. received £69 640 from the Government, more than half this
sum went on the salaries paid by the Central, District and Village
Administrations (Emir £6556, District Heads £20 910 and Village
Heads £13 940); most of the remainder was saved, though £500 was
made as a 'special grant for economic development'! It was in 1912 that
the policy of investing these reserves through the Crown Agents was
suggested by the Governor, Sir Hesketh Bell, and accepted by the Colonial
Office (PRO, CO 446, 14); it was most curious that the argument that
such invested funds would be available for immediate famine relief was
seriously advanced. The long-term result was the accumulation of ever-
rising, huge, reserves which, until recently, were hardly touched.

It might be supposed that the Colonial Office rested all its hopes of
economic development on that single great project the northern railway
which was built over a period of about four years, finally linking Kano
with both Southern Nigeria (and Lagos) and with Baro on the river
Niger in 1911. (The cost of the railway did not fall on the Treasury but
was met from a loan raised on the credit of Southern Nigeria – see Hyam,
1968). Winston Churchill was much impressed with this project – in
1907 he wrote of it as 'Napoleonic both in compass and precision' (PRO,
CO 446, 63); like others he saw its main justification as political and
military, not economic. As Governor Girouard put it in a despatch of 30
May 1907 (PRO, CO 446, 63), it was because 'the people are not
attached as yet to our rule' that it was necessary to maintain 2000 troops
in the North to restrain their fellow countrymen – and armies need lines
of supply.

Lugard's successor, Girouard, did not arrive in Northern Nigeria until
1907. In his early months he spent much of his time at the railway construction camp near Baro, and it was not until the end of 1908 that he
was able to set off on a grand tour of inspection of Kontagora, Sokoto,
Kano, Bauchi and Zaria Provinces. That this tour resembled a voyage of
discovery is evident from his interesting report (PRO, CO 446, 82) which
has not received the attention it deserves. In part his prior ignorance of
conditions in the northern Emirates was personal to a man who owed

his appointment to his experience as a railway engineer; but it also reflected Lugard's unfortunate choice of a capital town, Zungeru, which lay so far south of the centre of gravity of the population as to be right outside Hausaland. Rural Kano Emirate came as a revelation.

The 14 great districts which radiate like the spokes of a wheel, with Kano as a hub, have populations of from 100,000 to 180,000. Any one of these districts will eventually support a light railway. As in Egypt...so in Kano the extra rentals which could be derived from districts served by a light railway would not improbably pay interest and sinking fund upon the capital raised for its construction. Kano as an agricultural and industrial country requires to be visited to enable one to fully appreciate its possible future expansions. In the interests of its millions such a visit on the part of an officer of the Colonial Department is highly desirable prior to amalgamation [of Northern and Southern Nigeria] (PRO, CO 446, 82).

Of course no such light railways (other than that to Bauchi which served the tin mines) were ever built, or contemplated – the grossly inadequate road network which developed in later years linked the great cities without serving the districts. Girouard would be amazed if he knew that the potentialities of rural Kano Emirate as an agricultural (if no longer an industrial) country remain to this day unappreciated.

No one had previously told Girouard of the grand possibilities of increased grain production in densely populated northern localities such as Kano Emirate, where he estimated that an acreage equal to that of Scotland was under permanent cultivation, and he was soon strongly urging the Colonial Office to agree to the establishment of a Department of Agriculture. (While ignorance regarding such mundane matters as agriculture was natural enough, the Colonial Office was critical of Girouard's unfamiliarity with matters Islamic. In Sokoto he found that 'the dignified bearing and manners of Chiefs, Scribes and Priests', and 'the Arabic language of the learned' composed a picture which was 'unexpected in British West Africa'. Italicising these last five words, R. L. Antrobus commented: 'It is curious how little Sir P. Girouard seems to have realized what he would find in Nigeria.' (*ibid.*) This is likewise indicated by a lecture Girouard gave in July 1908 before his grand tour in which, apropos of the railway, he argued that it would be 'dangerous to move the native mind at anything like express speed'. 'Hitherto they have moved about as far as the seventh century by our reckoning – I am not sure but that some are positively antediluvian' (– Girouard, 1908, p. 335).

A slightly later voyager in Zaria, Kano and Katsina Emirates was G. C. Dudgeon, who held the preposterous post of Superintendent of

Agriculture for the whole of British West Africa (see Omosini, 1968). (In 1908 when Dudgeon had held the temporary post for three years, the West African governors were still unanimously opposed to appointing him permanently – PRO, CO 446, 74.) In 1909 the Superintendent, also, was astonished by what he saw. Like Girouard he recommended the appointment of an Agricultural Officer to Northern Nigeria. Several decades ahead of his times, he advocated the introduction of ploughing – though (see below) he thought that the employment of Indian ploughmen would be necessary. However, his reference to 'a careful and intelligent class of farmers' was refreshingly at variance with stereotyped images of lazy and improvident countrymen.

If, as I consider possible, Northern Nigeria is to become very largely productive of agricultural crops for the home markets, the employment of cattle for ploughing should be introduced. This should not be difficult among a careful and intelligent class of farmers such as is found in parts of the country...No more suitable implement is at present required than the Indian or Egyptian plough, which can be made or repaired by the cultivator himself (PRO, CO 446, 83).

Like the Food and Agricultural Organisation in a report on Nigerian agricultural development published in 1966 (see *R. H.*, p. 252), Dudgeon unrealistically urged the necessity for massive population movements out of densely populated Kano Province to more sparsely populated regions. (However, he was wrong in regarding 'the natural disinclination of a people to settle under another chief or king' as the main obstacle.)

Perhaps exhausted by his extensive touring, Dudgeon was invalided from his post in 1910. Governor Sir Hesketh Bell took the opportunity of casting doubt on the value of 'flying visits', insisting on the need for 'a detailed and leisurely enquiry into the economic condition of the country, its products and its possibilities' (PRO, CO 446, 90): of course, no such enquiry was ever undertaken. After much delay the Colonial Office, in December 1911, did finally agree to recommend the appointment of P. H. Lamb, Chief Agricultural Officer in Uganda, as Director of Agriculture in Northern Nigeria. What one territory gained another lost for it was stated (PRO, CO 446, 100) that Lamb would be a great loss to Uganda, where he was just getting the cotton industry into shape.

The only Northern Nigerian crop in which the Colonial Office had taken any serious interest before Lamb's transfer was cotton – the Lancashire industry required new sources of raw material. Progress had been slow and in a despatch of March 1909 (PRO, CO 446, 82), Governor Girouard had stated that increased cultivation for export would necessitate the intervention of the overworked Political Department for the British

Cotton Growing Association (BCGA) had previously only operated far south in the Lokoja area. The BCGA's manager, Mr Percival, had toured Hausaland in order to assess the possibilities of increasing the area under cotton cultivation. He had not been impressed with the possibilities at Zaria owing to the extent of 'exports' to Kano and elsewhere. Governor Bell reported that 'the most unfavourable aspect of the whole problem lies in the comparatively high price for which cotton sells in the local markets' (despatch of September 1910, PRO, CO 446, 92) – even 2d or 3d a lb against 1d offered by the exporting firms! So at the end of the period under review no agricultural developments had affected the Hausa states. There had been no change since 1902 when Lugard had reported (PRO, CO 446, 85) that he could not furnish a report on agriculture (as had been required by a Circular Despatch) because owing to 'the absence of any Economic, Botanical or Statistical Department' he had no one 'to compile the available information' – as though any such existed! (The Colonial Office thought that Lugard had been typically pedantic in replying to the Circular at all.)

Lugard must surely have had his tongue in his cheek when he telegraphed to the Colonial Office in August 1904 (PRO, CO 446, 40) regarding the need for famine relief, for even had immediate funds somehow been made available, the administration would have been powerless to assist the countryside. (In fact the Treasury informed the Colonial Office *unofficially* that 'any famine relief must be met from savings'.) In 1908 there was a serious pre-harvest famine in Kano Emirate. On that occasion the Governor made no appeal to the Colonial Office for the very good reason that he had learnt of the famine for the first time in 1909 upon reading the 1908 Annual Report on Kano Province (NAK, 472/1909). When challenged, the Acting Resident was unabashed: 'Yes the mortality was considerable but I hope not so great as the natives allege – we had no remedy at the time and therefore as little was said about it as possible.' (*Ibid.*)

Two subjects, above all, exercised and interested Lugard as High Commissioner: slavery and taxation, each of them matters tied up with land policy. I deal with these questions elsewhere – see Chapter XIII and Appendix II(1) – and now turn to consider whether there were any other 'improvements or developments' which affected the general living standards of the rural population. I also examine the notorious caravan tax imposed by Proclamation in 1903.

Given the prevailing philosophy regarding the need for colonial self-sufficiency and the necessary lack in Northern Nigeria of that conventional colonial prop, the revenue from customs duties, Lugard was faced with the absolute need to raise revenue from country people. So understaffed was the political Department that the prospects of immediately and substantially increasing the yield of the 'land tax' (at least that part of the yield which actually accrued to the central administration) were poor; the obvious solution was a tax on long-distance trade which could be readily justified as replacing the arbitrarily levied existing caravan tolls.

Lugard started collecting the caravan tax before getting official permission from the Colonial Office, who were worried about its 'propriety' (PRO, CO 446, 30). Until shortly before its abolition in 1907, the yield of the tax was very poor, both because of staff shortage and because traders avoided the main trade routes and were generally deterred by the tax. In Kano Emirate the great main roads became overgrown and sometimes impassable, the Resident regarding their maintenance as a waste of time in the circumstances (*ibid.*). There was much blackmail and corruption: 'I find it very difficult to get traders to understand the percentage system' complained Acting-Governor Wallace (despatch of 7 October 1905, PRO, CO 446, 46). A well-informed article by 'Africanus' ('Natives Overtaxed and Industry Stifled', *Daily Chronicle*, 5 April 1906, PRO, Co 446, 47) asserted that everything was subordinated to the raising of revenue: 'Sights have been seen as that of a Political Officer in charge of a huge province, sitting at a table in full view of the populace, collecting shillings from unfortunate hawkers like any old Fulani tax-gatherer and detested in consequence with an even greater detestation.'

As a strong opponent of the tax Wallace urged its abolition in 1906, so that more time and energy could be devoted to acquiring 'a better knowledge of the inhabitants and an insight into their needs, habits and customs' (PRO, CO 446, 55). Although the yield had by then increased to some £40 000 annually (or about 40% of the total local revenue), in January 1907 the Colonial Office finally agreed to its abolition on grounds of 'restraint of trade'. The Resident of Nupe Province, which lay astride the main trade routes from Hausaland to Lagos, reported that many Bida citizens would consequently resume trading with the Coast and that there had been great scenes of rejoicing on a ceremonial occasion when 20 000 people followed their venerable old Emir in prostrating themselves 'as a mark of profound gratitude' to the colonial administration for removing the tax (PRO, CO 446, 61).

However, owing to understaffing, little attention was paid to lines of communication in Kano Emirate until late 1908 when a few main roads were 'cleaned' by order of the Emir. In 1910 it was reported by an Intelligence Officer who toured Kano Province that there were no bridges there (PRO, CO 446, 91). (The first important road bridge was, in fact, built at Wudil as late as 1928.) The whole tone of the officer's brief and casual report suggested a sortie into a peaceful undiscovered country, where there were fortunately few rifles in the hands of the natives which were in a 'serviceable condition'.

Although the administration was reluctantly obliged to employ many 'natives' to collect the caravan tax (despatch of 7 October 1905, PRO, CO 446, 44), in general it entrusted very little responsibility to such few Northern Nigerians as were on its pay roll, most of whom were, presumably, interpreters. It was because the general run of native was considered unskilled and untrainable (except as a soldier) that Lugard sought permission to employ Indian craftsmen and 'transport attendants'. His first request, in 1904, to purchase a consignment of mules from the Argentine and drivers from India or South Africa, was rejected by the Colonial Office (PRO, CO 446, 38), but later on a few Indian craftsmen, clerks and others were recruited – a despatch of 27 November 1908 (PRO, CO 446, 76) referred to two Indian carpenters, fourteen transport attendants, one shoeing smith, two blacksmiths, two saddlers and one Veterinary Assistant, all of whose contracts were due to expire. But the Colonial Office felt uneasy on the matter and G. C. Dudgeon's recommendation relating to the employment of Indian ploughmen was deleted from the printed version of his above-mentioned report. The first large-scale employment of responsible officials of Northern Nigerian origin (*mallamai*) was possibly in connection with the revenue survey which – see Appendix II(I) – was introduced in parts of Katsina and Kano Emirates in 1909.

Whatever view may be held about the 'exploitation of the natives' by expatriate trading firms, one of the incidental benefits of colonialism was commonly the opening up of the countryside by these firms. But the Niger Company, the principal firm in Northern Nigeria, operated on a very small scale. So in 1911, when the firm opened branches in Zaria Province, thus providing 'an unlimited demand' for agricultural and sylvan products (PRO, CO 446, 105), its principal purchases, apart from cotton, were hides worth only £3200 and shea nuts – £7000. And there were continual complaints about barter terms of trade (salt or manufactured cottons being exchanged for raw cotton as late as 1910 – PRO, CO 446, 92), which the Colonial Office was obliged to take rather seriously. Nor were cheap imported wares in evidence:

The great markets of the principal centres are full of wares of all sorts, and on every highway one meets a constant stream of petty traders carrying, from East to West and from North to South, the products peculiar to their districts. But everything is of local make or production. With the sole exception of Manchester cotton goods, hardly an article of European origin is to be seen. (Despatch of 14 November 1910, PRO, CO 446, 96.)

It seems likely that at that time, and for some years to come, most market-trade was still being conducted in cowry shells. As late as 1911 the land tax in Kano Province was still being collected in cowries, and in 1912 the Kano Treasury held something like 20 000 bags of cowries, worth some £7000, which were fast depreciating (Annual Report on Kano Province for 1912, NAK, SNP 10/1, 134P/1913). It was not until 1911 that subsidiary coinage in the form of nickel pennies and tenths of pennies was put into circulation and began gradually to displace the cowry as the usual medium for local transactions.

This examination of the improvements and developments affecting rural areas which were introduced by the British up to 1912 is rather brief: there is nothing very much to report.

PART 2: THE ENDEAVOUR TO REFORM INDIGENOUS RURAL
ADMINISTRATION IN KANO EMIRATE

Far from regarding the taxation of impoverished rural populations as an unnecessary evil arising from the extreme parsimony of the Colonial Office and their masters the Treasury, Lugard regarded it as a 'moral benefit', which stimulated industry and production.

Hitherto the male population has been largely engaged in tribal war and the men have depended on the labour of their women and the great fertility of the soil to supply their needs in food. Where taxes were formerly paid (as in the Kabba Province) and have lapsed, I am informed that large areas have gone out of cultivation, and the male population, deprived of the necessity for producing a surplus to pay their taxes, and of the pastime of war, have become indolent and addicted to drinking and quarrelling. (*Memorandum on Taxation*, 1906, p. 87.)

Whereas the pressure of population was the 'corrective' in most countries, he considered that owing to the devastations of war and slave raids no such pressure existed in Northern Nigeria, so that it had presumably been easy for individuals casually to earn their livelihood – despite the extreme harshness of natural conditions and the admitted vagaries of the climate. On the one hand, men would not work hard unless external stimulation was applied to them; on the other hand, direct taxation was 'the moral charter of independence of a people' (*ibid.*, p. 86) for it involved 'State recognition of the rights and responsibilities of the individual' (*ibid.*, p. 89).

From the outset, and for many years thereafter, the aim of good government in its positive aspects was virtually equated with a fair and efficient system of rural taxation. Given the existence of complex, centralised taxation systems in the large pre-colonial Muslim Emirates (the notable exception being Sokoto), as well as the obligation under indirect rule to utilise and improve the existent machinery of tax collection, the administration's most urgent task was to study the systems it was obliged to reform. Lugard set about this work with the greatest enthusiasm and many of the ideas he formulated in his fascinating, groping, muddled and premature *Memorandum on Taxation* (1906) provide the basis for much present-day received thinking on such matters as urban–rural relationships and the nature of the institution of District Head. His principal bequest to Northern Nigeria on his resignation as High Commissioner was intended to be the Native Revenue Proclamation of 1906, which aimed at the substitution of a 'general tax' for the multiplicity of taxes previously in force in many Emirates – but which was wholly inoperative in Kano Emirate for five years to come.

That the 'Districts' were to be reorganised and that 'chiefs' were to be appointed *for the very purpose of reforming taxation* was made explicit in the 1906 Proclamation.

Para. 8. *For the purpose of this Proclamation* [my italics] a Resident may from time to time divide his province into districts, and may place any one or more of such districts under the supervision of a district headman, and may place any community in or any portion of a district under the charge of a village headman.
Para. 9(a). A Resident may from time to time appoint chiefs or other suitable persons to be district headmen and village headmen *for the purpose* [my italics] of supervising and of assisting in the collection of tributes and taxes under this Proclamation.

The earlier Land Revenue Proclamation (1904) had referred merely to 'chiefs', defined as 'any person who is in receipt of the profits, or any part of the profits, arising out of any land whether as tribute, taxes or rent'. The change in the definition amounted to a recognition that those who had received the tribute were either 'unsuitable' or not chiefs at all.

All this being so, Lugard's interest in the more detailed aspects of existent District or Village administration derived almost entirely from his concern with taxation: he was uninterested in any rural administrative functions which had no bearing on taxation. In particular, he was entirely vague about the practicalities of land tenure. Postulating, as he was bound to do, that ultimate rights over land resided in the Emirs, he presumed that the pre-colonial *hakimai* were full *territorial magnates* (in his *Memorandum on Taxation* he even referred to them as absentee landlords) to whom land-allocating functions had been transferred by the Emir; but at the same time he never asked whether land was actually allocated in the countryside and, if so, by whom.

When an Emirate was annexed, Lugard proclaimed in his letter of appointment that ultimate rights in land had been transferred from the Fulani rulers to the British. But in retrospect he admitted that no attempt had been made at that time to define those rights '*in so far as they were held by the Fulani dynasty as conquerors*' (Lugard's italics, Kirk-Greene, 1970, p. 344). In a despatch of 24 April 1903 (PRO, CO 446, 31), he judged that there was 'nothing inherently unjust' in the transfer of land: 'I explained fully to them [the Emirs of Sokoto, Kano and Zaria] that what they had won by conquest they had now lost by defeat. . .In this they acquiesced as a matter of course, and as an obvious and recognised result of conquest.' As pointed out by A. McPhee (1926, p. 176), Lugard's Land Registry Proclamation of 1901, whereby native landholders were entitled to register their holdings with the government in return for certificates which would be accepted as true titles to land, had never been put into effect owing to lack of staff; this Proclamation is perhaps the supreme example of the failure to realise the implications of the low ratio of staff to population.

W. F. Gowers and H. R. Palmer in their evidence to the Northern Nigeria Lands Committee were the first political officers to appreciate that the *hakimai* were not territorial magnates. 'I am still unable to regard the "fief-holders" of this country as having estates in the lands ruled administratively by them', said W. F. Gowers (HMSO, Cd 5103, p. 39). Palmer spoke of the private estates of *hakimai* as having been 'mere toys' (*ibid.*, p. 70).

District 'reorganisation'

In 1905–6 Dr F. Cargill, the Resident of Kano Province, turned his attention to the task of forming his Districts and of appointing the 'headmen'. In his last *Annual Report* on Northern Nigeria for 1905–6 (HMSO, Cd 3285, 1905), Lugard optimistically reported that Cargill had been most successful – which was far from being the case.

As in most other provinces, he [Cargill] found that the fief-holders owned towns vicariously scattered over the whole province, but unlike most other provinces, he found no difficulty in re-distribution. Taking the principal town under each fief-holder, he grouped around it in one homologous district a sufficient number of towns to yield a revenue equivalent to the former revenue of the fief-holder, and appointed him 'District Head' of this self-contained District. He even succeeded in giving to the most important chiefs the districts furthest from the capital, where their responsibility would be greater, retaining the villages close to Kano itself under the direct rule of the Emir. To avoid too drastic and hasty a reform, it was found necessary to allow the Emir to place some of these under his head slaves as a temporary concession.

In the course of this work Cargill was reported to have visited 'every single town and village in the Kano Emirate numbering upwards of 1,100' (*ibid.*). But as no report on his touring has been preserved, and as it is impossible to define 'villages' in areas of dispersed settlement, the statement is obscure, especially as many of the old *hakimai* would have had no towns in their 'territories'. However this may have been, Cargill created thirty-three consolidated Districts, about half of the *hakimai* he appointed being members of the royal Sullubawa clan (many of whom were close relatives of Emir Abbas), three being royal slaves and only two being of local origin.

As a result of this detailed exploration, Cargill became convinced of the lack of respect of the Kano peasantry (*talakawa*) for their former *hakimai*: 'It was the entire absence of any local feeling for the Hakimai and the somewhat honorary nature of their offices due to the absorption of power by the Emir's slaves that led me to push through the District scheme in 1905.' (Annual Report on Kano Province 1907 by F. Cargill, part of a rejoinder to the Acting Secretary's comments, NAK). Cargill thought that the last few Emirs of Kano had been in the habit of making arbitrary appointments, 'ousting hereditary families in favour of their own relatives, transferring towns at will from one Hakimi to another, and undermining their position by concentrating the power in the hands of their palace slaves' (*ibid.*).

In terms of the collection of revenue the new scheme was not a success. Although the Native Revenue Proclamation had laid down that the Districts should be 'Resident assessed' (on the basis of the estimated annual value of lands, produce, profits from non-farming occupations, flocks and herds), no such assessments were made and taxes continued to be collected on the old 'native assessment'. Tax yields, so far as they were revealed to the administration, remained very low, the land tribute (*kudin kasa*) rising from £6024 in 1903–4 to only £8110 in 1906–7. While some of the newly appointed District Heads reluctantly spent part of their time in their Districts, the power of the tax-collectors (the *jakadu*) remained undiminished, for they merely followed their new overlords into the countryside.

Returning to Kano in October 1907, after more than a year's absence due to illness, Cargill undertook a most drastic reform, which he made no attempt to justify, reducing the number of Districts in Kano Emirate to only fourteen, each comprising three to five Sub-Districts. As Fig. 1 shows, all the small Districts around Kano city, including Kumbotso – then called Dan Isa – were formed into one large District under the Emir's eldest son, the Ciroma. Resolutely attempting to follow Lugard's *Memorandum on Taxation*, Cargill absented himself from Kano city and dealt

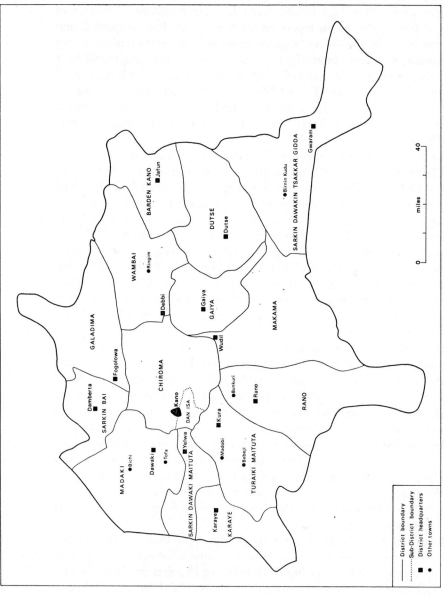

Fig. 1. The fourteen Kano Districts created by Cargill in 1907–8, showing Dan Isa Sub-District in which Dorayi is situated. (From a map dated 30 June 1909, in the National Archives, Kaduna, the spelling being unamended.)

directly with the *hakimai* on the matter of tax assessment, though even so he was obliged to retain native systems of taxation (PRO, CO 446, 61). The results of such flaunting of the first principle of indirect rule were foreseeable, especially as Cargill had destroyed all previous monthly and quarterly reports on Kano Province – which he had unsuccessfully argued should be renamed Hausa Province. The Acting Secretary reported on Cargill's state of health to the Colonial Office, which concluded that he was suffering from 'peculiarity of character' (*ibid.*). After an abortive attempt had been made to transfer him to Kabba Province, Cargill was permanently invalided.

Cargill's positive actions infuriated the Governor who considered that 'such a general resolution' should have been referred to him 'in particular terms' and who was concerned that the authority of Emir Abbas had been undermined (Annual Report on Kano Province for 1908, NAK 472/1909). It was to him scandalous that Cargill should have summoned all the District and Sub-District Heads before him and redistributed them on the basis of his personal knowledge.

It was not until C. L. Temple was appointed Kano Resident in January 1909 (after Cargill's removal the post had been occupied successively by W. P. Hewby and A. H. Festing) that, as we shall see, any serious consideration was given to Village (as distinct from District) administration. As an earnest student of land tenure – Perham, (1960, p. 474) has described him as 'a rather speculative and individual kind of Socialist' – Temple was the first Resident to realise the futility of imposing ignorant aristocratic outsiders on Districts which lacked all internal coherence. In order to reform taxation it was necessary to *create* a system of Village administration: 'Administration and taxation are so inter-dependent and interlaced that it is impracticable to consider one without at the same time considering the other' (Report on Kano Province for Half Year ending June 1909, NAK, SNP 7/10, 3635/1909).

Temple agreed with the Governor (Preliminary Report on Kano Province for 1909, NAK, SNP 6/5, 44/1909) that fourteen District Heads were insufficient for a population then put at two million and further considered them to be effectively Sub-Emirs – despite the fact that Sub-District Heads often communicated with the Emir direct. He hoped to create about sixty Districts (far more than ever came into existence), though as there had already been so many changes of policy he would introduce his own changes very gradually and with the greatest caution. (As it turned out, Temple was Kano Resident for only a year, and it was not until 1916 that the number of Districts was increased to twenty-four.) But not until Village authorities had been strengthened would anything have been changed, for the *jakadu* were still emanating from a central authority. 'The Village Unit has nowhere been constituted except perhaps in Kazaure. The central authorities have been changed; they used to be Emirs at the Capitals, they are now the District Heads. But this does not affect the principle.' (*Ibid.*) Temple did not approve of this apparent devolution of authority to the District Heads; as one of the staunchest of all the believers in the philosophy of indirect rule – H. R. Palmer wrote that 'Indirect Rule was Temple's religion and that at times he verged on the fanatical' (Perham, 1960, p. 476) – he thought that Emir Abbas had been monstrously treated. By dealing directly with the Emir's subordinates the administration had deprived him of all power and influence and had then proceeded to blame him 'because orders not his own and not given through him were not executed' (NAK, SNP 7/10, 3635/1919) – which prompted an annotation of 'extraordinary' from Governor Girouard.

Perhaps with a view to counteracting any tendency Temple might have had to give the Emir too much freedom, Governor Girouard advised him (in a confidential preliminary report of March 1909, NAK, SNP 6/4, 111/1908) of the 'unwisdom and even danger' of inculcating Emirs 'with the idea that they are sovereign rulers over independent States'. The Emirs should be regarded as the Governor's 'Wakils' (deputies) and must be guided by the Resident 'who speaks, hears and sees for me when I am absent'. He justified this by a rare reference to the Caliph: 'The Serikin Muslimi [*sic*, i.e. Caliph at Sokoto] alone might consider himself an independent sovereign, but as you know, his own religious law will not tolerate the assumption of such power.' (*Ibid.*)

Writing in retrospect in 1921 about the period up to 1909, H. R. Palmer, then Acting Lieutenant Governor, said:

At the time of the British occupation in 1903–4 the actual power at Kano was wielded almost entirely by slaves. The free Hakimai by custom never or hardly ever saw one another, and only as a rule saw the Emir for purposes of salutation...The demand of Government that the Hakimai should go out into the districts was met by sullen refusal, and it was only after great difficulty that they were got out in 1905 for half the year. To get this done at all the districts had to be 'satrapies' in size...

By about 1907 the Hakimai had begun to see that there were certain advantages in having 'satrapies' away from the court, while the court on the other hand was not much inclined for progress and reform...The Resident of that time [Cargill] was almost forced to go behind the Emir to the Hakimai in order to get anything done. The Hakimai responded so readily that in a few months the power of the Emir and his Slaves was almost reduced to nothing, and the Emir told Sir Percy Girouard quite truthfully that he had nothing to do and no power.

It may be noted that up to about this date the people of Kano Province never believed that we would stay in the country – they thought we were a visitation sent by God which would shortly be removed.

It was the initiation of the Baro-Kano railway which changed this belief. . . so that when Mr Temple came to Kano in 1909 he found the Emir already inclined to repent his previous attitude of passive resistance, and a population who at last understood that we were something more than a temporary plague. . .

The 'satrapies' however remained, and so did the Palace Slaves as the effective agents of the Central Native Administration. . .It was useful having 12 big men whom the Resident could see fairly frequently and whom the Emir could play off against his Slaves. (Comments by H. R. Palmer on the Report on Kano Province for the fifteen months ending March 1921, NAK, SNP 10/9, 120P/1921.)

Emir Abbas died in 1919 and, according to Acting Resident A. C. G. Hastings (*ibid.*), Kano Emirate fell into 'a state of maladministration and chaos' at the beginning of 1920. While regarding this as overstrong language, H. R. Palmer did think that great opportunities of reform had been missed on the Emir's death.

Various administrative reforms were proposed by Hastings, most of them involving the Village Heads. Palmer was very scathing:

I hope that the Acting Resident does not think that this is the first time reforms on these lines have been made; if so he is quite mistaken: the fact that [official] salaries are paid to a few messengers [*jakadu* – as had been proposed], will not in itself ensure that they are the only agents a District Headman uses . . .This report reads as if most of it was not very first-hand information. I note that Mr Hastings was only able to get on tour 16 days.

By 1924 when (see below) the reorganisation of the Kano Village Units was regarded as complete, the number of District Heads had risen to thirty, nearly half of whom were members of the royal Sullubawa clan who were close relatives of the Emir (see Paden, 1973, pp. 244 *et seq.*), many of the remainder being strangers to their Districts. Lugard's advice (as given in the citation below) was impracticable so far as the need to appoint local 'chiefs' was concerned and was otherwise ignored, as transfer from one District to another was (and has remained) standard practice in most cases.

The men selected for appointment as District Headmen should be chiefs with local influence, and it may often be advisable that as far as possible the appointment should be retained in the same family. District Heads will very rarely therefore be transferred from their own district to another, merely because the new appointment carries higher responsibility and increased salary. For the new holder of office would know nothing of the district. (Lugard, *Political Memoranda*, 1919, Kirk-Greene, 1970, p. 314.)

As late as 1930 it was reported that the District Heads of Kano Emirate,

all look far too much to Headquarters, treading delicately and with circum-
spection without taking action and showing a sense of responsibility. This has
always been very noticeable in Kano and is a tribute rather to the power of the
ruler than an indication of lack of ability in his subordinates. It is also a heritage
of the slave regime abolished in 1928, up till when the District Heads were in
the pockets of palace favourites. (Annual Report on Kano Province for 1930,
by H. O. Lindsell, NAK, SNP 17/2.)

As for village administration, 'there was much room for improvement':
'unfortunately District Heads and Village Heads seem to engage in a
perpetual game of bluff with one another' (*ibid.*).

Village 'reorganisation'

Soon after assuming charge of Kano Province in 1909, C. L. Temple
said (NAK, SNP 7/10) that he had a confession to make, namely that
in 1908 when he had given evidence to the Northern Nigeria Lands
Committee he had been unaware that a radically different taxation system
existed in Kano Emirate: whereas in Bauchi, Bornu and Sokoto the
villagers paid their taxes to the head of the village in which they *resided*,
in Kano Emirate taxes were paid to 'the head of the group of farms in
which a man's farm is situated wherever his dwelling may be'. He explained that the entire Emirate was 'divided up into coadunate groups of
farms in place of coadunate groups of habitations', the natural result of
such a system being [my italics] '*that village heads have not and never
have had any real authority*'. He claimed that the Fulani Emirs, and
probably their Habe (or Hausa) predecessors also, 'were alive to the fact
that the village heads having no authority some kind of authority must
be set up' – this taking the form of 'an army of remarkably able, if
unscrupulous envoys from the capital', namely the *jakadu*. (As the
jakadu were almost invariably abused by the British it is worth citing, in
this connection, the following statement by H. R. Palmer, relating to
Katsina Emirate:

The Jakadas had wonderfully good memories and when you went to them they
would tell you the taxes of many hundred towns down to the smallest details. . .
They would tell you in a wonderful way what each village produced. When it
came to the actual collection, if there was a short harvest or anything special
they would strike off a certain number of taxes (*Minutes of Evidence* of the
Northern Nigeria Lands Committee, HMSO, Cd 5103, 1910, p. 69).

– which suggests that the *jakadu* might have been more efficient and less
harsh than the customary portrayal.)

What could Temple have meant when he said that taxes were paid to 'the head of the group of farms'? Considering that concepts of clan or lineage land were lacking and that the farms comprising an individual's farm-holding were often widely dispersed, it is doubtful whether Temple's new ideas were any more realistic than those he was rejecting. Perhaps he was merely noting that when men migrated to towns from areas of dispersed settlement they continued to pay taxes to their former *dagaci* (Village Head)? However this may have been, his statement raised doubts about the effect of migration on tax payment and the relationship between nucleated and dispersed settlements. Although Cargill had done so much touring that he must surely have been aware of the ambiguities involved in the concept of Village Unit, it was Temple who was the first to appreciate the practical implications. 'The native system of taxation' Temple asserted 'does not lend itself readily to the creation of village authorities' (NAK, SNP 7/10). At the same time such authorities had to be *created* (*ab initio* as it were) in order that the stranglehold of the *jakadu* over ordinary farmers should stop: 'The organisation of the Village is to my mind quite as important as the assessment of the tax.'

In his 1906 *Memorandum on Taxation*, Lugard had been very sanguine about the prospects, even in Kano Emirate, of abolishing the *jakadu* when once the taxes had been Resident-assessed (para. 64). At the same time he gave little thought to the constitution of Village Units, which was surprising considering that he was realistic enough to recognise that 'the Sub-Chiefs under a District Headman' varied greatly in degree, from the powerful chief 'of a large town having many subordinate towns and villages under it' to the 'Headman of the small farm-hamlet consisting only of half a dozen huts' (*ibid.*, para. 28).

In his similar, but not identical, *Memorandum on the Taxation of Natives* (HMSO, Cd 3309, 1907), Lugard had been even more sanguine about prospects of reorganisation in Kano Emirate where, owing to the high population density, the 'territorial claim' tended (as it did not elsewhere) to supersede 'the clan claim' – he had vaguely defined the 'clan' or 'tribe' as a group of individuals 'however scattered'. Perhaps he had half-glimpsed the possibility that there was a lower proportion of settled Fulani (who unlike the Muslim Hausa have a clan organisation, though no concept of clan land) than elsewhere in Hausaland? Anyway, he argued that the Kano clan organisation could easily be swept away in order to 'reconstitute the districts *de novo*'.

In writing about the clans or tribes in relation to village organisation Lugard, had, typically, been jumping in where no one else dared venture, and it was not until Temple was transferred to Kano that there was any further serious discussion (at least in Kano Annual Reports) of the nature of village authority in Kano Emirate. (In 1905 Resident Cargill, as we have seen, had acted without knowing what he was doing.) In their endeavours to facilitate tax collection the hard-pressed political officers were guided only by their innate presuppositions regarding the nature of village organisation. What did they assume a village to be?

In Kano Emirate, as we know, the bulk of the population, especially in the Kano Close Settled Zone, lived in dispersed farmsteads surrounded by farmland; although, especially in some localities, there were some walled towns dotted about the countryside, their total population was relatively very small (nearly all of them being unimportant places) and there were vast townless tracts, which may even have lacked coagulations large enough to be denoted 'hamlets'. On the basis of their knowledge of English villages and possibly, also, of Indian village organisation, political officers probably tended to assume that nucleated villages were surrounded by satellite settlements and farmsteads – that each hamlet adhered to, or was a component part of, a larger, more densely settled, unit. But there was another possibility (one which would have been more compatible with the existence of so few walled towns), namely that the towns had crystallised out of the general matrix of dispersed settlement by means of migration. In Temple's discussion there may have been implicit recognition of this latter alternative. But not so with Lugard who failed to realise the implications of his own 'clue' – that while walled towns in Kano might have two or three villages under them, they were more usually 'singular' (*Memorandum on Taxation*, 1906, para. 64, Kirk-Greene, 1970).

So, when writing in retrospect, Lugard overtly accepted the former concept. Thus, in his revised *Memorandum on Taxation* (1919) he defined a village community as 'comprising a village with its outlying farm hamlets, all under the control (whether effective or not) of a single Head' (p. 185): however, the parenthesis should be noted. In *The Dual Mandate* (1922, p. 244) he went further in regarding hamlets as necessarily 'emanating' from towns or villages.

In an advanced civilisation like that of England, the State has a personal account with each individual citizen, but in tropical Africa (as in India) the village must be the unit of taxation. For this purpose scattered groups of tenements, which cannot even be dignified with the name of 'hamlets', must be considered as forming part of the town or village from which they emanated, and to which in association they belong.

Forgetting Temple's findings in Kano Emirate (or perhaps it would be more charitable to suggest that he found them generally irrelevant?), Lugard resorted to the familiar argument that dispersed settlement was due to the Pax Britannica.

The village is the administrative unit. It is not always easy to define, since the security to life and property which has followed the British administration has caused an exodus from the cities and large villages, and the creation of innumerable hamlets, sometimes only of one or two huts, on the agricultural lands (*ibid.*, p. 202).

Temple, as we have seen, did not explain his assertion that taxes were paid to the 'head of the groups of farms', but his important (and oft-quoted) example of the town of Chiromawa in Kura District, in the Kano Close Settled Zone, provides one clue. In this case the inhabitants of the nucleated village had clearly not colonised the surrounding farmland: on the contrary, people from the surrounding farmland had taken refuge, maybe temporarily, in the village, retaining their socio-economic links with their kin. Of the 309 compounds that were counted in Chiromawa, 179 'paid allegiance' to the headman of Chiromawa, the remaining 130 to one or other of four headmen of lesser settlements (NAK, SNP 7/10).

Temple regarded it as axiomatic that the unit for administrative purposes must be the village, which he somewhat unrealistically defined as

a coadunate group of habitations of convenient size for administrative purposes, i.e. not so large that the various members of the group are not living more or less in daily contact, and not so small that the weight of the combined opinions of the various members of the group becomes insignificant (*ibid.*).

He had come to realise that a village might be 'one of the quarters of a large town or a number of farm houses scattered over an area of, say, four square miles'. The immediate task was to render each existing Village Unit 'coadunate'. Temple gave little indication as to how he thought this could be done. But it was on his advice that a standard 'compound tax' – see Appendix II(1) – was introduced: this tax was designed to enhance the authority of the head of the community in which the taxpayer *resided*, for it was directly payable to him.

In the course of his despairing analysis, which affected District as well as Village organisation, Temple failed to mention the interesting case of Gaya, perhaps the largest town in Kano Emirate, for here was a town (a rare one) which contradicted his assertion regarding the incompatibility of native systems of taxation and orderly Village authorities. Resident Cargill having apparently destroyed all his records relating to his touring, it is fortunate that his account of his assessment of Gaya in 1905, was preserved by Lugard: it is summarised (not cited) below. (It is a pity that in his post-war discussion of village organisation Lugard failed to buttress his arguments with memories of this report.)

Taking the Waziri of Kano (a son of the Emir) with him, he arrived in Gaya and interviewed the sarki, informing him that he had come to assess Gaya 'with a view to doing away with the Jakada'. He then called together the twelve Hamlet Heads (*masu unguwoyi*) who collected tax within the town, each of whom brought with him the farmers belonging to his quarter. The Hamlet Heads were asked to state how much revenue they collected under each tax heading and each individual farmer was asked what he paid. The assessment and census of Gaya was completed in two days. The sarki then summoned all the Hamlet Heads from the district outside Gaya and they were interviewed by two of his own clerks and two Mallams brought by the Waziri. He then went on a tour, which occupied three days, of all the eight walled and fenced towns under Gaya, and found that the clerks had completed their lists (of tax collected) on his return. The Waziri was then told to leave one of his Mallams, assisted by one of Sarkin Gaya's Mallams, to go round the district and to collect much information about each farmer, as he had done in Gaya town. Altogether seven days were spent at Gaya: 'the result is map, census and assessment of one district completed, and one Jakada abolished'. (*Annual Report on Northern Nigeria for 1904*, HMSO, Cd 2684, 1905, para. 33.)

Although as many as thirty-three 'villages', as well as eight 'towns', paid taxes to Gaya, Cargill was confident that the sarki could be trusted to collect the tax directly, thus dispensing with the *jakadu*. But the accuracy of the data collected by such a method (which is reminiscent of certain types of village enquiry today) must be extremely dubious.

Following Temple's departure in 1910 there is so little reference to Village organisation in the Annual Reports on Kano Province for the next few years that it is difficult to judge what progress, if any, was made. Commenting on the Governor's remarks in the Annual Report for 1912 (NAK, SNP 10/1, 134P/1913), the Resident, W. F. Gowers, noted that the average Village Head got about £2 per year from the government – or one-sixth of the pay of a private in the Northern Nigerian regiment. However, in 1915, Acting Resident Palmer decided 'after exhaustive enquiries' (Annual Report on Kano Province for half year ending June 1915, NAK, 382P/1915), that very few of the Village Heads (*dagatai*) got a cash share and that the sum of £11 500 ear-marked for the Village Heads went into the pockets of the District and Sub-District Heads. By 1916 it must have been clear that the policy of creating Village Units had failed for it was in that year that the Governor instructed Palmer (Annual Report, Kano Province, 1915, NAK, 170P/1916) 'to go through the units at present known as Group Heads and hamlets with the object of forming "Village" units'. He did not define such units, or give any indication of the principles involved, but requested Palmer to bear in mind that the Village Head must not be so important as to be above the control of the villagers, or so unimportant as to be without 'influence and power'. Village Heads were to be paid; as for the subordinate Hamlet Head, 'he should live on the prestige of his post'.

Not surprisingly, the Resident, W. F. Gowers, who returned to his post in October 1916, after an absence of twenty months, was very critical of the reconstitution of units throughout Kano Province carried out by Palmer.

> Further experience has made clear that the reorganisation was carried out too hastily...Nor was the vital principle (often insisted on) sufficiently recognized viz. – that the administrative unit – the village – should not be so large that the village headman cannot be in close touch with every part of it, without the use of 'jakadas' and other intermediaries. (Annual Report on Kano Province for 1917, NAK, 179P/1918.)

One unidentified Divisional Officer (who was not necessarily in charge of Kano Emirate) wrote of the system as being 'too prescribed and in-elastic to admit of success', and reported that those Village Heads who had been given far more villages than they could look after were employing large staffs of servants to do the work for which they had been paid (*ibid.*).

With many setbacks the policy of increasing the sheer numbers of Village Units was thereafter successfully followed. In 1921 there were 459 'salaried *dagatai*'; in 1924, when the number had risen to 1175, the average Unit was about thirteen square miles in area and had a population of 1632. After twenty years' struggle the organisation of the Village Units was regarded as 'complete'.

As for the efficiency of the organisation, this remained highly dubious; and scarcely any information was made available as to who the Village Heads were. Begging the important issue of principle raised by Temple in 1909, E. J. Arnett plaintively asserted in 1922 that of all the links in the administrative chain that connected the ordinary man with his District Head, the Village Head, oddly defined as 'the Head of an historically and territorially associated group of hamlets', *should* be the most important (Annual Report on Kano Province for 1921, NAK, SNP 548/1922).

The rapid increase in the numbers of Village Heads between 1922 and 1924 was only achieved by means of drastic action. According to the fascinating Assessment Report on Dawaki ta Kudu District of 1937 by D. F. H. MacBride, the process

> involved the disruption of long established village areas, particularly the original territories of the larger towns, and the promotion of agents or local hamlet heads to be digatai [dagatai] of units including other hamlets which had never

acknowledged their authority. It also produced a fresh crop of territorial anomalies, for the existing village and hamlet boundaries had not then been surveyed and the new grouping. . .often conflicted with the traditions and sentiment of the communities affected.

The Hausa word for this reorganisation was *yayyaga* (tearing asunder). In Ungogo District, where the number of Units was raised from fifteen to forty-seven in 1923, nearly all the old Village Heads had been deposed for embezzlement, their successors being mostly 'inexperienced and untried' (Assessment Report on Ungogo District by R. F. P. Orme, NAK, Kad Local Govt 525/1924).

The poor quality of village administration in Kano Emirate continued to concern the Residents. In 1926 it was reported that it remained 'indifferent' and that the quality of Village Heads (for once denoted as 'officials') compared unfavourably with that in neighbouring and smaller Emirates. In 1930 there was said to be much room for improvement – this was the year, as already noted, when District and Village Heads were reported as being engaged in a perpetual game of bluff. In 1934 it was noted that touring officers had compiled histories of *all* Village Headships in their areas (surely such a monumental task would have been altogether beyond their capacities) and had actually collected information as to which office holders had 'historical and/or sentimental claims to the position' (Annual Report, Kano Province, 1934, NAK, SNP 17/3 23586A).

In that year the wheel had again come full circle: 'More attention can now be paid to the selection of Village Heads and it is possible to ensure that the right man is appointed; that is to say the man who has long historical or strong sentimental claims to the position. . .Village Heads are beginning to realise that tax collection is not the be-all and end-all of their duties.' (*Ibid.*)

From this account of the prolonged struggles of the British administration in Kano Emirate to establish (*ab initio*) an hierarchical structure of authority linking the 'village' with the Emir, by way of the District Head, it is evident that (especially in areas of dispersed settlement) there was indeed a serious lack of 'chiefs' with 'long historical or strong sentimental claims' to the position of Village Head (*dagaci*) – that the pre-colonial *jakadu* (wrongly denoted 'messengers') were the indispensable civil servants (the political officers) who collected tax directly from individual farmers on the Emir's behalf, with the assistance of whatever 'local headmen' happened to exist. For many years the British concentrated on the problem of establishing a strong District organisation, without realising that most of the *hakimai* who had been appointed were aristocratic

Fulani who were to an even greater degree strangers (for their gaze was solely directed on the capital) than British District Officers would ever have been, had they been permitted to reside in and administer the Districts. Given the existence of these *hakimai* the great need was to *create* strong, indigenous, village authorities, who were capable of acting on their own initiative and standing up to the *hakimai*, not merely of obeying their instructions. In applying the policy of indirect rule to a regime which was almost solely concerned with the downward transmission of centralised orders rather than with facilitating the upward projection of rural demands, the British inadvertently allied themselves with 'direct rulers' who favoured the establishment of very small inoffensive Village Units which would cause no trouble.

Whether, in the end, the British were successful in establishing a reasonably efficient and incorrupt rural taxation system has never been seriously investigated; but the principle that the responsibility for tax payment lay with the village community as a whole (whose representatives fixed the sum payable by each individual) was certainly calculated to increase the coherence of Village Units. What is not in doubt is that the present-day system of village administration, which basically resembles that created in the 1920s, is even more unsatisfactory in terms of the need to decentralise decisions regarding rural economic development than it was in colonial times though it remains to be seen whether the new local government system will ultimately improve the situation.

APPENDIX II(1)
The reform of the local taxation system in Kano Emirate, 1903–13

Although the Native Revenue Proclamation of 1906 had laid down that the reorganised Districts should be 'Resident assessed', Kano Province remained under 'native assessment' of taxation until 1910–11, most of the old taxes remaining in force up to that date. During that period the British had introduced two new taxes, the notorious caravan tax (1903–7, see above), and the compound tax (1909, see below). Also in 1909 a start had been made in replacing the customary farm tax (*kudin kasa*) in certain populous Districts with a tax based on farm area (*taki*). The general aim (which was perhaps not achieved much before 1918) was to replace the multitude of different taxes with one consolidated tax (*haraji*) levied on the sedentary population (individual rates being determined by Village communities themselves), though the traditional cattle tax (*jangali*) would still be payable by Fulani (and not by Hausa) cattle-owners. The following notes relate to the traditional taxes and also to the compound tax and the tax based on farm areas; a note on the cowry currency is also appended.

Kudin ƙasa

Much less was known about variations in pre-colonial taxation systems within Kano, and other Emirates, than Lugard supposed. In his *Memorandum on Taxation* (1906) he stated, most misleadingly, that *ƙurdin ƙasa* (more correctly known as *ƙudin ƙasa*, lit. 'land money'), which was always supposed to have been the most important tax in terms of yield, had been levied at the same rate in Kano Province since 'time immemorial', having been from 6d to 1s per acre – it is almost needless to add that there were no indigenous units of area. In fact the evidence, slight though it is, indicates that during the reign of Sarki Bello (1883–92) attempts were made to fix a uniform rate of 4000 cowries per farm in Kano Emirate, rates having formerly varied according to the size and value of the farm – Barth may have been mistaken in asserting that in 1851 every 'head of a family' paid 2500 cowries (Barth, 1857, II, p. 144). However, opinion differed about the results of this attempt at standardisation. Generalising about Kano Emirate in 1908, W. P. Hewby (Report on the Kano Emirate, NAK, 111/1908) stated that the tax was a fixed rate on 'holders' of grain farms, whether they were under cultivation or not, and that every farmer knew his 'personal rate' which varied, according to district and size of farm, from 2000 cowries (about 1s 3d) to 10 000 cowries – though 'in certain few quarters' it was generally 4000 cowries. Writing in 1909, C. L. Temple (NAK, SNP 7/10, 3635/1909) referred to Sarki Bello's standard rate, but appeared to think that when farms were subdivided the tax was usually subdivided also. In an Assessment Report on Dan Makoyo District (now part of Ungogo) in 1910 (NAK, 451/1911), it was asserted that the total raised by *ƙudin ƙasa* was no higher than it had been twenty years earlier although there had been much subdivision of farms. A 1909 Assessment Report on Dawaki Tsakkar Gida District (in south-eastern Kano) stated that the tax varied in different localities and that newcomers were charged less (NAK, 5570/90).

Did *ƙudin ƙasa* fall most heavily on poorer farmers whose yields were lowest owing to lack of manure? Certainly, the evidence suggests that it was a regressive tax, unrelated to income, and for all we know poorer farmers may sometimes have been obliged to sell farmland owing to their inability to meet the tax. In this connection it is worth noting that in 1909 C. L. Temple (*op. cit.*) considered that *ƙudin ƙasa* did 'not reach the full economic rent, for farms have a large transfer value as between individuals'. Could he really have meant that farming would have been unprofitable had an 'economic rent' been paid? Whatever his meaning, the idea of the sale of farmland was new to the Governor who annotated his surprise.

Except in those areas where the *taki* (farm measurement) system was introduced, *ƙudin ƙasa* continued to be levied until about 1917.

Kudin shuƙa

According to W. P. Hewby in 1908 (Report on the Kano Emirate, NAK, 111/1908), a tax known as *ƙudin shuƙa* (*ƙurdin shuƙa*) was paid on every plot or 'patch' (*fage*), varying in size from ¼ to one acre, which had been planted with non-grain crops such as sweet potatoes, groundnuts, cocoyams, sugar cane, cassava or yams, the rate varying according to crop, and as between localities, but generally being between one to two thousand cowries; he added that cassava farmers occasionally paid very high rates. It was reported that in Kura in 1909 (NAK, 2607/1909) the tax varied with the length of furrow (*kunya*), those less than ten yards being exempt.

In 1909 the abolition of this tax (as well as *kudin rafi*) was recommended by C. L. Temple (NAK, SNP 7/10), on the grounds of embezzlement, arbitrariness and the need to encourage the cultivation of special crops, but whether it was everywhere abolished is not known.

Kudin rafi

Colonial officials sometimes inexplicably confused the tax on irrigated plots which was correctly known as *kudin rafi* with the tax on dyepits (*kudin karofi*). Like *kudin shuka*, *kudin rafi* was levied on plots which were actually planted, at a rate, according to Hewby (*op. cit.*, NAK, 111/1908) of some 2000 to 5000 cowries per plot – i.e. a higher rate than *kudin shuka*. The crops included wheat, onions, sugar cane, tobacco and henna.

Hewby considered that the two taxes on special crops accounted for a quarter of the 'land revenue'. He noted that cotton and indigo were never taxed and that vegetables such as okro and tomatoes were generally exempt.

Zakka

In his 1908 report (*op. cit.*) W. P. Hewby stated that the Koranic grain tithe *zakka* (or *zaka* or *zakat*) on guinea corn and millet had never been 'honestly levied or paid' and was 'the biggest channel for extortion and robbery of the whole taxation system'. He estimated that the yield of the tax represented about a quarter of the total extracted by means of the various 'land taxes', including *kudin kasa*. The tax had never been uniformly collected, but in 'haphazard instalments' throughout the year, the ordinary farmer never knowing when he might have 'to journey fifty miles with corn loads to Kano'. It was no wonder that much of the grain held back as *zakka* was sold or eaten, that the grain that was actually delivered tended to be sub-standard, and that one-third of the original bulk was lost in transit 'partly by robbery and partly by the carrier taking his daily ration from it'. No authority was responsible for appraising individual crops and opportunities for corruption at all levels were preposterously great. 'Not since 1903', complained Hewby, 'has the Administration, British or native, received anything like the amount returned as due.'

As late as 1910 (Kano Annual Report, NAK, 951/1911) H. R. Palmer arranged that *zakka* should again be paid in kind (not in cash) as in pre-colonial times: 'it would be a boon to have a great reserve of grain store, to be sold off gradually throughout the year, thus ensuring a constant supply of grain in the wet season, when, as is well known, there is often a serious shortage in Kano, unless the previous year's crop has been excellent'.

According to an estimate in an Assessment Report on Kura District for 1909–10 (NAK, 2607/1909) by H. Moreton Frewen, which was based on the doubtful assumption that that District was self-sufficient in grain, actual *zakka* payments represented but a seventy-sixth of the grain yield. Maybe the incidence of the tax was not unusually low there?

In the Kano Districts where the *taki* system was introduced in 1909 *zakka* was possibly officially abolished – i.e. absorbed into the new farm-tax. But the speed with which *zakka* was abolished elsewhere depended on the date of replacement of *kudin kasa* by the general community tax (*haraji*), a matter on which there appears to be little detailed information. (As late as 1917, W. F. Gowers reported in his Annual Report on Kano (NAK, 179P/1918) that some districts were still paying *zakka*.)

It is worth noting that Bargery, in his dictionary, defined *zaka* (*sic*) as 'a religious tax payable by the well-to-do'. Thus, on thirty bundles of grain or more, the tax was one-tenth; and on money or trade goods it was one-fortieth of the sum in excess of £20.

Kudin karofi

While Lugard believed (*Memorandum on Taxation* 1906) that 'every form of handicraft' without exception had its special tax, and that *kudin karofi* (the tax on dyepits) was the most lucrative, there is little firm evidence that such taxes, with the exception of *kudin karofi*, were systematically levied in the country-side, especially in areas of dispersed settlement where there were no craft heads. In 1909 C. L. Temple asserted (NAK, SNP 7/10, 3635/1909), maybe incorrectly, that there were no 'industrial taxes' at all. (In 1919 an attempt to reintroduce such taxes was abandoned when it was found that there were hardly any craftsmen who were not also farmers.)

Jangali

According to a note by H. R. Palmer in Temple's 1909 report (*ibid*.), the Emir of Kano had raised the cattle tax (*jangali*) to 5000 cowries per head after the great rinderpest epidemic of 1892, a rate which was reduced to 2500 cowries in 1905. In his 1908 Report on Kano Emirate, W. P. Hewby stated that the tax had been raised to 2400 cowries: 'in previous years this tax received practically no attention, no system was defined and the Returns were small'. He glossed over the question of what owners were liable to pay the tax, but noted that Hausa owners had previously paid *zakka* of one animal in thirty in place of *jangali*. Subsequently, the yield from the tax rose steeply.

Compound tax

On the recommendation of C. L. Temple a 'a compound tax' (*kudin gida*) – to which I have seen no previous reference in the literature – was introduced in Kano Province in July 1909, the rate being 1s 6d per compound except in three Districts (Wombai, Barde and Sarki Dawaki Tsakka Gida) where the rate was 1s. It was intended (see p. 45 above) that the tax should enhance the authority of the head of the community in which the taxpayer resided, for it would be directly payable to him. According to the unreliable testimony of the Kano Annual Report of 1911 by E. J. Arnett (NAK, 1114/1912), the efficiency of Village Headmen had been greatly increased by the introduction of the tax, even though opinion differed as to the appropriate definition of 'compound', and on whether account should be taken of the number of sleeping-huts.

On the first introduction of the tax, Temple had remarked in his Preliminary Annual Report for 1909 (NAK, SNP 6/5, 44/1909) that, on the one hand, 'the people seem to be paying without demur', but that on the other hand 'the exodus from Kano into Ningi and Zaria' is easily accounted for by the high incidence of the tax! According to a 1910 Assessment Report by N. M. Gepp on Dan Makoyo Sub-District (NAK, 451/1911), the immediate effect of the tax had been to cause amalgamation of compounds. 'We shall hope to stop this by measuring compounds soon', commented the Acting Chief Secretary, adding that it 'is wonderful how quickly the population in this Protectorate reacts to altered conditions'.

This heavy-handed attempt at rationalising the taxation system in the interests of a system of rural administration which was not understood, was suddenly discontinued in 1917, no reason being given.

The 'taki' system

In 1909–10 it was decided to replace *kudin kasa* in a few areas by a tax on farms measured by means of pacing (*taki*), the rate in the inner ring of the Kano Close Settled Zone having been fixed at 1s 8d per acre – somewhat lower elsewhere; although the system was gradually extended to other densely populated districts, it never became the basis of assessment throughout the Protectorate as had been hoped in the early years (see *R. H.*, pp. 312–13). A cadastral survey being lacking, the farms had to be paced by men who received little training, and it was not until 1914, two years after strong protests had been made by the surveyor F. G. Guggisberg, that a Survey School was set up in Kano, after which the system was officially known as Revenue Survey.

A note on the cowry currency

In 1900 the cowry currency had had many different uses in Hausaland: in the villages it was suitable both for small local transactions, such as snacks sold by village women, as well as for major transactions for market-trade; it was an international currency indispensable for long-distance trade; inflation apart, it was a reliable store of value; and it was the currency in which taxes (other than *zakka*) were paid. Although in 1904, in a vain attempt to control the cowry inflation, Lugard (see Johnson, 1970, Pt. 1, p. 48) prohibited further importation of the shells, yet as late as 1911 *kudin kasa* was still being collected in cowries (Kano Annual Report, NAK, 951/1911) at the low rate of 6d per 1000 shells, the rate in Kano being 6d per 1300. It was not until 1911 that subsidiary coinage in the form of nickel pennies and tenths of pennies, with holes for stringing, were put into circulation (silver shillings had been imported somewhat earlier), so that it is not surprising that in 1912 (Kano Annual Report, NAK, SNP 10/1, 134P/1913) prices were still generally quoted in cowries in Kano markets, the main unit having been 1000 shells. The fact that the rate of exchange in relation to silver continued to depreciate was attributed by W. F. Gowers (*ibid.*) to 'the conservatism of the country-people and their ignorance of exchange values'!

As emphasised by Johnson (*op. cit.*), in savannah West Africa cowries were not strung as they were in the south, but were laboriously counted afresh for each transation; certainly loose cowries provided a useful local currency in rural Hausaland (where a *daddawa* cake might have cost five cowries, or much less than a tenth of a penny), and it is no wonder that the shells continued to circulate there alongside coin for many years.

III

The Kano Close Settled Zone

Although the very densely populated farming area around Kano city, which is commonly known as the Kano Close Settled Zone (KCSZ), is very much larger and more populous than any other comparable region in savannah West Africa, its existence is somehow taken for granted. Perhaps it is inevitable that the largest and most prosperous city in the Central Sudan in the nineteenth century should have been surrounded by such a vast and ancient area of dispersed settlement – in which case it is worth reiterating that the population of the city, until quite recently, was but a trivial proportion of that of the Zone. Until the Zone has been intensively explored by historians, archaeologists and others, our ignorance regarding its origins, development and relationship to Kano city must remain profound. While one purpose of this chapter is that of placing Dorayi (see Chapter IV) within its general geographical context, it is also an attempt to pose a few of the historical questions about the recent history of the Zone which cannot yet be answered.

The most prominent recent writer on the KCSZ is the geographer M. J. Mortimore who undertook the first systematic socio-economic survey of certain localities there (Mortimore *et al.*, 1965) and who has followed this up with a long series of publications, the more important of which are listed on p. 226. (It is appropriate that, as he recently told me, he was accidentally responsible for coining the term Kano Close Settled Zone.) Having noted that the population density gradient, on the basis of the 1962 population census, noticeably steepened if followed outwards from the city at a density of about 350 per square mile (Mortimore, 1968, p. 298), he defined the Zone as being bounded by that gradient. He estimated the total population of the Zone at about 2.4 million (Mortimore, 1967), with an average density, excluding Kano city, of some 500 per square mile – figures which should be regarded as indicating orders of magnitude only owing to the well-known unreliability of the 1962 census (see *R. H.*, p. 310).

The Zone, as thus defined, is seen (Fig. 2) to be an irregularly-shaped

ellipse, extending some sixty miles from Kano city to the south-east and
only some thirty to forty miles in other directions. Roughly half of the
total recorded population of Kano Emirate lived there in 1962 – a proportion which will since have fallen owing to the subsequent vast expansion
of Kano city which, at the time of writing, may be inhabited by some half a
million people, many of them non-Hausa.

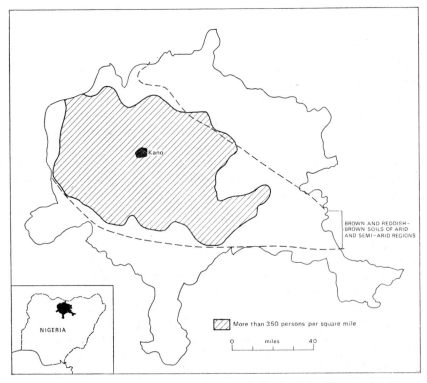

Fig. 2. Outline map of Kano Emirate showing the limits of the Close Settled Zone
(from Mortimore, 1967, p. 678).

Mortimore emphasises the favourable pedological conditions in the
KCSZ which (see Fig. 2) lies wholly within the limits of distribution of
soils which are classified as 'brown or reddish-brown of arid and semi-
arid regions' and which are 'light, freely draining, sandy loams, which
have proved highly amenable to intensive cultivation; situated on a gently
undulating plain at about 1500 feet above sea level, and drained by
seasonal rivers, these soils have developed on windblown sands derived
from acid crystalline rocks of the Basement Complex' (*ibid.*, p. 677). So

far as is known (information from Mr Mortimore), a high water table of some twenty-five to thirty feet is general (though not universal) throughout the Zone, a level which was found to be astonishingly stable during the severe drought of 1972–4. Domestic water supplies, which are mainly based on wells dug inside house-compounds, are consequently excellent.

Although it may be very generally stated that most cultivable land within the KCSZ is actually under cultivation during the farming season, being kept in condition by plentiful application of organic manure, small scale population density maps tend to indicate a greater uniformity of density than actually exists, for in terms of such matters as farm size, and the extent of grazing land, there is a surprising degree of local variation – see Appendices III(1), IV(5). While population dot-maps show that densities are highest within an inner ring of the Zone, which lies (according to direction) within some five to ten miles radius of the built-up area of the city (this has now extended several miles outside the ancient walls to the north-east), any tendency for densities to decline uniformly outside that ring, as distance from the city increases, is not striking. In the inner ring rural densities may substantially exceed the astonishing figure of 1000 per square mile – as at Dorayi.

In the inner ring, but not elsewhere, a large proportion of the organic manure (*taki*) which is applied to the farmland consists of household and roadside sweepings from the city, the main value of which is derived from the droppings of small livestock and from ashes, loads of which are fetched by the farmers with their donkeys. (Some lorry loads of rubbish are bought by farmers from the municipality, but they tend to be of very poor quality, including much discarded enamelware.) According to surveys undertaken by Mortimore in 1965 and 1969 (Mortimore, 1972, p. 875), some 85% to 90% of the manure of city origin was applied within some five miles of the edge of the built-up area, at an average application of the order of one ton per hectare. The usage of chemical fertilisers within this inner ring was negligible in 1972 (owing to manpower problems affecting distribution, it was probably negligible in most areas of dispersed settlement), and such high population densities would be quite unsustainable were it not for the Kano sweepings. However, this curious type of dependence on the city is nothing new: in the first decade of the century (as, presumably, much earlier) farm-slaves were commonly engaged in transporting manure from the city.

Owing to the entire lack of general historical fieldwork in the Zone (such as has been undertaken in Katsina Emirate by Y. B. Usman), the main historical sources are the writings of European explorers and travellers. Clapperton, the first explorer to traverse the Zone, emphasised the intensity of cultivation there. Near Sarina, which is situated (see Fig. 3) in present-day Wudil District some forty miles south-east of Kano city, he noted numerous plantations which were 'as neatly fenced as in England' (Bovill, ed., 1966, p. 639) – and fencing or hedging (see *R. H.*, p. 303) is an indication of permanent cultivation of manured farmland; and south of Dawakin Kudu, he reiterated that the country was 'clear of wood, well cultivated and divided into cultivations' (*ibid.*, p. 641).

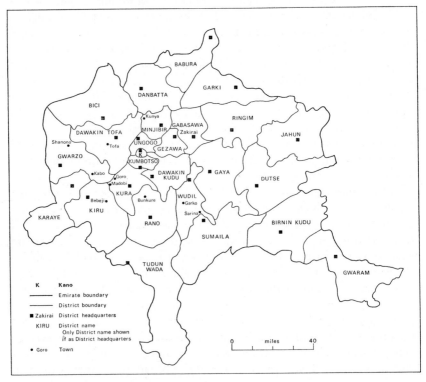

Fig. 3. A map of the 25 present-day Kano Districts showing District capitals and 9 other towns mentioned in the text.

The explorer Heinrich Barth was more expansive. He was impressed not only by the intensity of cultivation and by the hedging, but also by the extent to which the population lived dispersedly – and by the beauty of the inhabited countryside, which afforded a pleasant contrast to Kano city that 'picturesque but extremely dirty town' (Barth, 1857, v, p. 360). The original map of Barth's route in 1851 notes 'farms without interruption' between Bici (see Fig. 3) and Kano city where he remarked that 'the villages are here scattered about in the most agreeable and convenient way, as farming villages ought always to be, but which is practicable only in a country in a state of considerable security and tranquility.' (*Ibid.*, II, p. 94.) Again, before reaching Gezawa, north-east of the city, he commented that 'small clusters of huts and detached farms' were spread over the countryside (*ibid.*, II, p. 143) and that tobacco fields were just in flower: the fields, which were shaded by luxuriant trees, 'looked fertile and well cared for, while the clusters of neat huts scattered all about had an air of comfort' (*ibid.*, p. 151). It is interesting, too, that in recording information about a southerly route, which he had not himself followed, he took the trouble to note that at Garko (near Sarina, visited by Clapperton) there was little *jeji* (or uncultivated bush) to be seen (*ibid.*, p. 571).

Later travellers included that astute observer E. D. Morel who (Morel, 1911, p. 234) presumed that the system of permanent cultivation of manured farmland was an ancient practice passed down the generations (see also, *R. H.*, pp. 303–6). After eulogizing Kano cultural systems he noted that for miles and miles around Kano city, 'one passes through a smiling country dotted with farms, riven by fine, broad native roads lined with hedges of euphorbias and other plants.' (1911, p. 235.) C. L. Temple presumed (without giving any reasons) that the KCSZ was very old. 'Round the city of Kano there live about one million natives on small holdings, with an average density of population of some three hundred to four hundred persons to a square mile, entirely supporting themselves from the produce of a soil which is none too fertile and which has been under close cultivation for five hundred years at least.' (Temple, 1918, p. 147.)

As early as 1904 a large scale map (four miles to the inch) of Kano and other northern Emirates was drawn and issued – I have found no previous reference to it in the historical literature. It shows (see Fig. 4) the main routes radiating out of Kano city, but the intervening countryside was not mapped. Various expressions on the map, such as 'open country many farms and hamlets', denote dispersed settlement in the KCSZ, and another description applied to the countryside west south-west of the city, viz. 'cultivated lands small farms', also indicates long-standing cultivation, as does the term 'park-like farms' around Rano to the south. Nowhere within the KCSZ is there any reference to 'bush', as there is further south, notably in the south-east of Kano Emirate where 'thick' or 'close' bush is recorded. Although the expression 'villages', which may mean dispersed settlement with some clustering, is only casually and occasionally employed, it happens that one instance is provided by some of the 'villages' I denote Dorayi. Unfortunately the map gives no indication of the relative sizes of towns (thus an important town like Gaya is marked with a mere dot), but it does at least record the existence of numerous named settlements on certain routes, notably those from Kano to Zaria via either Bebeji or Korai (Karaye), and on an east–west route from Bonkuri (Bunkure) south of the city, through Kura and Kabo and on to Gworoso (Gwarzo). However, the likelihood is, as we shall see, that most of the settlements were very small.

Nineteenth-century historical material on towns in the KCSZ is very scanty. Clapperton (1829, pp. 165–7) was much impressed by Baebaegie (Bebeji); he estimated its population at 25 000, which was perhaps too high, especially as he added that most of the inhabitants were 'refugees' from Borno and Wadai and their descendants, all of whom were engaged in trade. (Dr Ibrahim Tahir informs me that Bebeji was a very important commercial centre in the mid-nineteenth century, with many resident merchants and strong links with Kano city.) Barth provided (1857, II, pp. 558 *et seq.*) a list of twenty-eight walled towns in 'Kano Province', about half of which lie within the KCSZ; his list of other 'considerable places', which he admitted was incomplete, ran to seventy-three names – many of these cannot be identified but assuming that about half of them were in the KCSZ, the total number of listed towns there would have been about fifty.

In his *Annual Report* on Northern Nigeria for 1904 (HMSO, Cd 2684, 1905) Lugard reported that there were forty walled towns within thirty miles of Kano city. If – see Appendix I(1) – the total population of that portion of the KCSZ was at least one million, and if – see Appendix III (3) – the forty walled towns had had a total population as high as 100 000, then only about 10% (probably much less) of the total population would have lived in such towns. (This is not to say that there had not been more walled towns in earlier times as archival Assessment Reports often suggest: thus in 1910 (NAK 451/1911) it was reported that there had formerly been three walled towns in Dan Makoyo Sub-District (now in Ungogo District) which by that time was town-less.)

In 1920, according to the *Kano Gazetteer* (in Kirk-Greene, 1972), the only town in the KCSZ with a population exceeding 5000 was Kura; and the corresponding number of towns according to the 1931 census was only three. But there is a very important technical reason for supposing that there may have been no towns of this size at all.

Nearly all publications (including all official reports on population censuses) which are concerned with the sizes of Northern Nigerian towns according to the 1921 and all subsequent censuses, including that of 1963, are marred by a grave oversight, namely the failure to admit that urban 'enumeration areas', except in the cases of cities and very large towns, have always included considerable portions of the surrounding countryside – over which (as we have seen in Chapters I and II) towns, at least in Kano Emirate, seldom held sway. The result has been a general and considerable overstatement of the size of towns relative to that of the total population – overstatement which may often have more than counteracted the general tendency towards undercounting in the census – see Appendix I(1). And there is an additional and even worse error of presentation, namely the tendency to identify all enumeration areas with populations exceeding certain figures as towns, irrespective of whether there is any nucleation! – see Appendix III(2). Accordingly, the results of the only Nigerian census of any reliability for which detailed statistics have been issued, viz. that of 1952, have to be very carefully scrutinised, on the basis of knowledge derived from other sources (such as maps), before the incidence of urbanisation is even roughly estimable. As I think that it is reasonable to assume that the great majority of men resident in towns with populations smaller than 5000 are partly or wholly dependent on farming or farm-labouring, only towns exceeding that size are here regarded as 'urban' – an arbitrary definition, especially as there is usually a considerable area of cultivated land within the walls of all towns and cities including Kano itself.

Careful scrutiny of the 1952 census report for Northern Nigeria suggests that there were as many as five Districts in the KCSZ, with a total recorded population of 321 000, in which there was no town with a recorded population of 5000 or more, after deduction of outlying areas. (The extent to which all recorded populations represented undercounts is another issue, which has already been discussed in Appendix I (1).) These Districts were Gabasawa, Gezawa, Kumbotso, Minjibir and Ungogo, all of which (see Fig. 3) lie close to Kano city. Then there were three very populous Districts (Bici, Dawakin Tofa and Gwarzo), with a total recorded population of 562 000, each of which possibly had no more than a single town of that size. Only four other Districts (Dawakin Kudu, Gaya, Kura and Wudil) were slightly more urbanised: certainly no more than 15% of their recorded populations lived in such towns. (Rano District, with its recorded population of 130 000, is omitted owing to lack of information, as are a number of other Districts lying mainly outside the KCSZ.) No town except Gaya (12 996) had a recorded population exceeding 10 000. At least a half of all these towns are old, having been in Barth's list.

Commenting on the 1921 census report, for which he had been responsible, the anthropologist C. K. Meek, who knew the countryside well, stated that 'one of the most striking features in the distribution of the population of the Northern Provinces of Nigeria is the comparative absence of large towns' (Meek, 1925, II, p. 173). But he might also have remarked on the absence in many districts of towns exceeding the modest size of, say, 2000. Nowadays there are regional clusters of small towns in a few sections of Kano Emirate outside the KCSZ, for instance in Kiru District near Zaria Emirate, and perhaps there had been more in earlier times, as Y. B. Usman's study suggests had been the case in Katsine Emirate; but such clusters are generally lacking in the KCSZ, except possibly in Wudil District. What makes the phenomenon of population dispersal so remarkable in the KCSZ, at least at first sight, is its association with very high population densities. There appears to be little tendency for towns to crystallise out of the general matrix in response (merely) to high population density.

I have sought in vain for literature which deals in broad, general terms with the factors which determine the tendency for agricultural populations to live dispersedly (as so commonly in savannah West Africa) or in compact towns or villages (as in China, with the sole exception of the Szechwan Basin). In recent years locational geographers, who might have been expected to fill the gap, have perhaps been mainly concerned with central place studies; and earlier works on village communities, such as *The Origin and Growth of Village Communities in India* by B. H. Baden-Powell (1899), which was strongly influenced by H. S. Maine, tend to be outmoded. Nor, so far as West Africa itself is concerned, have there been many writers concerned with the general distinction between dispersed and nucleated settlement patterns. It is indeed true that we 'cannot yet claim to be fully clear as to why some West African populations are addicted to a dispersed settlement pattern, whilst others have opted for life in large, compact villages.' (Horton, 1971, p. 97.) Moreover, the idea that dispersal was necessarily a consequence of the Pax Britannica is still nearly as strong as in the days of Governor Hesketh Bell:

The humble peasant who, up to quite recently, was completely at the mercy of his chief, now feels that, in case of oppression, he can always appeal to the British official and be sure of obtaining a fair hearing. The people who, in days gone by, used to be penned within the walls and ditches of their fortified cities, are now spreading over the broad plains and building homesteads wherever their fancy pleases (Bell, 1911).

In discussing the nature of dispersed settlement within the KCSZ, it is ironic that it should be necessary to turn to R. Horton's inspiring article on 'stateless societies' – for are not the large Hausa Emirates usually considered to be West African states *par excellence*? However, Horton's 'four-point definition' of statelessness (*ibid.*, p. 78) has partial application to the KCSZ in terms of the manner in which life is actually lived by hundreds of thousands of people at the local level. His first point relates to the lack of rulers and has no relevance; his second point, that authority roles 'affect a rather limited sector of the lives of those subject to them' has (and I am using the ethnographic present) a degree of validity; his third point, that the wielding of authority is not a 'specialised full-time occupation', applies to all authorities resident in the KCSZ with the exception of some fifteen District Heads and the *dagatai* of a few large towns only – most other *dagatai* are largely occupied with farming; his fourth point, that people feel an obligation to settle their disputes within a 'small unit', had great relevance to the KCSZ in 1900, when (so far as we can tell) few disputes were referred to alkali's courts, and still has considerable relevance today, considering that most disputes are dealt with informally by unimportant *dagatai* – thus, very few inheritance or land cases (in relation to the size of the population), in fact, reach an alkali's court at the District capital, which is often far away, and it seems that a high proportion of marital cases are dealt with locally. It is largely because the population lives basically dispersedly and is mainly organised in very small 'Village Units' (as we have seen in Chapter II) that these three conditions apply – though poor communications with the wider world should also be emphasised. To take an extreme example, the population of Dawakin Tofa District, just north-west of Kano city, which according to the District Head in 1972 was thought to be the most populous District in the whole of Nigeria (as long ago as 1952 its population is likely to have been between 300 000 and 400 000), lives almost wholly dispersedly: apart from the small District capital, and three towns on peripheral main roads, there were (according to the District Head) only six small settlements worthy of being denoted *garuruwa* and most roads were remarkably poor. Life there is essentially lived on a local level.

Horton – who acknowledges a debt to Daryll Forde (Forde, 1947) – emphasises the radically different social situations which prevail in areas of dispersed and of compact settlement. He distinguishes between two types of dispersed settlement pattern for agricultural peoples: the first type (*ibid.*, p. 84) 'is properly applied where a society is organised from top to bottom in terms of a single, embracing genealogical scheme' which 'provides the sole or dominant principle of social organisation' (and which is commonly regarded as 'the veritable archetype of stateless organisation') – it necessitates (*ibid.*, p. 85) 'a readily accessible supply of extra land, distributed fairly evenly round the domains of this population'; the second type, which he denotes 'the dispersed, territorially defined community', exists where 'there are gross inequalities in the peripheral land supply' (*ibid.*, p. 93), so that those communities whose expansion is 'blocked' migrate through 'the territories of all their closer genealogical relations and end up begging land from groups to which they acknowledge distant or nil genealogical ties' – this he terms 'disjunctive migration'. Although his analysis of both types of dispersed settlement pattern relates to societies organised on a segmentary lineage basis, as Muslim Hausa society is not, and although he emphasises a distinction between 'landowners' and 'latecomers' which (given the lack of land-owning lineages) does not properly apply to the KCSZ, yet (rather absurdly) his discussion of the 'dispersed territorially defined community' has a certain relevance to a part of the world which, as I shall argue, has been magnetically attractive to agriculturalists from other savannah regions over the past centuries and which also attracted Fulani pastoralists.

Whereas with the 'pure type' segmentary lineage system 'it is very difficult to point to any level of grouping as "the political community"' (*ibid.*, p. 96), with the other type the autochthones and the immigrants see each other as interdependent parts of an organic whole: 'the "late-comers" need land from the "landowners" and the "landowners" need the "latecomers" to help them hold their land"' (*ibid.*, p. 95). Would it be too far fetched to regard the semi-sedentary and sedentary Fulani populations as representing the principal latecomers?

According to the 1952 census about a third of the population of the KCSZ was classified as Fulani – a proportion which is even higher in certain central Districts, notably Dawakin Tofa and Ungogo. Whatever allowance may be made for the tendency of informants to claim Fulani origin merely because of the prestige this is supposed to bestow, the pro-portion of the population which is wholly, or mainly, descended from Fulani pastoralists is indubitably high. Presumably most of this population is nowadays sedentary and agricultural, though there is still a fair number of semi-sedentary pastoralists who practise what Stenning (Stenning, 1959, p. 7) has called 'a restricted cycle of transhumance' – as in Kirimbo, Appendix IV(5). Stenning regards semi-sedentarism as arising principally from widespread reductions in the size of herds below the level necessary for entire subsistence. As population densities increased in the KCSZ, so the degree of sedentarisation of the existent Fulani communities would have risen. There might also have been a tendency for pastoralists from elsewhere who had suffered loss of cattle through disease or any other cause, or who had wanted to live in more peaceful conditions, to migrate to the area – as they did to Dorayi in the last half of the nineteenth century. Each of these groups might be equated with latecomers who both com-peted with the indigenes for farming land and enjoyed a symbiotic re-lationship with them, thus cementing the territorial community. As pointed out by Y. B. Usman (Usman, 1974), the commonly expressed view that pastoralists and cultivators are in perpetual conflict is an over-simplification: in the KCSZ the farmers have a particular need for cattle manure, and the pastoralists require the highly nutritious fodder of the corn stubble.

In considering the relationship between the growth of Kano city and of the KCSZ, two hypotheses may immediately be dismissed. Given the small population of Kano city relative to that of the KCSZ in earlier times, as well as the composition of its population, we cannot regard the city as a crystallisation out from the matrix of the Zone, or the Zone as an overflow from the city – a species of water meadow.

The much admired speculative writings of H. F. C. (Abdullahi) Smith on state formation in Hausaland, dateless though they are owing to the entire lack of archaeological investigation, are relevant here. He regards the basic characteristic of the Hausa *birni* as having been the cosmopolitan nature of its community and considers these settlements as having emerged as centres of immigration from distant places rather than as a result of the natural increase of a single community (Smith, 1970, p. 341 and 1971). He insists that a scientific explanation of the foundation of the states must recognise the different types of migration which have taken place over the centuries both within Hausaland and from outside. He suggests that migration within Hausaland was 'a more important factor in the foundation of states than invasion from outside'. (Smith, 1970, p. 343.) 'Migration within Hausaland occasioned by the search for better means of livelihood, by conflict between expanding groups over the use of land, by disputes of a family nature, by any sudden development which made life intolerable in a particular place, must have been a common phenomenon over the centuries' (*ibid.*, p. 344). I now pursue the hypothesis that the KCSZ resembled the city in being a centre of immigration in its own right and that this was partly the consequence of its high population density.

Three main types of immigration into the KCSZ in, say, the last half of the nineteenth century may be distinguished: first, there was the introduction of tens, if not hundreds, of thousands of farm-slaves mainly from non-Muslim regions; second, there was an increase in the population of partially sedentarised Fulani; third, was the immigration of Hausa and non-Hausa peoples from other savannah regions, who were desirous of settling in a fertile farming zone which offered such exceptional opportunities for craftwork and trading.

The involuntary immigrants, the farm-slaves, whose descendants have since been absorbed into the free population of Kano Emirate (see Chapter XIII), were mainly purchased by private farmers whose prosperity enabled them to invest large sums in these productive workers. As for the free strangers, my suggestion that immigration was substantial is based on my fieldwork in Dorayi, on archival evidence, on P. J. Shea's thesis (1975) which emphasises the importance of immigrant textile workers and agents (who would also have been farmers), on surmise regarding the sedentarisation of pastoralists, and on sundry other sources, such as P. E. Lovejoy (see p. 15 above). As for outward migration, the likelihood is that the 'failure' to remove to less densely populated farming areas in recent decades (see Chapter IX) is nothing new.

What were the factors which accounted for the Zone's power to attract and hold its population? Considerations of defence must immediately be dismissed, for such was the vast size of the rural population that there was no possibility for most people of taking refuge in Kano city in times of war. Nor did the Emir maintain a large army which could effectively defend the rural population against raiding, as bitter experience with Ningi and Damagaram marauders showed. Adamu Fika (1973) refers to the extreme weakness of Kano's military machine. There was probably much less slave-raiding in the KCSZ than in many regions. However all this may have been, the main attractiveness of the Zone must have been its economic prosperity which was associated with the fertility of the soil, the high water table, its central position within the vast trading area of the central Sudan (which constituted a huge market for grain and other crops produced, in large part, by the farm-slaves), its flourishing textile industry, its proximity to Kano city, and with many other factors.

The notion of a vast *rural* community being attractive to immigrants from far less densely populated localities may seem so startling to demographers that it is necessary to emphasise that the KCSZ was by no means unique in this regard. The KCSZ is remarkable because of the very high population densities in its inner ring, because of its great size, because of the degree to which the population lives dispersedly (despite the high densities), and because of its (presumed) antiquity; but there were many other West African regions where farming, craftwork and trading went hand in hand – to the point that, in very general terms, this may be regarded as a significant characteristic of West African rural communities, differentiating them from communities in certain other regions of the world where traders and craftsmen tend to be distinct groups.

Moreover, there are other (smaller) high-density rural zones in Hausaland which may have been likewise attractive to immigrants. East of Katsina city, north and south of Sokoto city and to the north of Zaria city (see Mortimore, 1970) are zones which are as densely populated as the KCSZ outside its inner ring; and the demarcation of the KCSZ is somewhat arbitrary, there being high density areas northwards in Katsina and Kazaure Emirates which might be regarded as part of the same whole.

Many aspects of the general economic relationship between the city and the Kano countryside in 1900 were discussed in Chapter 1: it now remains to consider this relationship for different sectors of the KCSZ. Within a radius of some seven or (in some directions) ten miles of the city wall there were no sizeable compact settlements or market-places and no especially notable centres of textile production, though there were many weavers. The special relationship of this zone to the city derived mainly from the possibility of making the return journey by donkey, or on foot, in a single day with some time to spare. Although it supplied some grain to the city in 1900 (most of it probably grown by city residents who owned slave estates there), it was a large net importer of grain from less densely populated localities, which probably lay mainly outside the KCSZ. (It is even possible that the city, also, drew most of its supplies from outside the KCSZ.) Its inhabitants were especially favourably situated (as they still are today) to supply city dwellers with bulky produce such as fodder, cornstalk, thatches, building materials and even with water – though probably with little firewood (if trees were then as generally scarce as they are reported to have been in Dorayi), with fresh vegetables, including cassava, and with groundnut oil, which is awkward to transport. Owning many donkeys, members of the free and slave populations had good opportunities of working as transporters and minor traders in the city. Possibly the most important centre of long-distance trade (*fatauci*) lay to the east of the city, in and around the present Village Area of Kawo (some three miles from the city wall and now being encroached on by the expanding suburb of Nassarawa), where caravan-leaders (*madugai*) lived and where caravan-members from rural areas assembled; in general, however, it seems that few long-distance traders lived in the countryside within easy reach of the city.

Outside this central core the nature of the relationship was much more variable, according to the direction of trade and cattle routes, craft specialisation, accessibility and so forth – as already noted, there is (and probably was) no marked tendency for population densities to decline uniformly as the distance from the city increased. The most famous of all trade routes was, of course, the Kano to Zaria road which ran through Maidobi and Bebeji in the KCSZ (see Fig. 4); another route to Zaria lay further west, passing through Kabo and Karaye. It is possible that the principal westerly route ran through Tofa and Shanono; and the route to Katsina certainly went through Bici (Bichi).

The official maps were presumably compiled by army surveyors who moved out from Kano city and who were uninterested in routes which linked towns within the countryside: it follows that Fig. 4 gives an altogether false impression of Kano as a trade hub. Some curious data which

I collected in certain central Districts of the KCSZ possibly have a bearing
on the direction of trade routes. I learnt of the existence of fifteen market-
places which open every alternate day – not on one or more fixed days
of the seven-day Muslim week, as nearly everywhere in Hausaland. Four
of the five alternate-day markets in Dawakin Tofa District (to the west of
Kano city) lay on a straight line running west of the city to Madobi in

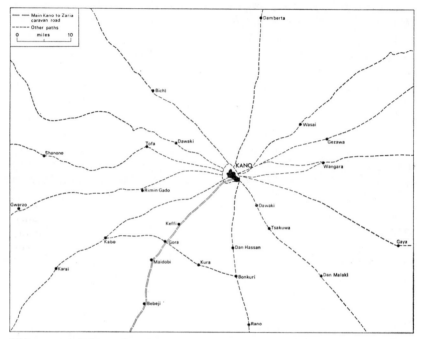

Fig. 4. A map showing the principal caravan routes and paths centering on Kano
city in 1904. (From an official map of a much wider area on the scale of 1 : 250 000
in the Cambridge University Library, ref. MAPS 470.04 62B).

the south and two other sets of three such markets lay on straight lines
running through Kura, but not from the direction of Kano – neither of
them being the Kura route shown on Fig. 4. These market schedules
are always reported to be very old, and I venture the opinion that such
frequent opening resulted from their situation on trade or cattle routes
which did not run through the city.

The KCSZ, like many other areas of dispersed settlement, is badly
served with market-places, except in a few Districts away from the centre,
such as Wudil. In Dawakin Tofa District, for instance, a population of,
say, 400 000 is served by only thirteen markets, many of them very small;

and my lists for six other central Districts (Dawakin Kudu, Gezawa, Kumbotso, Kura, Minjibir and Ungogo) suggest that the average population per market is very high by West African standards, although few of the markets are at all large. For reasons which I have discussed in Chapter 1, regular attendance at a market is by no means necessary for the ordinary householder; were this not so, many markets would be situated in the open countryside, whereas nearly all of them are in compact settlements – few of them being central places of any significance. (An interesting exception was one of the few markets to be commented on in early Assessment Reports on central Kano Districts (NAK, 4055/1912), viz, Yankatsari, some five miles north-east of Dawakin Kudu, which was set in open countryside; very large and ancient, it presumably owed its existence to its situation on trade routes.)

Perhaps, after all, there is no mystery about the persistence of dispersed settlement as population density increases, so long as the people are obliged to continue moving about mainly on donkey back and foot owing to the very poor road network in the Districts which, as I have already suggested, would amaze Governor Girouard, who presumed that the building of light district railways was already justifiable in 1909. It is evident that a very high proportion of the population of the KCSZ, especially in some Districts, lives more than, say, five miles from a lorry road. Nor has the building of important main roads, such as that from Kano to Zaria (which runs well to the east of the old caravan road), had a significant effect, so far, on the geographical distribution of the rural population – it has not even resulted in the 'clotting' of many road-side settlements of any size.

Having concluded this brief and speculative account of the recent history of the KCSZ, I now turn to examine present day socio-economic conditions in the exceedingly densely populated locality in the central ring of the Zone which I have called Dorayi, where the general way of life, apart from the absence of farm-slaves, would hardly surprise the explorer Clapperton.

APPENDIX III(1)
Variable conditions in the Kano Close Settled Zone

The very fact of denoting the densely-populated farming area around Kano city as the Kano Close Settled Zone is apt to suggest a greater degree of ecological and socio-economic uniformity than actually exists and to convey the idea that all sections of the Zone are to some extent focused on the city. As, in addition, there is a risk that conditions in Dorayi will be regarded as typical, I feel bound to remark on a few of the variables which I have found particularly striking following visits to some twenty localities, all situated within about thirty miles of the city (see also, Appendix iv (5) on Kirimbo).

Population density

In some districts there are marked local variations in population density which presumably mainly reflect variations in soil fertility, water supplies and accessibility, as well as historical factors such as the presence of settled or semi-settled Fulani communities. Very large farm plots of maybe twenty acres or more, exist in some localities; and there is great variation in the extent both of uncultivable land, some of which is too rocky, stony or marshy to be used for grazing, and of marshland (*fadama*) where dry-season crops may be grown. Large cattle herds are found in some localities, but whether these are mainly transhumant is not known; and donkeys are reared for selling in some areas. Conditions near the few large rivers, which lie south of the city, are very variable according to the possibilities of irrigated farming, to accessibility and so forth. Except after heavy rain has fallen, these rivers are usually dry on the surface, making it necessary to dig for water.

Dependence on Kano city

Communities situated more than ten miles (or so) from Kano city, especially those which are not close to a motorable road, often have very weak links with the city, either because they look mainly in other directions (such as Malumfashi, Zaria or Gumel) or because their trading links are mainly with other rural areas – as they may not have been in former times. It is probable that Zaria and Kaduna, rather than Kano city, are favoured by migrants from southern sections of the KCSZ outside the inner core. Since there is still a flourishing intra-rural trade in grain based on donkey transport, most grain-selling within the Zone may bypass the city, which is probably mainly dependent on supplies drawn from further afield.

Craftwork

While there are few male weavers or dyers in most localities, these crafts sometimes continue to flourish on a very localised basis or in some of the most renowned old centres such as Kura, which still exports much black glazed cloth to the Niger Republic. In Gezawa District over 10% of all male tax-payers were officially recorded as being weavers in 1971, of whom half lived in six of the fifty-eight Village Areas. Unfortunately, official District statistics relating to the non-farming occupations of men are much too unreliable for close comparisons to be possible, but it is clear that craft specialisation on a geographical basis affects other occupations besides weaving, e.g. mat, pannier or sieve making, leather working, tailoring and calabash decorating. (It is possible that some women weavers are found in most localities and that most potters are women – of course many localities lack suitable clay for potting.)

Long-distance trading

Enquiries show that communities varied greatly in the extent to which they were formerly engaged in long-distance trade (*fatauci*) and in the directions they followed, and it may be that, despite the changes in means of transport and wares, some of the famous old centres which are on main roads retain their pre-eminence; certainly, visits (among other places) to Kunya (some fifteen miles north of Kano city, nowadays a bustling town with which Dorayi contrasts most painfully), and to some centres in Wudil District suggested that this was so.

APPENDIX III(2)
The size of towns

The technical defects in Nigerian population censuses which make it impossible to assess the size of towns have been discussed on pp. 60–1 above. However, even though the recorded sizes of all towns (other than the very largest) are liable to have been inflated (by the inclusion of surrounding areas) in the census reports, certain figures in the *Report* on the 1921 census do at least justify a belief that most towns in Kano Province (which then included Katsina Emirate) were very small. According to that Report (Meek, 1925, Vol. ii, p. 170), the size-distribution of 304 'towns' in Kano Province of over 1000 inhabitants was as follows.

Population	Number of towns	Assumed average size	Estimated total population (000)
1–2000	244	1400	340
2–5000	56	3000	170
5–10 000	2	7000	14
10–20 000	2	14 000	28
	304		552

Note: The figures in the two right-hand columns are my own estimates.

As C. K. Meek used the terms 'enumeration area' and 'town' interchangeably, it is unlikely that all the 304 'towns' were, or even included, compact settlements, even though it was stated (*ibid.*) that Residents had been asked to make 'a return of all towns over 1000 inhabitants'. However, even if it is unrealistically assumed that the entire population of these 'towns' lived in compact settlements, their total population (on the basis of the recorded figures) would have been only 552 000 (say 600 000), as the estimates in the table suggest, compared with the recorded population of Kano Province of 3.44 million. If, in accordance with the estimates made in Appendix 1 (1), it is assumed that the population required upward adjustment of the order of 75%, the total population of Kano Province would have been some 6 million, compared with 1.0 million for the 304 'towns' which, it then has to be assumed, had populations of 1750 or more.

Most of the larger towns in the KCSZ are situated, like Bebeji, near the edge of the Zone, and it is certain that the average size of the forty walled towns within thirty miles of the city in 1904 (see p. 60 above) would have been smaller than the average 'town' in Kano Province in 1921: hence the estimate that no more than 100 000 people (at the outside) would have lived in such towns – the figure was probably very much lower.

The census figures continue to be misinterpreted to the present day. According to *Statistical Yearbook 1970* for Kano State there were twenty-five towns in Kano Emirate in 1963 with populations of 10 000 or more; it is, in fact, inconceivable that more than nine of the places named could have had populations anywhere near this size, enumeration areas having again become confused with towns.

IV

A brief introduction to Dorayi

The featureless, drab, farming area which I have arbitrarily denoted Dorayi lies in Kumbotso District some three-quarters to three miles south of the ancient wall of Kano city, just south of Bayero University College – see Fig. 3 and Appendix iv(1). It is roughly bounded to the west by the northern end of the famous old road from Kano to Zaria city (via Madobi and Bebeji), which was virtually impassable to cars in 1972, and it is bisected by the tarred road from the city to the municipal installations on the Challawa river. It was formerly crossed by several wide cattle tracks (*burtali*), the chief of which (see Fig. 5) skirted Kano city to the east, then running southward to the east of the Challawa road; once trodden by many animals these tracks are now grass-grown.

DISPERSED POPULATION

Dorayi is a typical section of the inner ring of the Kano Close Settled Zone: its population lives dispersedly on the farmland, as Fig. 5 shows, there being no nucleated settlement worthy of being denoted a hamlet. This does not, of course, mean that the individual houses are randomly scattered as though from a pepper pot, for (as Fig. 5 indicates) there are numerous small groups of houses, some densely packed, others loosely associated, and there are sizeable tracts of farmland on which no dwelling stands. The separate houses are not necessarily distinguishable on the aerial photograph which was used for mapping the farmland – see Appendix vii(1) – for a closely knit house-cluster (the largest of which consists of nine residences) might readily be mistaken for a single big house.

Various tendencies affecting the settlement pattern of this old-established area may be discerned. First, it is unusual for nearby houses within, say, a hundred yards of each other to be inhabited by non-kin (in the male line); second, when men hive off from a homestead (and, as we shall see, they usually do so as individuals not as members of kin-segments),

73

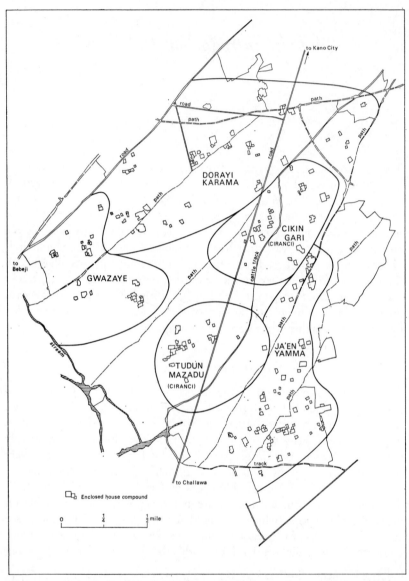

Fig. 5. A map of Dorayi showing the houses falling within each of the 5 Village or Hamlet Units; territorial boundaries are not shown as they are somewhat indeterminate. As the map was derived from an aerial photograph it was not always possible to distinguish the separate houses comprising a house-cluster.

they seldom remove more than a hundred yards (or so); third, the propensity to hive off is much lower than in less densely populated Hausa localities – hence (as will be seen) the phenomenon of the very big house; fourth, there appears to be a preference for living near to one of the main footpaths radiating out from the city. Members of the settled community found their wish for continued proximity to their kin outweighing other considerations when removing to a new site; newcomers, on the other hand, sought interstices which were large enough for the establishment of farms of several acres around their homesteads.

In newly-settled areas of dispersed residence most of the farmland cultivated by the members of any house lies around the dwelling. But as population density increases and as individual houses expand, transactions in farmland begin to occur, so that the various farm-plots owned by any individual tend to become scattered, farmland and dwelling becoming increasingly detached. In Dorayi this process has developed to the point that many houses are entirely surrounded by farmland owned by members of other farmsteads who are non-kin – one of the most evident advantages of dispersed settlement, viz. proximity to farmland, having therefore been lost; however, a considerable number of isolated homesteads in certain sections of the area are still mainly enclosed by their own farmland. There is no evidence that the residential distribution of the population on the land has tended to become increasingly uniform over time – indeed, rather the contrary owing to the growth during the past half century of many very big houses.

LACK OF 'CENTRAL PLACES'

As 'dispersed' may inappropriately convey the idea of diffusion from a source or centre, rather than approach from many directions, so the Dorayi settlement pattern is perhaps better denoted as scattered or non-coherent, especially as no significant focal centres have tended to develop over time – though some big houses effectively constitute nodes on the economic landscape (see Chapter XII). However, in the north of Ja'en Yamma there is an unimportant centre where a small number of butchers, sitting in a group, retail meat which they have bought in the city, and where a few blacksmiths finish knives and other implements while sitting in the open air; here, too, is one of the few mechanical grinding mills in Dorayi, though it was in disrepair in 1972. Neither there, nor elsewhere in Dorayi, are there any shops, although a few 'table-sellers' (*'yan tebur*) have regular positions. As most Dorayi men, other than some traders, seldom go to market except for making a special purchase, such as a donkey or a gown, the lack of any rural market-place within convenient walking distance is not seen as a hardship – and is not to be explained by the proximity of Kano city. The demand for consumer goods, including cloth, is mainly satisfied by itinerant traders, and a wide range of basic foodstuffs, including grains and groundnuts, may be bought from local farmers and produce traders at their houses. Few men attend a Friday mosque in Kano, for numerous house-rooms, where prayers may be led by local imams, are made available as small mosques.

THE VILLAGE AND HAMLET AREAS

The right to cultivate, or acquire, farmland is unrelated to the particular Hamlet or Village Area in which a man resides, and the boundaries of these Areas (especially the Hamlet Areas) are somewhat indeterminate: as one farmer put it, it is the general directions of the boundaries, rather than their actual positions on the farmland, which are known. There is, therefore, no formal sense in which population can be properly related to farmland. However (see Fig. 5), the various houses comprising the different Hamlets or Villages are situated in distinct localities which are not interlaced, so that no arbitrariness attaches to the demarcation of residential communities as distinct from their farmland. For the purposes of this work the population of Dorayi was defined as comprising the residents of five contiguous Village or Hamlet Areas (see below). In order to relate this population to a particular area of farmland the only practicable procedure was to map all the farmland within an unnecessarily large surrounding area and to pare off the edges of the map where most of the farms proved to be cultivated by non-Dorayi farmers: this is why our map of the Dorayi farmland (Fig. 6) has frayed edges, corresponding to the boundaries of individual plots. As farmers sometimes cultivate land several miles from their houses, so it was necessary to face the fact that some of the mapped farmland is cultivated by non-Dorayi farmers.

some Dorayi farmers owned land outside the mapped area – and that

South of Kano city the Village Areas stretch outwards in a curious longitudinal way, perhaps because the colonial officials who originally had a hand in creating or reorganising them moved out radially on horseback. Since it seemed preferable to study the population of a solid block of land rather than of a long strip, Dorayi was defined (see Fig. 5) as including the residents of one entire Village Unit (Dorayi Karama) together with four Hamlets – Ja'en Yamma (a Hamlet in Ja'en Village), Cikin Gari and Tudun Mazadu (both Hamlets in Ciranci Village), and Cikin Gari (a Hamlet in Gwazaye Village, which is denoted as Gwazaye on Fig. 5). The Hamlet in which the Village Head (*dagaci*) resides is commonly, though not invariably, known as Cikin Gari; it is the centre of habitation because the Village Head lives there, not for any spatial reason – see Appendix 1(2). It is indicative of the lack of interest in Village boundaries that the most up to date official map of Kumbotso District, which was revised in 1966, should fail to record the existence of Ciranci Village although it had been carved out of Ja'en some forty years ago.

The Dorayi population, according to our house-to-house enumeration, was 3499 – see Appendix iv(2). Relating this figure to a mapped area of some 1660 acres (Fig. 6), the population density is about 1400 per square mile (540 per square kilometre). That this figure is considerably higher than any hitherto recorded in the KCSZ is due both to the fact that Dorayi is a very small area situated close to Kano city where densities are highest, and to our ability (unlike that of official enumerators) to repeat our population counts – which yielded successively higher figures before they finally stabilised!

Of course it would have been interesting to have related the Dorayi population to the area of land it actually cultivated, but the farms outside the mapped area were far too scattered for this to be practicable; indeed, many of them lay outside the area covered by the aerial photograph we used for mapping. However an adjustment was made for farmland cultivated by men resident in Kano city: it was found that they owned about 161 acres, some half of which was the property of Dorayi men who had migrated to the city retaining their land. If this area is deducted then the population density is about 1500 per square mile (580 per square kilometre). Some 162 acres of the mapped farmland was cultivated by non-Dorayi people living in neighbouring Hamlets, but as we do not know whether this area was smaller or larger than that cultivated by Dorayi people outside the mapped zone, no further adjustment to our figures was possible.

The likelihood that immigration, including the arrival of farm-slaves, substantially increased the population of the KCSZ in the nineteenth century has been generally discussed in Chapter iii. As for Dorayi, scanty oral evidence, which includes information relating to the founders of certain houses, suggests that the population in the mid-nineteenth century was far lower than today. Mahamman Lawal, the Hamlet Head of Cikin Gari (Ciranci), said that when his paternal grandfather migrated to Dorayi from Jahun, in Eastern Kano, there were few houses there and none at all in Kwari Hamlet (Ciranci) which lies further south. Nowadays Dorayi farmers own no herds of cattle, but in the latter half of the nineteenth century many beasts were owned by resident Fulani who came from

Fig. 6. A map of the Dorayi farmland showing farm boundaries, roads, main paths, houses and house-clusters. The Emir's large farm (see p. 214) consists of the six rectangular portions, together with surrounding farmland, to the north-west. It having been impossible to map some of the smallest farms around the houses these are included in the house areas, a few of which are therefore larger than those shown in Fig. 5.

Jahun, from Shanono (in Gwarzo District) and from elsewhere. A fair number of present-day houses which are near to the city in northern Dorayi Karama were founded by twentieth-century strangers when restrictions on building houses close to the city wall were relaxed.

It was reported that in 1900 there had been little uncultivated land at Dorayi. Then, as today, most farms were manured and cultivated every year, large quantities of organic manure being fetched from Kano city by free men and slaves to supplement local supplies, which included latrine manure (*takin masai*) (see *R. H.*, p. 289). The community was already dependent on grain 'imported' by local traders from southern Kano and Katsina.

Perhaps the population density in 1900 was lower than today, but this is uncertain for (see Chapter XIII) a considerable proportion of the population then consisted of farm-slaves (and their dependants), many of whose descendants subsequently migrated. It is indeed a sad reflection on our ignorance that we should find significance in Mahamman Lawal's remark that 'everything was more in former times, including the rain, sheep and goats and donkeys'. (But, as he added, the water table has risen, and a virtually treeless landscape has been transformed into 'farmed parkland' by the planting of useful trees – see Pullan (1974) for some excellent aerial photographs of such parklands.)

Fortunately we are on somewhat firmer ground when considering population changes in Dorayi during the past forty years, when it may be – see Appendix IV(3) – that the average annual growth rate (based on estimated rates for Kumbotso District and for Ja'en Village Area) has been something of the order of $\frac{1}{2}$% to 1% – an estimate which is so tentative that it should really be regarded as no more than a conviction that the population has neither remained stable, nor declined, nor grown as fast as, say, 2%. Throughout my discussion of the consequences of high population density, I shall at least feel justified in referring to the 'persistent and intensifying pressure of population on the land'.

It might be expected that, in recent years, mortality rates would be lower in Dorayi than in the KCSZ generally owing to the possibilities of having medical treatment in the nearby city. But despite the lack of a nearby rural clinic, very few Dorayi people ever attend hospitals or clinics in the city and, as in Batagarawa, hardly anyone receives modern medical treatment during their terminal illness. In 1971 cholera struck heavily in Dorayi, leading to a fair number of deaths – which, since no one was hospitalised, went unrecorded in the official statistics, though an injection team was aware of the outbreak and toured the area. The attitude to death is most fatalistic and not only in relation to infants: a stranger who is in touch with the community for a year is much struck by the large number of sudden deaths which occur among younger adults, as in Western Europe in the nineteenth century.

Nowadays most Dorayi people regard themselves as Kano Hausa (Kanawa), and it is only in special circumstances that Fulani or Kanuri descent (for example) is mentioned; this applies as much to those of slave as of free origin, for although many of the former were descended from non-Hausa slaves, they have become thoroughly integrated into the community over the generations (see Chapter xiii).

The sociological detachment of Dorayi from the city is very marked: those who doubt this statement should note that only 3% of a large sample of 324 Dorayi wives were of city origin – 60% of the sample having been born in Dorayi, 30% in neighbouring Hamlets within a radius of some five miles. While Dorayi is certainly a peculiar type of farming area, it is not a suburb. Hardly any men ever remove from the city to live in the countryside, the population being entirely of country stock. While (see Chapter ix) about a hundred Dorayi men are known to have migrated to Kano city in the past few decades, none of them ever returns home to live and their daughters seldom marry Dorayi men.

THE VILLAGE AND HAMLET HEADS

The District Head of Kumbotso is not well known in Dorayi, and has little influence on events there. Consistent with the historical findings reported in Chapter ii, the four Village Heads (*dagatai*) who reside in Dorayi are unimportant people, in terms of status, wealth, charisma, power and the position of their sons – very nearly all of whom, like they themselves, have had no modern schooling. The unimportance of the office itself, in a society where status and age are so closely related, is shown by the fact that none of them had attained middle age when first appointed, older men having apparently been uninterested in seeking office – because, for instance, it might have interfered with their work as produce buyers. (I find their youthfulness at appointment typical of dispersed communities in the KCSZ, where I have even met *dagatai* who had not yet married.) While there is no rule that a *dagaci* should be succeeded by a son or other kinsman (in former times in Dorayi the office often passed to brothers and sometimes to non-kin), it happens that each of the present office-holders had succeeded his father – in one case the father had been a servant who had succeeded his former master. Unimportant though the office is, there is yet a fair amount of competition for it among younger men, and two of the present four *dagatai* had been obliged to sell most of their farmland to meet the expenses of the contest: they are, therefore, virtually landless, for there are, of course, no farms attached to the office. Nowadays in Dorayi (though not, I think, so much formerly) the chief benefit of office, apart from the small official salary, derives (see Chapter VII) from commissions on the sale of farmland. The unattractiveness of office is enhanced by the frequency of dismissal: there are three dismissed *dagatai* in Dorayi, each known by the title Murabus.

The *dagatai* in Dorayi and neighbouring localities are not necessarily on good terms with their subordinates the Hamlet Heads (*masu unguwoyi*), who may be much closer to the people. In 1972 there were only four Hamlet Heads in Dorayi – there having been none in Dorayi Karama or in Cikin Gari (Gwazaye); and by January 1976 no successor had been appointed to fill the vacancy caused by the death of Mai Unguwa Cikin Gari (Ciranci) more than a year earlier. The unimportance of the office, as such, is shown by the frequency with which it lapses if no obviously suitable candidate spontaneously emerges. In 1972 all the Hamlet Heads were ordinary working farmers, one of whom, an elderly impoverished man, did not hesitate to demean himself by working, at times, as a farm-labourer.

CROPS

As in rural Hausaland generally, the main crops in Dorayi are basic grains – bulrush millet (*gero*) and guinea corn (*dawa*) – which are grown both for household consumption and for sale, the guinea corn stalk (*kara*) having a high value. While the production of groundnuts was considerable in 1971, it has since declined; no part of the crop was then sold to licensed buying agents of the Marketing Board for export overseas, the farmers having found it more profitable to sell the nuts to Dorayi women for processing into groundnut oil (*man gyada*) and cake (*kulikuli*), which is sold locally or in Kano city – where it is headloaded, chiefly by girls, who are often forestalled *en route*. Two other important crops are henna, which – see Appendix IV(4) – is marketed in Kano city and much further afield, and onions (see pp. 101 *et seq.*), which are grown on irrigated plots in Tudun Mazadu and Gwazaye only. No sweet potatoes (*dankali*), yams, rice, cotton or tobacco are grown, and cowpeas (*wake*) are less important than in some Hausa areas. The principal subsidiary crops include: cassava (*rogo*), grown on numerous small, fenced or hedged plots; tree-crops, of which the most important are locust beans (*kalwa*) and mangoes – there are very few baobab trees (*kuka*), not many kapok trees (*rimi*), and no shea butter trees (*kadanya*); thatching grass (*cibci*), which is sometimes grown as a sole crop on small farms; hemp (*rama*), for making rope; sugar cane, grown in damp places and sold for chewing; firewood, rightly considered a 'crop' since trees are deliberately grown for felling; and various small vegetables, such as tomatoes and pepper. Most of these subsidiary crops are grown almost entirely for selling, either in Dorayi or elsewhere, though some better-off households consume their own cassava.

Like all communities in the inner core of the KCSZ, Dorayi is far from being self-sufficient in grain which is brought into the area by local grain traders, who obtain large supplies from Rimin Gado market some fifteen miles to the west (it may be approached either by donkey or by lorry), some of them also travelling much further afield: other basic produce, such as rice, is also 'imported'.

CROP STORAGE

In Batagarawa we counted as many as 571 clay and cornstalk granaries used for storing unthreshed grain and other produce, but in Dorayi, with a population about three times as large – see Appendix v(1) – the number was very much smaller, most of them being small ramshackle structures made of cornstalk. In Dorayi much grain is stored during the long dry season on the open farmland, often some distance from the homestead, merely covered by long cornstalks which form a conical shape known as a *ƙiriga*. (If one ascends Goron Dutse hill, just inside the western wall of Kano city, around the turn of the year, hundreds of these cones are seen embellishing the hedged farmscape below.) Unthreshed groundnuts, also, may be piled in the open air for some months after harvest. Among other reasons for the relative lack of granaries are: the lack of space within the house walls; the small number of specialist builders in mud – in Dorayi, unlike Batagarawa, most men build and repair their own mud houses; the practice of storing threshed grain in sheds or rooms; and finally the relative poverty of Dorayi which means, as will be seen, that there are fewer rich men who store large quantities of unthreshed grain for a price rise, and that a great proportion of the population is dependent throughout most of the year on buying threshed grain.

LIVESTOCK

As already noted, there are no longer any resident herds of cattle owned by Dorayi men and no transhumant Fulani herds traverse the fields. Nor are there any ploughs or plough-oxen. However, donkeys are of even greater importance as beasts of burden than in Batagarawa, owing to their use for fetching manure from Kano city and for transporting many types of ware there for sale. A rough count suggests that there were about 500 donkeys in Dorayi, or about two for every three married men – all of them being males which had been bought mainly at markets. As for sheep and goats, every household aspires to own some of these animals, which are usually reared for selling to traders and others, and which are a valuable source of manure; forage presents a serious problem during the farming season when the animals have to be kept inside house compounds, and there are no large herds as in former times. Fowls are kept at many houses, and there are also some guinea fowl and ducks – most birds and their eggs are probably sold outside Dorayi.

FARMLAND

In Dorayi, as elsewhere in rural Hausaland, the farmland (see Fig. 6) is owned by individual farmers, many of whom own more than one plot (*gona*). Land-holding lineages being lacking and the sense of territoriality being weak, individual farmers are free, as they have been for generations, to sell their farmland outright to whomever they wish. For reasons which will be discussed in later chapters, the average size of plot is diminishing fast over time and there are many diminutive plots of a tenth of an acre or less, especially around homesteads. The distribution of farmland between men (who effectively control most of the farmland) is most unequal (see Chapter VI): about 2% of all men cultivate ten acres or more, and (if married sons are excluded) about one man in eight is virtually landless.

DOMESTIC AND FARMING ORGANISATION

Houses vary greatly in size (see Chapter XII). About a third of them are inhabited by one married man and his dependants, and about three-quarters by no more than four married men; but over a third of the population lives in twenty-four big houses, inhabited by seven or more married men, most of them related in the male line. The existence of such large Muslim (as distinct from pagan Maguzawa) houses has not hitherto been recorded in rural Hausaland. The larger houses are divided into separate residential sections; sons-in-*gandu*, and their dependants usually reside in the same section as their father.

The Hausa institution of paternal *gandu*, under which married sons work in a subordinate capacity on their father's farms in return for a share of the produce and/or general economic support, has been fully described by myself and others (see *R. H.*, Chapter III). For a variety of reasons, which are discussed in Chapter VIII below, sons-in-*gandu* in Dorayi enjoy much less economic freedom than in rural Hausaland generally. Few married sons formally leave *gandu* or migrate, and the abnormally close economic relationship between fathers and sons usually persists throughout the father's lifetime.

MUSLIM SECLUSION AND THE POSITION OF WOMEN

Insofar as the strict control exerted by fathers over married sons is seen as a function of the rigours of poverty, so it is tempting to regard the unusual severity of Muslim wife-seclusion in Dorayi, which has developed quite recently, as part of the same anxiety syndrome. In 1972 no girls (and very few boys) attended the nearest Primary School, which lay just off the northern boundary of Dorayi, and the age at which girls were 'married off' by their eager fathers, and other male kin, had recently fallen fast. Little pre-nubile girls of nine and ten were being thrust into full purdah (*kulle* – lit. locked), never to be allowed outside their husband's compounds during the day except (with permission) on special occasions or, at planned intervals, to visit their parental home. Older wives, too, usually remained secluded, to the point that any sixty-year-old seen walking towards Kano city was almost certain to be husbandless.

In rural Hausaland generally this terrible restriction on individual liberty, which (see *R. H.*, p. 279) is non-traditional and possibly unique in the rural Muslim world, is partly intended as a demonstration that rural people are as socially sophisticated as city-dwellers: it is a demonstration which fails, the strictness of rural seclusion not being generally appreciated, particularly by the educated elite who are apt (somewhat indignantly) to deny its existence. On another level, it is the fear of being taunted by other men if their wives are *seen* outside their houses in daylight that makes all husbands conform. (Much divorce is instigated by women, and there is no evidence that the divorce rate, which is very high in Dorayi, is much affected by seclusion.) Until quite recently only the wives of the more notable malams were in strict purdah, and the reasons for the development of universal seclusion in most rural communities during the past few decades are unclear, though were it not for the high water table (which permits the building of many wells in house compounds) and the ubiquity of the donkey, it would not be possible for men, at no inconvenience to themselves, to excuse women from performing their traditional functions as beasts of burden. Nor is it known why there are a few communities in the KCSZ (one of them being Dambare, some two or three miles west of Dorayi) where women are allowed to move about freely (though they do not cultivate the land or go to market), their marriage system being known as *auren fita* (lit. 'marriage of going out'): these are certainly Muslim, not pagan Maguzawa, communities.

While the Dorayi community as a whole suffers from a surfeit of male labour in relation to land, the poverty of some households is much ex-acerbated by the refusal of husbands to permit their wives to farm. How-ever, in Dorayi, as elsewhere in rural Hausaland (see Hill, 1969), most secluded wives have gainful occupations, which they pursue entirely in-dependently of their husbands – the most lucrative and common of which are the making, for sale, of groundnut oil and cake and of locust bean cakes (*daddawa*). But Dorayi wives have less scope for their enterprise as house-traders than Batagarawa women, this being partly a consequence of dispersed residence – see Appendix xi(3).

THE NON-FARMING OCCUPATIONS OF MEN

The types of non-farming occupations pursued by men are examined in Chapter vi and elsewhere. Suffice it here to note that there is a great degree of under-utilization of labour and that an unusually high pro-portion of men are not regularly occupied as skilled craftsmen or traders, but derive most of their income from casual work, such as labouring, transportation or the making of crude cornstalk beds – see Appendix xi (2) – for sale in the city. Only a small range of occupations is open to poor men, nearly all of whom lack the finance to engage in trade, which is the main occupation of Dorayi men, other than those wage earners who work at all regularly in the city.

Only about 17% of all Dorayi men (exclusive of sons-in-*gandu*) gain part of their livelihood in the city – and most of them live in northern Dorayi close to the city wall. The main industrial estates lie some distance away to the east of the city and hardly any Dorayi men have succeeded in getting factory jobs. Enquiries I made in Kawo Village Area, a farming area close to the estates, showed that nearly a half of all married men there had regular work in the city, a third of them being in factories; in great contrast to Dorayi, in as many as four-fifths of all Kawo houses there was at least one man who worked in the city. Only about 7% of all Dorayi men work for regular wages in the city or at nearby Bayero University College: most of them are young men (known as 'labourers' in Dorayi) who work as gardeners, watchmen and porters – their wages are low and their positions insecure. Apart from this work, which is so hard to find, there are few openings for impoverished Dorayi men in Kano city: by and large, only better-off men benefit substantially from living so close to the metropolis.

AMENITIES AND POSSESSIONS

In 1972 there were no public amenities of any kind in Dorayi or in the surrounding countryside: there was no clinic, no pumping windmill, only two cemented wells (most households being dependent on wells which they had dug for themselves), no market-place or slaughter slabs, no other assembly place and no publicly owned mosque. There was indeed little justification for the levying of the community tax (*haraji*), which in 1971 varied arbitrarily between about £2 and £3 7s per tax payer (no account being taken of wealth), the equivalent of about 10s per head of the population. (Since that date the general rate of community tax in Kano State has been roughly halved.)

Farm tools, which are all made by local blacksmiths, are of simple, traditional design, and there are no oxen-drawn ploughs or carts, or modern storage facilities, and very few (hand-operated) mechanical groundnut decorticators. Apart from the general use of enamelware bowls and plates, the food processing and cooking equipment used by women is little changed since 1900 (or indeed much earlier), being based on pestles and mortars, grindstones, pots and open fires on the ground. Other property, apart from clothing, and wives' personal possessions, has little value, there being, for example, few radios and mosquito nets. But at least there have been two great changes for the better: people (especially men) own far more good quality gowns than formerly, and many younger men acquire bicycles for riding to Kano city.

'EXPORTS' AND 'IMPORTS'

Considered as though it were an 'island community', Dorayi is obliged to export goods and services to pay for nearly all the goods (including manure, grain, rice, meat, sugar, sour milk, clothing, sandals, donkeys, bicycles, salt and other condiments, kola-nuts, cigarettes, matches, soap, kerosene, lamps, cooking-pots and sundry personal items) which she is obliged to import from the wider world – for remittances from relatives are small. Her main exports include farm produce (onions, henna, cassava, vegetables, thatching grass, sugar cane, etc.), small livestock (sheep and goats), fowls and their eggs, tree crops (including mangoes) and firewood, fodder, foods processed by women (mainly groundnut oil and cake, and *daddawa*), craft goods made either by men (cornstalk beds, blacksmiths' wares, etc.) or by women (mats, panniers, etc.); 'invisible exports', which are not substantial, include wages from farm-labouring outside Dorayi, wage-earning employment and trading in Kano city, and transportation of earth, etc. by donkey. So in order that she may survive, Dorayi is obliged to export many wares, including groundnut oil and cake, small livestock, fowls and eggs, and cassava, of which there is a dire deficiency in the community.

APPENDIX IV(1)
Historical notes on Kumbotso District

As early as 1903, according to the Ungogo District Notebook, there was created a Home District around Kano city, consisting of Ungogo and Kumbotso which separated in 1905. In 1908, as part of the radical reorganisation of Districts carried out by Resident Cargill (see p. 36 above), Kumbotso was created a Sub-District, known as Dan Isa, being one of the ten Sub-Districts comprising the Home District of Chiroma (see Fig. 1). According to the Kumbotso District Notebook and to oral information, the first Sub-District Head was Dan Isa Mamman Mai Ruwa, a kinsman of the Emir, who was dismissed for corruption after two years. In 1916 there was a further reorganisation and Kumbotso became one of twenty-four Kano Districts. Between 1908 and the present time the District has had as many as twelve rulers, of whom nearly half were deposed for malpractices, most of the remainder having been promoted to more important Districts.

Not only was the small District (it had an area of some eighty-four square miles) a purely artificial creation, but its capital town, Kumbotso, was very small, maybe having a population of less than a thousand in 1903 – in 1952 it was recorded as only 1245. The only other old towns in the District were Hotoro and Mariri, on the north-eastern periphery, and they, also, were very small; needless to say, they had previously owed no allegiance to Kumbotso, as (presumably) had none of the rural *dagatai* much nearer to that town.

Although the main Kano-to-Zaria road ran through the District near its western boundary, crossing the Challawa River at a place called Challawa where there was formerly a ferry, very little has been recorded of the history of the District, partly because, like Ungogo District, it lay too close to Kano to be included in any District Officer's touring area, so that it was 'seldom visited except on evening drives' (J. Smith, 1968, p. 30).

In 1911, according to an uninformative *Assessment Report* (this was included in a Despatch of 18 July 1911, PRO, CO 446, 105), the tax revenue of the Sub-District amounted to £1260 made up of the farm tax (*taki*) at 1s per acre, which yielded £940, and of the compound tax at 1s 6d per compound – with a yield of £320, this corresponded to 4270 compounds. On the one hand it was reported that all farmland was manured and kept under permanent cultivation, on the other hand that no more than two-fifths of the total area was under cultivation – a scarcely credible figure (see below). The population was recorded as 27 760, a figure which should be disregarded, if only because it explicitly excluded 'the floating element': while this may have been the slave population (see p. 201 below), its definition ought strictly to have presented much difficulty considering that all children born since 1903 were legally free.

In 1920 the farm tax (*taki*) was raised to 3s per acre. On the basis of this rate the tax yield was £8223 in 1926-7, a sum which implied that some 95% of the total area was cultivated farmland — maybe the discrepancy between this and the 1911 figure was partly explicable in terms of the acquisition of land by freed slaves. In 1932 the area under cultivation was recorded as 93% of the total. If – see Appendix IV(3) – the population was about 60 000 at that time, this would have corresponded to about one acre per head of the population and to about four acres per working man.

The foregoing figures derive from an unusually informative Re-assessment Report on Kumbotso District (1932) by S. A. S. Leslie (NAK, Kano Prof 5/24, No. 764). In 1931–2 the farm tax raised £7292, and the *kudin sana'a* (or 'industrial tax' on non-farming incomes) yielded £636 – a total incidence per tax-payer of about 12s 9d. The author referred (see p. 215 below) to certain large tracts of land (some of them in Dorayi) which were lying vacant, having formerly been cultivated by slave labour, and commented that the owners had much difficulty in raising the farm tax.

The erection of the Power Station serving Kano city on the Challawa River in 1931 led to the building of a modern road through the District. This was, according to Leslie, 'the first event for a hundred years to enliven the annals of a District described in 1911 as "being fortunate in having no history" '!

Among other statistics presented in Leslie's report were the following: Manure was available in the city at 1d per donkey load. The number of compounds was 5464. The areas devoted to the principal crops were estimated as: guinea corn (*dawa*) 46%, groundnuts 20%, millet (*gero*) 13%, cassava (*rogo*) 5% and *maiwa* (a type of millet which does not respond to manure) 5%, sweet potatoes (*dankali*) 3%. (No mention was made of cotton which was reported as having been grown throughout the area in 1911.) Some twelve to twenty bundles of thatching grass per acre (worth some 1s to 2s) were obtained from fallow land. There were five markets in the District, all of them very small. Of the total of 565 dye-pits, as many as 460 were at Unguwar Rimi to the extreme south-east. There were recorded as being 1095 weavers, 277 'corn traders' ('*yan kwarami*), 245 tailors and 237 dyers. The average size of farm-plots was 1.9 acres for the whole District, being as high as 2.7 acres for Ja'en Village Area, which then included Ciranci.

The author was impressed by the scale of dry-season farming, both on non-irrigated *rafi*, which produced valuable crops of wheat and sweet potatoes, and on irrigated farms along certain streams to the east of the District and along the Challawa River, where onions, wheat and pepper were grown.

In 1932 there were thirty-four Village Areas compared with forty-four in 1971. The first primary school was opened in about 1932 in Kumbotso town. (In 1971 there were ten primary schools in the District, three of them with one class only.)

APPENDIX IV(2)
The Dorayi population

Notes on Table IV.1

A house-to-house enumeration was carried out several times by my assistant, M. Musa, successive counts having always yielded higher figures. I also checked many of the figures myself with the aid of third-party informants in an effort

Table IV.I   The Dorayi population

	Married men (1)	Wives (2)	Other women (3)	Children (4)	Unmarried youths and men (5)	Total M	Total F	Total T
				Numbers				
Ciranci: Cikin Gari	98	131	19	206	40	254	240	494
Tudun Mazadu	67	101	10	134	32	168	176	344
Gwazaye: Cikin Gari	85	111	23	158	40	205	212	417
Dorayi Karama	218	265	41	383	84	497*	494*	991
Ja'en Yamma	249	320	57	475	152	637	616	1253
Total	717	928	150	1356	348	1761	1738	3499
				Percentages				
Ciranci: Cikin Gari	20	26	4	42	8			100
Tudun Mazadu	19	29	3	39	9			100
Gwazaye: Cikin Gari	20	27	6	38	10			100
Dorayi Karama	22	27	4	29	8			100
Ja'en Yamma	20	25	5	38	12			100
Total	20	27	4	39	10			100

* Adjusted figure (see Notes)

to improve the accuracy of those relating to 'other women' (see below), children and unmarried youths and men. It is to be noted that the tax lists were found to be reasonably reliable so far as concerned male tax-payers and their wives, but quite useless for all other categories. In all areas except Dorayi Karama, the sexes were reasonably balanced; but as it appears that far too high a proportion of children in that locality were reported as being boys (perhaps some of them ought to have been classified as unmarried men), the totals of males and females in that area have been adjusted to correspond with those elsewhere. Otherwise the consistency of the various percentages relating to the five areas suggests a reasonable degree of accuracy. The experience of undertaking this work has made me more than ever convinced that, especially in localities like Dorayi where many people live in big houses, official house-to-house enumerations for census purposes are apt to involve serious under-counting – though the 'cooking' that may occur at later stages is another matter – see Appendix 1 (1).

Column (1). 'Married men' are those who have ever been married, whether or not they were married when enumerated. Considerable difficulty was experienced in enumerating all the men excused tax on grounds of age, illness, deafness (which is very common) or other disability.

Column (2). A 'wife' is defined as a woman married to a man in the house where she is living. (The wives of elderly, ill or disabled men who are excused tax tend, like widows, to be excluded from population figures based on tax records.)

Column (3). 'Other women' are women who have formerly been married, but who are not now married to anyone living in the same house. Very great difficulty was experienced in persuading household heads, and other informants, to include all these women, the numbers of whom constantly increased as our work progressed, and it is to be presumed that most of them are omitted from official censuses. But our final figures are possibly reasonably correct, for they show that the ratio of such dependent relatives to married men was one to five – a very high proportion considering the large numbers of sets of brothers with the same mother. Of the total of 150 such women as many as 113 were reported to be widowed mothers of married men, and ten were widowed sisters – one woman was described as a 'retired wife', as she was living with her son in the same house as her divorced husband.

Column (4). 'Children' were defined as including all unmarried girls and all boys under the age of about fourteen to sixteen – but see notes on Column (5). Only about 8% of all children were recorded as having fathers not living in the house; considering that a wife's child by a former husband (*agola*) is included in this category, the proportion seems to be too low.

Column (5). Very great difficulty was experienced (in other localities, as well as in Dorayi) in counting the unmarried (or 'never married') young men, most of whom were found to have been omitted in earlier stages of the work. Whether Dorayi informants' reluctance to admit the existence of such young men is partly due to the fact that they are not taxed in Kumbotso District I still cannot say, but another explanation may be the fact that they usually have no proper sleeping place, so that insofar as a householder attempts to count those in each sleeping hut, in order to arrive at a total, they will tend to be omitted. It was, therefore, gratifying to find that the percentage of the total population in each of the five areas that fell into this category varied only between 8% and 12%. In discussion, these young men or youths were denoted *samari* (sing. *saurayi*), a vague term as the following definition drawn from Bargery's dictionary shows: 'A *youth*, strictly one between about 15 and 25 years of age, i.e. unmarried and beardless. But it is loosely applied especially as a term of address to any one considerably younger than oneself between 12 and 40 years of age.' In Batagarawa the definitions 'ex school-boy' or 'old enough to have left school' could be utilised, as was not possible in Dorayi, where we sometimes used the definition 'old enough to work regularly on the farm'. However, given the extreme youthfulness of many girls on first marriage, and the small excess of boys over girls according to our figures, it seems that some boys aged twelve, or even less, were regarded as *samari* by our informants, although it is doubtful whether they do much farming. (The age of first marriage of youths, like that of girls (see p. 84 above), appears to have fallen recently, but there is still sufficient discrepancy to sustain a high incidence of polygyny, which is not made possible by any unbalance of the sexes.)

APPENDIX IV(3)
Estimated population growth in Kumbotso District and Dorayi,
1932–72

S. A. S. Leslie, author of the 1932 Re-assessment Report on Kumbotso District – see Appendix IV(1) – enumerated the population of the District, with the following result:

Table IV.2   *The population of Kumbotso District*

	Leslie's 1932 count		Official 1931 count based on tax returns	
	(000)			
Adult males	12.9		12.5	
Adult females	15.6		11.9	
Children	19.1	39%	9.1	27%
Sick and infirm	1.6		0.5	
	49.2	100%	34.0	100%

On the realistic assumption that the 1932 enumeration was not an overcount, then the official 1931 figure needs stepping up by about 45%, mainly because of the omission of large numbers of children and some women.

But was the 1932 figure itself an undercount? According to our own count in 1972 – see Appendix IV(2) – children accounted for about 39% of the Dorayi population and unmarried youths and men for about 10% – a total of about 49%. Assuming that the term 'adult males' related in both counts to married men only (a realistic assumption since unmarried men were not subject to taxation in this District, and the 1931 figure, which is very close to that of 1932, presumably related to taxpayers only, as do the official figures based on tax returns today), then unmarried youths and men had been omitted from the 1932 count. As, in addition, it is hard to believe that the 1932 count was an exception to the rule that 'all counting is undercounting' (the enumeration could scarcely have been checked in the short time in which the survey was undertaken), I suggest the correct figure for 1932 could scarcely have been less than 60 000, which would mean that the upward adjustment which has to be made to the 1931 figure was of the order of 75% – as has been assumed for Kano Emirate generally, see Appendix 1(1).

If our own enumeration is reliable then the official figures for Cikin Gari (Ciranci) and Tudun Mazadu which were based on the 1971 tax returns require stepping up by some 30%. Applying this percentage to the whole of Kumbotso District the official figure of 62 335 is raised to about 81 000. On the basis of these extremely rough estimates, the population of Kumbotso District rose by about 35%, from 60 000 to 81 000, in thirty-nine years (1932 to 1971) – an average of roughly 1% a year.

According to the 1932 count the population of Ja'en Village Area (which then included Ciranci) was 2449 – the figure recorded in the 1931 census having been 1736. If the 1932 figure is raised by the same proportion as that for Kumbotso District, the amended figure is 3000. In 1971 the official figure for that same area (assuming the boundaries had been unchanged) was 2876. If it is assumed that this figure should be raised by 30% – as for Cikin Gari (Ciranci) and Tudun Mazadu – then the correct figure was of the order of 3800, which represents an increase of about 27% since 1932, i.e. an annual rate of increase of between ½% and 1%.

APPENDIX IV(4)
Henna

There are many miles of henna (*lalle*) hedges, serving as farm-boundaries, in Dorayi, the leaves from which provide both men and women with a useful income. This shrub (*Lawsonia inermis* or Egyptian privet) is readily propagated by cuttings and lives for many years. The leaves are pounded and made into a paste which is applied as a reddening cosmetic to women's nails and other parts of the body, both in everyday life and in marriage and childbirth rituals. As the shrub is planted only in certain regions of northern Nigeria, there is a flourishing long-distance trade, in which Dorayi traders participate to a small extent.

Henna leaves may be stored (either on the stalk or plucked) in rooms, sacks or granaries throughout the dry season, but not for long during the rains when the price is apt to rise steeply – from say 4s to 5s per sack (of leaves) to

12s. Local men and traders from the city, and elsewhere, occasionally buy the leaves on the bush; more often they buy plucked, dried leaves (*ganye* or *samfera*), frequently arranging for the leaves to be pounded by Dorayi women. Some three to four sacks of leaves convert into one sack of powder (*garin lalle*), which varies in price from, say, £1 to £2 5s. Women receive between 6d and 8d for pounding a sack of leaves: by pounding three bags in her spare time, or in the evening, or five bags during the day, a woman may earn from 1s 6d to 3s 4d in a day.

Many Dorayi men and women store the leaves for a price rise; others, who are in immediate need of money, sell immediately after plucking and drying, which takes about three days. Some people employ labourers to pluck a certain length of hedge for an agreed sum. The shrub may be pledged, the creditor being entitled to pluck the leaves until the debt is repaid. A farm may be sold without the henna boundary, the value of a bush averaging about 3s 6d. Although it is admitted that the yield from a henna farm would be much greater than that from the same area of groundnuts, there are no pure stands of henna in Dorayi (as there are in some Hausa districts), for farmers do not like to commit themselves to the long term cultivation of this perennial crop. During the growing season when the fresh green bushes bear small flowers, which perfume the air, henna is a delight to the senses, as well as being one of the most useful boundary plants known to man. As bushes are seldom unnecessarily uprooted and as adjoining farms are sometimes consolidated, false boundaries occasionally confuse the research worker – a minor drawback considering that without the henna it would have been altogether impossible to have mapped the farms with the aid of an aerial photograph, *gamba* grass boundaries (such as existed at Batagarawa) being generally lacking around Kano city.

APPENDIX IV(5)
Kirimbo

For comparative purposes, I made some intensive enquiries in Kirimbo Village Area (an area of dispersed settlement comprising three Hamlets, Gasau, Gafiyawa, Kirimbo) which lies some five miles south of Dorayi, on the north bank of the river Challawa and to the west of Kumbotso town; it lay astride the old route from Kano city to Kura, the renowned centre of cloth production.

Scenically, parts of Kirimbo present a remarkable contrast to Dorayi, the farmed parkland of Gasau Hamlet, with its many large trees, being exceptionally attractive and tranquil and there being wide infertile tracts near the river. On the basis of my count of married men (who totalled 242), I think that the Kirimbo population density may be of the order of 700 per square mile, or about half that of Dorayi; however, the density varies greatly, and it may be that in the two northern Hamlets it approaches 1000 per square mile for the riverside Hamlet (Kirimbo) is rather sparsely populated.

As Kirimbo lies some six to eight miles from the city wall and is not on a main road, its economic links with the city are weaker than those of Dorayi. Few men commute there for regular daily work or as traders; less manure is fetched from the city; no city men have bought Kirimbo land; and no bulky cornstalk beds are produced for sale. However, firewood is transported to the city by donkey and elderly women and girls headload groundnut oil and cake there for sale.

A fair proportion of the population of Gasau Hamlet, including the Dagaci of Kirimbo who resides there, count themselves (with good reason) as of pastoral Fulani origin; a few men own considerable numbers of cattle which (together with some sheep) are driven south for grazing during a few months of the dry season. More men than in Dorayi are *'yan ƙwarami* who buy grain in remote areas, travelling with their donkeys.

For some time Buzu traders from the Niger Republic have been accustomed to basing themselves during several months of the dry season on Gafiyawa Hamlet where their camels and donkeys graze; they mainly sell palm fronds (*ƙaba*) which are used for making mats and panniers, returning home with various purchases including henna, dried boabab leaves and pepper. About a fifth of all Kirimbo men were recorded as making panniers for sale – apart from six cap makers and six weavers, there were few other craftworkers.

The main non-farming occupation of 22% of all Kirimbo men (excluding sons-in-*gandu*) was recorded as being *ƙaratu* (Koranic learning and/or teaching), compared with only 6% in Dorayi.

About 36% of the Kirimbo population lived in big houses (the homes of seven or more married men) against 38% in Dorayi; however, the largest house was much smaller than in Dorayi, for only twelve married men dwelt there. It was estimated that one-fifth of the inhabitants of Gasau Hamlet were of slave-descent, against 26% in Dorayi. (According to Mai Unguwa Kirimbo (born c. 1885) whose father had owned many farm-slaves, there had been several big slave-owners in the area, and many slave-descendants had migrated.)

As for migration, figures relating to recent departures from Gafiyawa and Gasau Hamlets suggest that the incidence of migration was somewhat higher than from Dorayi; it was particularly interesting that the incidence of migration of sons with living fathers was much higher than in Dorayi. As Table IX.1 (p. 153) shows, proportionately far fewer Kirimbo, than Dorayi, migrants went to Kano city, and far more to Hausa Emirates other than Kano.

In 1971–2 people in certain sections of Kirimbo were much distressed by being threatened with the compulsory acquisition of their houses and farmland owing to the projected building of an industrial estate by the Greater Kano Planning Authority.

V

The consequences of persistent population pressure: a summary

It is impossible to comprehend the present-day sociological stability of stagnating, impoverished, long-established, overcrowded rural communities in the Kano Close Settled Zone, such as Dorayi, without grasping the basis of their earlier prosperity. Prolonged contact with the outside world, over many centuries, had resulted by 1900 in the creation of a semi-autonomous economic system such as was no longer primarily stimulated by an outside system, though it was to some degree tributary to it (see Chapter I). Based on production for, and participation in, long-distance trade, on the cultivation of cash crops which were traded over a wide area of the Central Sudan, and on farm-slavery, this system permitted individuals to accumulate wealth (mainly in the form of livestock, farm-slaves and grain stocks) during their life-times, though for a variety of reasons, one of which was the lack of fixed productive capital resembling paddy fields or cocoa farms, there was a strong tendency for wealth to be dissipated on death. For numerous political, demographic and other reasons, including (in particular) the lack of an hierarchical system of village administration (see Chapter II), Emirate governments lacked the power to control economic activities in the countryside, despite the existence, in Kano Emirate in particular, of well-developed systems of individual taxation – see Appendix II(1). Such *laissez faire* conditions helped those who helped themselves, and the situation was characterized by marked economic inequality. In denoting the wider rural economy as prosperous, it is important not to overlook the existence of much individual poverty among the free as well as the slave population, in the harshly inegalitarian, heavily-taxed world of 1900 where, as I was told, poor (free) men often sold farmland to slave-owners because they had no food, and where in densely populated areas, such as Dorayi, uncultivated farmland was already very scarce.

The process by which the slave-owning economy of Dorayi was converted into an economy of free farmers (the richer of whom started to employ farm-labourers) is dealt with in Chapter XIII. By 1925–30, when few farm-slaves remained and when many slave-descendants had already departed, it may be that the Dorayi population was smaller than it had been in 1900, and it is certain that economic inequality had become less pronounced. Textile production was already declining owing to increased competition from European cloth, and the long-distance donkey caravans were gradually giving way to lorry transport. However, farmers with their donkeys still ranged widely as traders in grain, groundnuts, cowpeas, locust beans and other farm produce; and the cultivation of groundnuts for export overseas, which had begun with such a flourish in 1912 with the completion of the railway to Kano (see *R. H.*, p. 258), was slowly increasing – though insofar as such exporting deprived rural communities of much-needed proteins in the form of groundnut oil, it is by no means clear that they benefited. Otherwise economic life continued much as usual.

Since the early 1930s, by which time it seems that the exodus of slave-descendants had largely ended, the persistent and intensifying pressure of population on the land has been the main factor affecting living standards in Dorayi. As an introduction to the following several chapters which deal both directly and indirectly with the socio-economic consequences of such pressure, I here summarise my main conclusions.

Past statistical records and documentary material are lacking; there is a notable lack of key-dates (see p. 110); informants necessarily lack the power of quantification when contemplating the past (thus, having no units of area, they cannot accurately report on changes in the price of farmland) – for these and other reasons I cannot trace the changes that have occurred in Dorayi by means of graphs and similar respectable devices, though I can discern certain trends. I am, therefore, obliged to base my conclusions to some extent on comparisons of Dorayi with Batagarawa, where the population density may be arbitrarily regarded as no more than about one-sixth of that in Dorayi – see Appendix v(1). This I had always intended for, as Daryll Forde pointed out long ago (and as I have reason to know from my own more recent experience), the economy and society of Hausaland have sufficient 'underlying uniformity' (Forde, 1946, p. 119) for such comparisons to be justifiable; but it is a pity that the population density in Batagarawa in 1967 was so much lower than that in Dorayi in the 1930s.

ECONOMIC INEQUALITY AND THE SIZE OF FARM-HOLDINGS

What has been the effect of the 'persistent and intensifying pressure', which has been associated with a net annual population growth rate of, perhaps, ½% to 1% – see Appendix iv(3) – on the distribution of farmland between farmers – in practice between men, since women, who are in full Muslim seclusion, sell, or otherwise lose control over, most of the land that they inherit?

Comparing Dorayi with Batagarawa two conclusions clearly emerge: (1) Inequality is equally pronounced in terms of the proportion of manured farmland effectively owned by the richest farmers. If farmers are placed in rank order in terms of the size of their holdings, then it is found that in both places the 'top 5%' owned about a fifth of all the farmland, the corresponding proportion for the 'top 15%' being about 45%; (2) Inequality is very much more pronounced in Dorayi in terms of the proportion of farmers who own little or no farmland. Difficulties of mapping made it impossible to place the smallest farmers in rank order, but it seemed that one-third of all Dorayi men owned less than one acre, against about one-tenth in Batagarawa – see Appendix vi(1) – and that about 12% of all fatherless Dorayi men were virtually landless – see p. 174 and Appendix xi(4) – though some of them had borrowed (*aro*) land.

Reverting to (1), the comparison with Batagarawa tends to confirm the Dorayi farmers' own statements about the declining size of large holdings, and this despite the fact (see Chapter xi) that most of the farm-buyers in recent years have been rich farmers. Considering the existence of many large slave-run estates in former times, it is quite likely that the 'top 5%' owns a considerably smaller proportion of the land than in 1930. Nowadays no Dorayi farmer owns more than twenty acres, against a maximum of thirty-nine acres of manured farmland in Batagarawa – bush farms (see *R. H.*) are excluded from the latter figure. The 'top 5%' of farmers owned an average of only eleven acres in Dorayi, against twenty-three acres in Batagarawa – see Appendix vi(1) – the corresponding areas for the 'top 15%' having been seven and sixteen acres.

In Batagarawa there was a very close relationship between a man's general economic situation in life and the size of his farm-holding (*R. H.*, pp. 75–6 and Chapters vi and x below): a connected point was the fact that the most lucrative types of non-farming occupation were pursued by the largest farmers and *vice versa*. That present-day Dorayi is a real farming area, not a mere suburb, is partly illustrated by the fact that this relationship is still quite strong there, though it is less marked than in Batagarawa. Only 6% of all rich men in Dorayi own less than three acres, against 74% of all men; and those with very small holdings seldom pursue the more remunerative types of non-farming occupation (see Chapters vi, x and xi).

LAND-BORROWING (*'aro'*)

In response to the intensifying land pressure, the willingness of richer Dorayi farmers to lend farm-plots (*aro*), on a short-term basis, has greatly increased (see Chapter VII), so that in terms of utilisation, rather than ownership, the distribution of land is significantly less unequal than the latter figures suggest. Whereas in rural Hausaland generally a high proportion of land-borrowing involves kin or affines, this is no longer so in Dorayi where, it is said, reliable men are usually able to find somebody willing to lend to them. While this important new safety valve eases the situation of a fair number of men with little or no land, it does less than might be expected to assist the very poorest men, many of whom are regarded as poor risks or lack the capacity to farm effectively (see Chapter XI). In its failure to provide for the land-needs of many of the poorest members of the population, the process of agricultural change in Dorayi does not resemble the type of 'agricultural involution' described by Clifford Geertz for Indonesia.

THE SIZE OF FARM-PLOTS

The average size of farm-plots (farms) in Dorayi, which is now 1.0 acres, has decreased greatly within living memory, and the proportion of tiny plots has greatly increased: this is clear enough from oral evidence and receives partial confirmation from the 1932 Report on Kumbotso – see Appendix IV(1) – which states that average farm-size in Ja'en Village Area was 2.7 acres. At least two-thirds of all Dorayi plots (probably significantly more) are under one acre, compared with about a quarter in Batagarawa; and a mere 1% of all Dorayi plots exceed four acres, against 13% in Batagarawa (see Table VII.1). While this diminution is partly a function of the 'persistent and intensifying pressure', the process is bound to develop with special intensity in any long-established locality where bush land is lacking, whether the population is increasing or not. This is because farm-plots, which tend to be widely dispersed, are never consolidated as a result of inheritance, but are apt to be divided (see Chapter VII), so that provided there are some men in the community who have more than one son (as obviously there are bound to be) and provided some of these brothers divide the farm-plots on death (rather than sharing them out), the number of plots is bound to increase, their size to diminish. Whereas in Batagarawa inheriting brothers usually desisted from dividing small plots of under one acre (see *R. H.*, p. 185), choosing rather to share out their father's plots between them, this safety valve operates less often in Dorayi, and it is partly for this reason that many tiny plots, of a tenth of an acre or even less, have been created. However, as will be seen, such division still occurs much less often than the principle of 'equal division among sons' would lead one to expect.

THE PRICE OF FARMLAND

Whereas in 1930 the price of farmland in Dorayi may have been little higher than in Batagarawa, say £2 to £3 per acre, during the past twenty or thirty years it has risen so steeply that it may now be some twenty times higher, say £60 per acre – though there is much variation in both places (see Chapter VII). While this increase is certainly mainly due to the persistent and intensifying pressure, the purchase of farmland by rich men from the city has become, very recently, an aggravating factor.

THE POSITION OF MARRIED SONS

The sociological stability of Dorayi is best understood in terms of the position of married sons – i.e. married men with resident living fathers. The remarkably close economic relationship between fathers and sons (see Chapter VIII) is a direct consequence of the persistent and intensifying pressure: it is reflected in the astonishingly low rate of outward migration of sons (only twenty sons of seventeen fathers now living in Dorayi have migrated); in the almost invariable co-residence of fathers and sons (in great contrast to Batagarawa, only four of the total of 211 married sons live separately from their fathers); in the unusual strength of the *gandu* relationship – which even involves sons in passing over part of their earnings from non-farming occupations to their fathers, as has not been recorded elsewhere; and in the strong tendency for rich retired fathers to have rich sons and *vice versa* (see Table VIII.3). In Batagarawa the sons of poor fathers had a notably high propensity to migrate, but in Dorayi (where only 20 out of a total of 231 married sons are thought to be living elsewhere) this is not so, with the result that many sons become inextricably entangled in their father's poverty. (It is doubtful whether the general propensity to migrate has increased in response to the persistent and intensifying pressure (see Chapter IX); as in former times, no married sons or other men ever migrate in the capacity of farmers.)

WEALTH, POVERTY AND AGE

Perhaps the most interesting finding is that the persistent and intensifying pressure places great obstacles in the way of the advancement of younger men, only a small proportion of whom (see Table VI.1) are classified as 'rich'; whereas 27% of all old men (*tsohuwa*) and 22% of older middle-aged men (*dattijai*) are so classified, the proportions for the two younger age-groups are only 11% and 4%. (Although the population of Bata-garawa was too small for comparable figures to be meaningful, there is no doubt that proportionately more younger men flourished there.) It is partly because married sons are so closely tied to their fathers and own so little farmland (in Dorayi, unlike Batagarawa, sons-in-*gandu* are nowadays seldom granted the traditional private plots – *gayauni*), that the dice are so heavily weighted against younger men, few of whom have been able to afford the very high price of farmland in recent years. It is, also, very interesting to note that even in former times there were many men who failed to prosper as their age advanced: the incidence of extreme poverty is little related to age, being about 25% for all age-groups (see Chapters VI and XI).

INCIPIENT ECONOMIC STRATIFICATION

Upward economic mobility has recently been reduced in Dorayi to the point that the society, unlike Batagarawa, may be regarded as incipiently, if not actually, economically stratified on the basis of land ownership (see Chapter x). But such stratification is not of a familiar European type. This is partly because it does not correspond to social inequality: rich and poor often live in the same houses or house-sections and have similar ways of life; respected malams (religious scholars) may be quite poor – though seldom severely impoverished; authority systems do not bolster the rich; there are no occupational classes or systems of long-term clientage; and the matter of slave-descent has become irrelevant. Also, the polygynous system, which is associated with high rates of divorce, and which provides older richer men with an unfair advantage in competing for wives, tends both to enhance the inequality of brothers (of different mothers) and to promote the dissipation of property (other than farmland) on death, granary stocks being run down and livestock being sold. While the proportion of virtually landless men is bound to continue increasing (though possibly at a slower rate than formerly, as the high price of land inhibits the willingness to sell), it does not follow that the largest land-holders will necessarily come to own more of the land for (again owing to the polygynous system) their holdings constantly diminish in size, and it may be that, despite much land buying, their share of the total has already begun to decline (p. 97 above). Although in the longer run most rich men will prove to have had rich fathers, yet most of the sons of rich fathers will not become rich. As P. C. Lloyd puts it for Yorubaland, 'a high degree of polygyny, together with the inheritance laws, renders it impossible for a man to perpetuate his status in most of his children' (Lloyd, 1974, p. 54). This conclusion is aptly illustrated by Table viii.3 which shows that whereas as many as eight out of eleven rich sons had rich retired fathers, only eight of the sons of twenty-seven rich retired fathers were themselves rich. I think such a qualified type of economic stratification may tend to develop everywhere in West Africa where inheritance is partible and where land has become very valuable, either because it has been planted with permanent crops (such as cocoa) or because the persistent, intensifying and severe pressure of population on the land has not been relieved by migration. But the evidence regarding the ease with which slave-descendants formerly established themselves as free farmers (see Chapter xiii) shows that it was not until the price of land had risen very steeply that this situation developed. With present land prices stratification is indeed a reality in the sense that those who inherit no land can seldom hope to become land-owners.

BIG HOUSES

The growth of very big houses (see Chapter xii), inhabited by seven or more married men and their dependants, which are not known to exist in the Hausa countryside elsewhere than in the centre of the KCSZ, is a direct consequence of the persistent and intensifying pressure: the search for security in a harsh environment not only causes fathers to cling to their sons, but also impels most resident brothers to remain together after their father's death. (Most atypically, only 18 of the 298 fatherless married men who have married brothers in Dorayi are not resident with them.

INTENSIFICATION OF AGRICULTURE

Given the primitive nature of farming technology in rural Hausaland (where, as in most regions of West Africa, 'The small-scale technology of Eurasia is lacking' – Goody, 1971, p. 75) and given, also, the general shortage and high cost of chemical fertilisers, any possibility that the developing pressure of population on the land in Dorayi might have led to the general intensification of agriculture there was necessarily precluded; and owing to the lack of natural marshland (*fadama*) and of irrigable river banks, Dorayi farmers are not well situated to respond to the growing demand for irrigated crops from Kano city, which yield a far higher income per acre than grains. However, the recent development (see Chapter vii) of small-scale onion-growing, on specially-manured plots irrigated by wells from which early millet (*gero*) has already been harvested, is a minor positive response to high population density – the kind of intensification which might be taken for granted in certain Asian circumstances. But profitable though it is, such onion-growing has developed only in two small sections of Dorayi; and no labour-saving pulleys or beams (*jigo*), such as have been utilised for centuries on river banks, have been installed on the wells by the onion-farmers, who painfully lower buckets or calabashes on ropes. (That general farming technology in Dorayi – or indeed in the KCSZ – has not been improved in response to the persistent and intensifying pressure is obviously no judgment on the farmers, who must remain dependent on hand tools made by local blacksmiths until external authorities positively decide to introduce improved technology and to assist its acquisition. And, in this connection, it must constantly be borne in mind that the KCSZ is but a small portion of a vast and culturally homogeneous area *in which land is generally not scarce*. As for the oxen-drawn metal plough, which was the sole technical innovation for cultivators which was successfully introduced by the British (see *R. H.*), I do not know whether there are good agronomic reasons why none are in use in Dorayi and its environs.)

The profound inefficiency of an agronomic system which depends on the annual application of, say, 50 000 donkey loads of poor quality household sweepings, enriched with the droppings of small livestock, to the surface of the land, requires no emphasis, though the extent to which this manure (*taki*) is blown as dust in the wind before the start of the planting rains is seldom mentioned. Since Dorayi farmers no longer own any cattle and since it is likely that the population of sheep and goats has shown a long-term decline, Dorayi's dependence on household sweepings brought in on donkey back from the city is probably increasing as the years go by (see p. 169 for manure costs). However, such dependence on the city is nothing new, for it was one of the important duties of farm-slaves to fetch household sweepings, as well as latrine manure (*takin masai*), from the city. Although it is usually believed that the use of 'night soil' is abhorrent to the ordinary West African farmer, Dorayi farmers, like those in many Hausa localities, (see *R. H.*, p. 289), have long been accustomed to apply dry latrine manure to their land, most of which is produced by sealing their own house latrines with earth and ashes for a year or so, when a black, odourless 'earth' may be extracted (see *R. H.*, p. 289).

UNDER-UTILISATION OF MALE LABOUR

If circumstances relating to the supply of farmland and of finance are so favourable that every working man in a Hausa rural community cultivates the maximum possible acreage during the farming-season, then available information suggests (see *R. H.*, p. 239) that the average acreage per working man might be of the order of five to six acres; thus in Batagarawa the working men in the seventeen richest farming-units together with their farm-labourers cultivated on average about four and a half acres of manured farmland (see *R. H.*, pp. 62 and 121) or possibly about five acres if bush farms are included. Whatever allowance may be made for the cultivation of land outside the mapped area, the potential Dorayi labour force of about 940 men (a figure which excludes those who commute to the city, as well as retired men and those who are unwell) certainly cultivates less than two acres per head. Agriculture having been little intensified, individual men, especially poorer men, spend less and less time on cultivation as the population increases. Since the opportunities of pursuing other types of work have simultaneously diminished, so the available labour force is more and more under-utilised as time goes by.

Apart from some young men who find a little work as farm-labourers (*kwadago*) outside Dorayi or who secure poorly-paid regular jobs, e.g., as gardeners or watchmen in Kano city – see Appendix xi(1) – most of the poorest men who own little or no land increasingly resemble their counter-parts in the informal (non wage-earning) economy of the city. They waste much time looking for local work and contacting people; they are never fully employed for any length of time; and they commonly eke out a living by following a number of different occupations such as farm or general labouring, the collection and transportation of produce and manure, and the making of cornstalk beds – unlike richer men, some of whom are part-time traders in the city, their work is mainly locally-based (see Table vi.5). The multiplicity of ill-paid, part-time occupations (most of them of a petty nature) which are open to such men, ensures (I think) that few of them become a burden on the community as a whole, unless they are ill or old and lack close relatives who help them (see Chapter xi). Increasingly these men resemble a kind of rural proletariat – representatives of which exist everywhere in rural Hausaland, for (see p. 165) men do not necessarily flourish where land is plentiful.

Richer men who are traders are also much affected by the persistent and intensifying pressure (see Chapter x), for most of them either handle locally-grown produce, such as henna or sugar cane, which is severely limited in supply, or serve the local population whose demand for non-basic wares is very restricted – thus most households consume very little meat, the demand for which is mainly met by only six small-scale retail butchers who obtain their supplies of meat in the city. There are probably no more than about ten traders whose operations are wholly unrestricted by local limitations of demand and supply, for the reason that they buy produce in rural markets and sell it in Kano city (and elsewhere) as well as in Dorayi. As for the craftsmen, only the active blacksmiths, who number about thirteen, enjoy a significant external demand for their wares. (It is very curious (see p. 173) that secluded women, unlike their husbands, may have little difficulty in setting themselves to work: they often make groundnut oil and locust bean cakes, from 'imported' (as well as local) supplies of produce, for which there is an unlimited demand in Kano city; and it is they, not the men, who make large quantities of mats from palm fronds (*kaba*) brought to their doors by traders, on camel-back, from the Niger Republic.)

It is clear from this summary that we shall make no progress at all in studying present conditions unless economic inequality is one of the central themes. Let those who criticise the humble statistical endeavour outlined in the next chapter at least recognise that the recently aroused and profound interest in rural inequality in developing countries has not been matched by any significant increase in relevant statistical material.

APPENDIX V(1)
Notes on Batagarawa

As readers of *Rural Hausa* will know, Batagarawa is a compact, formerly walled, village (*gari*) situated on a minor road some six miles south of Katsina city – i.e. some hundred miles north-west of Kano city – on the edge of an area of dispersed settlement which is not unlike the less densely populated sections of the Kano Close Settled Zone. In 1967 the Batagarawa Hamlet Area, to which my enquiries related, had a population of 1395, of whom 1160 lived in the *gari*, the remainder dispersedly. Most of the manured farmland cultivated by Batagarawa men was situated in the mapped zone around the village which had an area of some 1110 acres; while the farmers had a strong preference for farming in this zone, many of them also cultivated unmanured bush farms situated within a few miles of the village where land was plentiful and could be freely appropriated. The total area of uncultivated, though cultivable, land having been unknown, it was not possible to estimate the effective population density: it has been arbitrarily put at 250 per square mile to make clear that it is considerably lower than to the south-east of Katsina city.

Batagarawa is the capital town of Mallamawa which is much the smallest District in Katsina Emirate. Unlike Dorayi it, therefore, has a ruling class (*masu sarauta*) consisting not only of the District Head and his wives and dependants but also of two prominent kinsmen of the District Head, namely the Village Head and the District Head's eldest son. These men, together with the appointed District Scribe, formed a class apart, and it was interesting that at least seventeen of the sons of the ruling family who had been to the Batagarawa primary school were either at secondary school or university or were civil servants or other professional men. Most Batagarawa boys and girls attended the excellent primary school, which had been founded as early as 1946. About a half of a sample of 130 surviving ex-schoolboys were still farming in Batagarawa, and about 15% (exclusive of members of the ruling family) were either students in higher education, teachers or government employees – these figures standing in great contrast to Dorayi from which only two men are known to have migrated for work in the 'literate sector'. Batagarawa also contrasts with Dorayi in that there was a substantial outward migration for farming.

Although Batagarawa is a compact village with a large ruling class (and a successful school), this class stood so detached that the general atmosphere of socio-economic life as it is lived by ordinary people is sufficiently similar to that in Dorayi to justify comparisons based on the demographic variable. The ordinary inhabitants of both places enjoy a remarkable degree of sociological detachment from their nearby cities, where a negligible proportion of the wives had been born. There was no market-place in Batagarawa (though many unsuccessful attempts had been made to establish one), most day-to-day requirements of food and other essentials having been bought from secluded women in their houses; and there was no alkali's court, most disputes having been settled locally. Nor was there any clinic, most Batagarawa (like Dorayi) people receiving no modern medical attention before death. (However, Batagarawa has a Friday mosque.) The institutions of wife seclusion and *gandu* are basically similar (though not identical) in the two places; and similar crops are grown. Batagarawa farmers do not fetch manure from Katsina city.

VI

The evidence for economic inequality

I start this chapter, which is concerned with the evidence for the existence of a pronounced degree of economic inequality in Dorayi, by considering the applicability to rural Hausaland of two models employed by P. C. Lloyd in his study of perceptions of social inequality among the Yoruba (Lloyd, 1974); I refer, in particular, to his chapter 'Social rank in traditional Yoruba society' which, while it purports to deal, using the ethnographic present, with conditions in pre-colonial times, evidently has much application to contemporary rural Yorubaland.

The first of these models, which he denotes the 'externalised analytic structure' (*ibid.*, p. 8), is such that the individual stands outside his own society (while at the same time noting his own place within it), seeing it as an integrated whole and being concerned with the inter-relationship between the constituent parts. In the second model, denoted the 'cognitive map', the individual is placed at the centre, surrounded by his personal network of relationships and sees displayed the goals available to him and the routes by which he can attain them. While each individual has his own cognitive map, the construction of an externalised view of society needs 'some level of intellectual skill' (*ibid.*, p. 9), which, as Lloyd holds, most individuals within the society possess in some measure.

Implicit in the thinking of Yoruba people is the belief in the inevitability of social and economic inequality: as Lloyd puts it (*ibid.*, p. 49), 'just as the fingers of the hand are of different length, so are some men older, healthier, richer, wiser than others'. So, while an outside observer may ignorantly regard the rural community as consisting of an amorphous mass of peasantry, the insider's externalised view necessarily emphasises heterogeneity.

In my work in Batagarawa, I had found that many individuals within the community are sufficiently intellectual to be capable of formulating externalised analytic structures (though some are very much more competent than others) and that the matter of economic inequality necessarily loomed large. On the other hand, many individuals, whether through failures of perception or otherwise, find it very difficult to formulate their own economic goals and the means by which they might achieve them, poverty-stricken people in particular tending to become very confused when contemplating their plight. As in Ibadan –

The poor are much concerned with themselves in an inward manner as they cling to the view that their society is an 'open society' in which achievement is possible and which carries considerable rewards. They blame 'the government' for their difficulties, but they also blame themselves – an attitude which has the support of the intellectuals and other members of the national elite. (Gutkind, 1975, p. 27.)

It is partly because the cognitive maps of the gravely impoverished tend to be so muddled (and misleading) that the study of individual (as distinct from community) poverty has been so neglected in rural Africa. Nor have the possibilities of relying on externalised views been sufficiently explored.

In Batagarawa I had found that it was possible to collect remarkably valuable information relating to the pattern of economic inequality within the community from a small number of carefully selected volunteers who were prepared to expatiate on the economic position of other married men. As a result I agree with Lloyd that the rationality exercised by the individual in constructing his image of his own society is normally understressed by outside observers, who tend to emphasise the 'homespun nature' of his concepts, the paucity of the information available to him and his inability to draw correct inferences from his experiences (*ibid.*, p. 9). I discovered that my informants were not only well capable of identifying the main variables which determine the living standards of individuals, but that they knew enough about the circumstances of many other members of the community to form quite positive judgments. When it came to the actual classification of married men in the community into four groups extending from 'rich' to 'very poor', their unprompted, independent judgments showed such a remarkable degree of conformity as to suggest (as subsequent analysis confirmed) that their views had much objective validity (see *R. H.*, Chapter IV).

As Lloyd emphasises (*ibid.*, p. 8), the outside observer's 'objective' descriptions of stratification systems based upon certain scientific measurements are not as free from personal bias and prejudice as is commonly supposed, partly owing to the need to select the variables to be measured. He goes so far as to claim that there is no intrinsic reason why the outsider's view of the system is more valid than that of individual members of society. Perhaps I go even further in claiming that this applies not only to stratification systems (which involve status and power as well as economic position), but also to studies of economic inequality which are supposed to necessitate formal quantification. I am sure that the ability of Hausa farmers to form expert judgments about economic variables which they cannot measure (such as relative areas of farmland) is normally disregarded – and they are, of course, far better placed than outsiders to assess the relative quality of land. Their knowledge and judgment enables them to make accurate and detailed comparisons of the standards of living of different farmers.

But there is another important point. It is usually not feasible in rural Hausaland for private investigators (as distinct from official organisations) to obtain sufficient detailed particulars relating, say, to income and expenditure, over a period which (for reasons of seasonality) must necessarily be as long as a year, from a population which is large enough to enable reliable conclusions concerning the relationship between standard of living and other factors, such as age and non-farming occupation, to be drawn. (I think that a population of at least 2000 must be covered, and I now see that, for certain purposes, the population of Batagarawa, some 1400, was too small.) And the only alternative is to rely, at least to some extent, on the judgments of informants regarding relative living standards.

If reliable statistical material relevant to economic inequality were easier to collect then, of course, many more anthropologists in West Africa would have adopted a statistical approach. (The very use of 'collect' betrays us, as though 'data' was a substance which fell off trees.) So rare are such statistical studies that even Daryll Forde's estimates of the yam production of individual Yakö farmers (Forde, 1964) are constantly quoted out of context. Certainly, also, the degree of reliance I place on the judgments of informants would not have seemed in the least respectable before the introduction of that new tool, the aerial photograph (showing farm boundaries), which enables us, in the savannah though not in the forest, to set these judgments within a framework of statistics on the size of farm-holdings.

In Batagarawa the degree of correspondence between my informants' 'subjective' assessments of living standards and the actual size of farm-holdings had been astonishing and very encouraging (*R. H.*, pp. 62, 76). It was not merely that average acreages of manured farmland for the four 'economic-groups' fell steadily from 19.5 to 8.4 to 4.2 to 2.8, but that there was little overlap – as many as twenty-seven out of thirty farmers with holdings of less than two acres had been placed by my informants in the two poorest groups.

Emboldened by my experiences in Batagarawa, I decided to rely mainly on third-party informants when studying economic inequality in Dorayi. For numerous practical reasons, including the fact that I was intent on studying a really large population, I was also obliged to derive most of my genealogical material and all my information on two sensitive subjects, migration and (erstwhile) farm-slavery, from five men who represented the various sections of Dorayi – and I am sure it was far more accurate as a result. (On one occasion, being accompanied by my usual assistant, I obtained all the genealogical material for a certain big house from the household head: I subsequently found that he had got his relationship to the thirteen other resident men in the house wrong in each case – admittedly he had no married sons.) For the first four months I worked only with the late Mahamman Lawal, the Hamlet Head (Mai Unguwa) of Cikin Gari (Ciranci), whose kindness, fearlessness and profound interest in the affairs of others (many of them outside his own Hamlet) made him the ideal informant. Towards the end of the work, the services of an extraordinary personality and well known Koranic scholar, Malam (subsequently Alhaji) Zawal of Ja'en Yamma, became available; seeing him striding fast across the countryside, it was hard to believe that he was well over eighty years old. The three other men were considerably younger: one, M. Ado, was a close friend of a Village Head; the second, M. Yahaya, was a brother of another Village Head; and the third, M. Jigo, was a very well informed, though unobtrusive, man of no particular position in life, who often acted as an intermediary for farm-selling. I am most grateful to them all.

My procedure in Dorayi was different from that in Batagarawa. Partly because I had much more time, and also because I was no longer nervous lest informants changed their judgments when faced with my opinions or my statistics on farm-holdings, we discussed various aspects of each married man's economic position before arriving at our classification, whereas in Batagarawa the original judgments had been unprompted and had involved no justification. In the course of this work a range of information on each man was elicited relating to such current matters as non-farming occupations, *gandu* position (if any) and property ownership, the whole being set within the context of a 'descriptive house genealogy' relating to married men only, which dealt with such questions as past migration, prosperity of certain former residents, and slave origin, and which usually covered several generations. The age of each man was assessed (see below) and in the last stages of the work informants were asked to classify each married man (with certain exceptions, see below) as either 'rich' (*mai arziki*, pl. *masu arziki*), or 'poor' (*matalauci*, pl. *matalauta*) – though the verb *sha wahala*, to suffer, was usually employed – or as 'neither rich, nor poor' (*ba arziki, ba wahala*). (My five informants agreed among themselves that they all fell in the last category.)

The problem of assessing the ages of the 717 married men in Dorayi was formidable. Concepts of numerical age are so poorly developed that were a thirty-year-old to be told that enquiries had revealed that he was fifty he would often not find this odd. Given the entire lack of age sets or grades and of school classmates, it is perhaps not surprising that my attempt to ascertain relative ages by reference to whether a man was older or younger than certain key individuals was a complete failure: informants returned different answers on different occasions and the number of key individuals whose ages could be ascertained with sufficient accuracy was too small.

The fact is that in Hausa areas of dispersed settlement the boundaries of life tend to be temporally as well as spatially vague. Village Heads, as we know, are usually unimportant men who leave little mark on society and are constantly subject to dismissal; and there are few external occurrences (key dates) to which individuals may relate salient events in their own lives, such as their marriages. The District Head of Kumbotso is hardly ever seen in Dorayi; few Dorayi men have much occasion to visit his headquarters – there was not even an alkali's court there until 1972, sixty-four years after the creation of the District; and owing to frequent transfers and dismissals there have been as many as twelve office-holders since 1908, most of whom have been forgotten. Finally, the Emir of Kano stands so aloof that ordinary people do not relate their humble lives to his term of office. While the famous Emir Abdullahi Bayero may have been an exception, it is unfortunate for dating purposes that he ruled for as long as twenty-seven years, during the salient period 1926 to 1953.

In fact the only key dates before 1960 which I found useful were: the arrival of Lugard (1903); the famines of 1907–8 and (much more notably) of 1913–14; the building of the nearby railway line to Kano in the years immediately before 1912; the influenza epidemic (1918–19); the accession of Emir Abdullahi Bayero (1926); the building of the Challawa road through Dorayi (c. 1930); the outbreak of the Second World War (1939) – though this is often confused with the later 'Burma War'; and Abdullahi Bayero's death (1953).

For the purposes of age assessment I was, therefore, obliged to resort to an age-cum-status classification, such as was spontaneously suggested by my informants. The four groups are:

Magidanci (pl. *magidanta* – abbreviated to MAG). Literally a 'householder', this term is used in the sense of a *mere* married man, without qualification, actually a young married man, perhaps under the age of about thirty-five or so, one who does not have a married son.

Matsakanci (pl. *matsakanta* – abbreviated to MAT). The term literally means anyone, or anything, of medim importance, size etc.. Such a man is neither 'young and unimportant' nor possessing the dignity of an older member of the community; he is betwixt and between. Most of those between, say, thirty-five and fifty years old are probably in this group, whether they are in *gandu* or not.

Dattijo (pl. *dattijai* – abbreviated to DAT). Although defined according to Bargery's dictionary as a man of 'about 50 years of age and upwards who comports himself as an elder should', Abraham, in his Hausa dictionary, is correct when he adds that the word denotes 'a respectable person of sound judgment whether of late middle age (as strictly denoted by the word) or not', for my informants allowed that a younger man who mainly associates with *dattijai*, or who has a white beard, may be prematurely so classified.

Tsoho (pl. *tsofaffi* – abbreviated to TSO). *Tsoho* is an old man, a venerable member of society who has not necessarily 'retired' from farming; as a strong man of sixty-five to seventy may continue to be regarded as *dattijo*, while a weak man of sixty may be regarded as *tsoho*, the concept cannot be attached to a minimum age, though it probably applies to most men over about sixty-five.

The five informants were agreed that two of them were old (*tsofaffi*), two were elderly (*dattijai*) and one was *matsakanci*, and I am sure that these were genuine age assessments. Such a wide spread was useful as men often have some general notion as to who is younger or older than themselves, so that the age element in the classification could be sometimes increased by reference to themselves. As the relative ages of brothers is necessarily always known to all and sundry (for x is never spoken of as the unqualified brother of y but always as his *kane*, younger brother, or his *wa*, elder brother), the existence (owing to the failure to migrate) of so many large sets of brothers facilitated the work of age assessment.

I think that in the end, after the classification of individuals had been repeatedly checked and rechecked, this grouping was sufficiently close to an age-classification for my practical purposes. It was certainly reassuring to find that the proportions of men falling into each group showed little variation as between different sections of Dorayi.

Before presenting the results of this enquiry, I must face some of the obvious doubts readers may feel about the ability of my informants to isolate economic factors when presenting their externalised views. Might it not have been, for instance, that a man enjoying high prestige in the community was automatically regarded as rich? Or that a miserly man was necessarily regarded as 'not rich'? (In rural Hausaland, as in Yorubaland (Lloyd, *ibid.*, p. 51), misers who are not free with their money or services are among those most despised.) Might it not have been that political power, such as is possessed in very small measure by the Village

Heads, was automatically equated with economic power? Does the Hausa concept of wealth (*arziki*) (see p. 155) relate specifically to economic well-being, or might not an elderly, popular man, with a bunch of active married sons, and three wives of varying ages, be held to possess this attribute, even though there were times when he went short of food?

The main reassurance I can offer is that in conversation the informants naturally distinguished economic from other factors, so that with reference to the last of the above questions they might have replied that such a father was 'rich in sons only', implying that he was poor in material senses. Commenting on the position of a much respected elderly man, whose father had been a slave-owner, they had remarked that owing to having so many brothers he was much poorer than his father had been. Then, the careful way in which informants discussed the relative living standards of retired fathers and their individual married sons showed that the wealth of a successful farmer was not necessarily seen as over-flowing to each of his sons, even though they all lived in the same house. As for the doubts about political office, only one of the four Village Heads (and none of the three Hamlet Heads) was denoted 'rich', and he is a doubtful case. Nor did headship of a big house necessarily signify wealth; and neither of the two richest men in the community are household heads.

Finally, I do not think that any serious circularity of argument is involved when I say that it is the internal consistency and coherence of the body of material collected which gives one most faith in the procedure. It is because the results as a whole make sense that one can even detect certain errors of judgment made by informants.

I now present in Sections A to E the bare bones of my findings on economic inequality, leaving general and detailed discussion for later chapters.

PROPORTIONS OF RICH AND POOR MEN

For the sake of clarity and brevity I shall use the terms 'rich', 'poor' and 'neither' (rich nor poor), without qualification, trusting that my readers will be aware, as my informants themselves constantly emphasised, that 'rich' means 'rich on village standards', and 'poor' implies notable impoverishment in a community where nearly everyone is highly penurious not only on 'Western standards' but also on the standards of certain other better-favoured rural West African communities.

I use the term 'wealth classification' in preference to any expression suggesting that a man's annual income determines his 'living standard' – another vague term. In fact informants took account of both presumed capital stocks (for instance in the form of grain) and earning power when judging a man's situation. They do not think in terms of income within a fixed period (and would not do so even if no produce were grown for 'own consumption'), though they may contemplate the presumed size of a man's harvest. The use of the word 'wealth' is meant to convey the importance of the economic security which its possession provides. Rich men 'own enough' to be able to help others as well as to look after their own affairs. Poor men were often described as 'owning nothing' – except (of course) some clothing, household implements and farm tools.

The total number of men who were classified as rich was 72 out of the 551 men to whom the wealth classification relates. As it is very unlikely that any of the 166 men who were excluded (see Note (i) on Table VI.1) were rich, about 10% of the whole population of 717 married men were so classified. It is, perhaps, of little interest that the proportions of both rich and poor men in the Dorayi and Batagarawa populations were roughly equal, but I feel justified in insisting that many of those classified as rich on Dorayi standards would have been similarly classified in Batagarawa. About 60% of the 551 men were classified as 'neither rich nor poor', and about 27% as poor: these percentages cannot be directly compared with those for Batagarawa where the classification was into three, not four, groups.

A. WEALTH AND AGE

Summarised comments on Table VI.1

(a) *Older men have a much greater chance of being rich than younger men.* More than a quarter (27%) of old men (TSO) are rich, compared with 22%, 11% and 4% of the three groups of younger men, the average for all groups being 13%.
(b) However, *the incidence of severe poverty shows little relationship to age*, being about a quarter for all age-groups.
(c) *Nearly two-thirds (60%) of all rich men are old or elderly*; the corresponding proportion for poor men is 30%.

B. WEALTH, AGE AND NUMBER OF WIVES

Summarised comments on Tables VI.2 (A) and VI.2(B)

(a) In this polygynous society, *the richest and the oldest men have on average significantly more wives than other men* – respectively 2.1 and 1.8 wives per husband, against 1.3 for all men.
(b) *The incidence of polygyny rises steadily with age.* The majority of the

oldest men (TSO) are polygynous (60%), as against 10% of the youngest men (MAG). As many as 14% and 13% of the two oldest age groups (TSO and DAT) have three or four wives, against only 3% and 1% of younger men.

Table VI.1 *Wealth and age*

	TSO		DAT		MAT		MAG		Total	
	(*Nos. of married men*)									
Rich	13	27%	30	22%	24	11%	5	4%	72	13%
	18%		42%		33%		7%		100%	
Neither	22	46%	77	56%	134	61%	94	68%	327	60%
	7%		24%		41%		29%		100%	
Poor	13	27%	31	22%	62	28%	39	28%	145	27%
	9%		21%		43%		27%		100%	
Total	48	100%	138	100%	220	100%	138	100%	544	100%
	9%		25%		40%		25%		100%	

Notes:
(i) Seven men whose ages were not known are omitted.
(ii) Men-in-*gandu*, 'labourers' in Kano and elsewhere, see Appendix XI (1), and those who are unwell are omitted from this and the following tables.
(iii) *Abbreviations* (see p. 111): TSO (Tsoho) is old; DAT (Dattijo) is older middle-aged; MAT (Matsakanci) is younger middle-aged; MAG (Magidanci) is young.

Table VI.2(A) *Wealth, age and number of wives*

Average number of wives per husband			
Rich	2.1	TSO	1.8
Neither	1.3	DAT	1.6
Poor	1.2	MAT	1.3
Sons-in-*gandu*	1.2	MAG	1.1
All husbands	1.3	All husbands	1.3

Notes:
(i) See notes on Table VI.1.
(ii) Men who were formerly married but are temporarily wifeless are omitted.

Additional summarised comments on Table VI.2(B)

(a) *Many rich men (28%) and hardly any poor men (2%) have three or four wives.*

(b) *Very few men in the two youngest age groups have three or four wives.*

Table VI.2(B)   *Wealth, age and number of wives*

No. of wives	Rich men	Poor men	TSO	DAT	MAT	MAG	All men
			Percentages of men with varying numbers of wives				
1	21	78	40	51	70	90	71
2	51	20	46	36	27	9	24
3	21	2	10	10	3	1	4
4	7	–	4	3	–	–	1
	100%	100%	100%	100%	100%	100%	100%

Note: See notes on Table VI.2(A).

C. WEALTH, AGE AND NUMBERS OF DEPENDANTS

It happens that forty-three older men (TSO and DAT) are rich, against forty-four such men who are poor. Table VI.3 compares the numbers of dependants of these two groups of men.

Summarised comments on Table VI.3

(a) *The average number of dependants of all categories is greater for rich than for poor men.* (The fact that rich men have more resident married sons than poor men is mainly to be explained by the higher proportion of poor men who have no such sons, 52% against 33% for rich men (see Chapter XI).)

(b) Apropos of the comments on Tables VI.2(A) and VI.2(B), it is now clear that *wealth not age is the principal determinant of the number of wives*: older rich men have 2.3 wives on average, against 1.4 wives for older poor men.

Table VI.3   *Wealth, age and numbers of dependants (Rich and poor older men (TSO and DAT) compared)*

	Older rich men (1)	Older poor men (2)	Ratio (1) *to* (2)
	Average numbers of dependants per man		
Wives	2.3	1.3	1.6
Children[1]	2.2	1.5	1.5
Unmarried working sons	1.0	0.7	1.4
Married sons	1.2	0.9	1.3
'Working sons'[ii]	2.1	1.2	1.8
All dependants	7.0	4.8	1.5

Notes:

(i) Including all unmarried girls and all boys who are too young to work; adopted sons, step-children (*agolai*), and brother's sons are included.

ii) 'Working sons' are generally available to help their fathers on their farms or in other work; sons who have left *gandu* or who work as 'labourers' in Kano city are excluded.

D.   WEALTH AND THE SIZE OF FARM-HOLDINGS

In Batagarawa, as already noted, there was a remarkably close association between the wealth classification and the size of farm-holdings. In Dorayi this association was somewhat less marked in terms both of average holdings and size distribution of individual holdings – see Table VI.4(A) – and considerably less marked in terms of acreages per head of (weighted) population – see Table VI.4(C). (See Appendix VI(I) on the size distribution of farm-holdings in Dorayi and Batagarawa.)

Summarised comments on Table VI.4(A)

(a) *The average holdings of rich men* (6.1 acres) *are much larger than those for the other two wealth groups* (1.9 and 0.9 acres).

(b) *Nearly all rich men* (94%) *have holdings of three acres or more*, whereas only 23% and 6% of those in the two poorer groups are in this position. (The corresponding proportions for five acres or more are 66% for the rich men against only 4% and a negligible figure.)

(c) *Nearly all poor men* (93%) *have holdings of three acres or less*, against only 6% of rich men.

(d) *All the farmers with holdings of ten acres or more are rich*, nearly a quarter (23%) of rich men being in this position.

Table VI.4(A) *Wealth and the size of farm-holdings*

Size of holding	Rich	Neither	Poor	Total
	Estimated percentages of married men			
Under 3 acres	6	77	93	74
3–4.9 acres	28	19	6	17
5–9.9 acres	43	4	neg.	7
10 acres of more	23	–	–	2
Total	100%	100%	100%	100%
Average acreage	6.1	1.9	0.9	2.2

Notes:

(i) The size of holdings is somewhat under-estimated as no allowance could be made for land outside the mapped area (see p. 77 above). However, all farmers whose holdings were known to consist to a considerable extent of farms outside Dorayi were omitted.

(ii) All land which is regularly cultivated by a farmer, whether he is the actual owner or not, is included in his holding; land which has been temporarily given out on *aro* (see p. 131 below) is necessarily included in the owner's holding, for it could not be mapped.

Summarised comments on Table VI.4(B)

(a) *A considerable proportion* (30%) *of those who own 5 to 9.9 acres are 'neither rich nor poor'.*

(b) *Only about a quarter* (24%) *of those who own under three acres are poor.*

Table VI.4(B) *Wealth and the size of farm-holdings*

Size of holding	Rich	Neither	Poor	Total
	Estimated percentages of married men			
Under 3 acres	1	64	24	100%
3–4.9 acres	22	68	10	100%
5–9.9 acres	70	30	neg.	100%
10 acres or more	100	–	–	100%

Note: See Notes on Table VI.4(A).

It is commonly assumed (see *R. H.*, p. 254) that a mixed population of men, women and children in Northern Nigeria requires about 1 lb. of unthreshed grain per head per day – an adult man about 2 lb. If grain yields, which are very variable, are arbitrarily put at 500 lb. an acre – see Appendix vi(2) – then about 0.7 acres per head is required to meet minimum grain requirements. Table vi.4(C) shows that more than three-quarters of Dorayi households are most unlikely to be self-sufficient in grain – a conclusion which occasions no surprise since the corresponding proportion for Batagarawa (omitting bush farms) was about one-third.

Summarised comments on Table VI.4(C)

(a) Depending on the quantity of groundnuts and other non-grain crops grown, *an appreciable proportion of richer households are in a position to be self-sufficient in grain.*
(b) However, *many of the richer households are certainly not self-sufficient in grain.*
(c) In interpreting Table vi.4(c), it should be borne in mind that *rich farmers apply far more manure to their land than poor farmers, so that their grain yields are correspondingly greater.*

Table vi.4(c)   *Acreages per head of weighted population*

	Rich	Neither	Poor	Total
	Percentages of households			
Under 0.7 acres	20	73	90	72
0.7–0.9 acres	37	15	9	16
1–1.9 acres	37	11	(1)	11
2 acres or more	6	1	(1)	1
Total	100%	100%	100%	100%

Notes:
  (i) In computing the weighted population of each household, children have been arbitrarily regarded as 'half-adults'.
  (ii) See Notes on Table vi.4(A).
  iii) Sons-in-*gandu* and their dependants have been included in their father's households.

E. WEALTH AND NON-FARMING OCCUPATIONS

The relationship between types of non-farming occupation (*sana'a*) and wealth is dealt with in Table vi.5.

Summarised comments on Table VI.5

(a) *Rich men are very much more apt to be traders than poorer men;* whereas over a third (39%) of all rich men are traders (few of them based on Kano city), the corresponding percentages for the two poorer groups are 16% and 4%.

(b) *Serious Koranic teachers and students* (who have no other more important non-farming occupation) *are seldom poor men.*

(c) *Nearly two-thirds (63%) of all rich men are traders and/or Koranic teachers or students* (in many cases one occupation is subsidiary to the other) *compared with only 23% and 7% for the two poorer groups.*

(d) Apart from fifty-one 'labourers' who work in Kano city (see Note (i) on Table VI.5) only 11% of men work regularly in the city; *the* (corresponding) *proportion of poor men who find work in the city is trivial (3%).*

(e) *Nearly a half (45%) of all poor men had no occupation other than labouring or transportation* (see Note (a) on Table VI.5) *compared with only 11% of rich men* – most of whom are retired.

(f) *Only 25% of poor men had any occupation other than labouring, transportation and the making of cornstalk beds.*

(g) If the making of cornstalk beds is excluded, *less than 10% of each wealth group is engaged in craftwork.*

Table VI.5   *Wealth and principal non-farming occupations*

Occupation	Rich No.	%	Neither No.	%	Poor No.	%	Total No.	%
(A) In Kano city:								
(a) traders	4		16		2		22	4%
(b) earth-carriers	4		14		2		20	4%
(c) other	–		19		–		19	3%
Total	8	11%	49	15%	4	3%	61	11%
(B) Not in Kano city:								
Craftwork:								
(d) cornstalk beds	3	4%	76	23%	44	30%	123	21%
(e) blacksmiths	1		11		1		13	
(f) builders	–		7		2		9	
(g) tailors	3		2		–		5	
(h) well-diggers	–		2		3		5	
(j) other	1		5		6		12	
Total crafts	8	11%	103	31%	56	38%	167	30%

Married men, exclusive of 'labourers' and sons-in-gandu

Table VI.5 – *cont.*

			Married men, exclusive of 'labourers' and sons-*in*-gandu					
		Rich		Neither		Poor		Total
Occupation	No.	%	No.	%	No.	%	No.	%
Traders:								
(k) 'special produce traders'	7	10%	6	2%	–	–	13	2%
(m) other	17	24%	30	9%	4	3%	51	9%
Total traders	24	33%	36	11%	4	3%	64	12%
(n) *karatu* (Koranic teachers and/or students)	17	24%	22	7%	4	3%	43	8%
(o) wood-cutters (*faskare*)	5	7%	33	10%	5	3%	43	8%
(p) other occupations	2	3%	34	10%	7	5%	43	8%
Total not in Kano city	56	78%	228	68%	76	52%	360	65%
(C) (q) 'no occupation' or not known	8	11%	56	17%	66	45%	130	24%
Grand total	72	100%	333	100%	146	100%	551	100%

Notes:

(i) Men who commute daily as 'labourers' (mainly as gardeners and watch-men) to Kano city or elsewhere – see Appendix XI (1) – are necessarily excluded as their wealth could not be assessed; fifty-one of these men go to Kano city.

(ii) As many men have more than one occupation, the choice of the principal occupation was often rather arbitrary, especially in the case of poor men (see Chapter XI). Occupations pursued during the dry season only are excluded.

(iii)   (a) These traders are concerned with selling (not buying) goods in Kano, some of them being brokers (*dillalai*) who act on behalf of others; they include sellers of locally grown vegetables (*'yan gwari*) and traders in cloth, fowls, kola, etc.

    (b) The earth is not carried to the city from Dorayi but within the city by teams of donkeys.

    (c) Other occupations include: flattery (*fadanci*), *tsubbu* ('magic'), carpentry, skin-cleaning, native doctoring, handcart pushing, portering, laterite digging.

    (d) Crude 'mats' for selling in Kano city which are made of cornstalk and string, see Appendix XI (2).

Table VI.5 – *cont.*

(e) The blacksmiths make knives as well as farm tools of traditional design.

(f) Specialist builders of houses, walls, granaries, etc., made from mud. (The numbers are so small because many men do their own house building and repairing.)

(g) Tailors who own sewing machines.

(h) Specialist well- and latrine-diggers.

(j) Other crafts include thatching, carpentry and cap-embroidery.

(k) These 'special produce traders' buy grains, groundnuts, locust beans, rice, cowpeas, etc. in other rural areas for resale from their houses in Dorayi or elsewhere (see p. 155).

(m) Other traders include: retail butchers (six, of whom five are neither rich nor poor), 'table traders' (*'yan tebur*), and traders in small livestock, henna, honey, sugar cane, *kaba* (palm fronds for mat-making), mangoes, etc.

(n) While Koranic students may receive no remuneration, they are still regarded as having a definite occupation (*sana'a*) if they are serious scholars. (The total number of men engaged in *karatu* is considerably higher than shown, as it is often a subsidiary occupation.)

(o) Firewood cutters may either buy trees for cutting or work with others who have done so (see p. 168).

(p) Other miscellaneous occupations include local administration (Village and Hamlet Heads), *bori* (spirit possession), musicians, *tsubbu* (magic), barbering, house service, *fadanci* (flattery), clothes washing, etc. – no occupation (other than administration) occupies more than a very small number of men.

(q) 'No occupation' means none other than farm or general labouring, or transportation of manure, produce, etc. (see Chapter XI).

APPENDIX VI(1)
The size-distribution of farm-holdings in Dorayi and Batagarawa

If farmers in Dorayi and Batagarawa are placed in rank order according to the size of their farm-holdings then, as Table VI.6 shows, the 'top 5%' and the 'top 15%' own roughly equal proportions of the farmland. (The average size of the largest holdings in Dorayi is about half that in Batagarawa.) In this very limited sense, therefore, economic inequality is no more pronounced in overcrowded Dorayi than in Batagarawa.

In terms of the proportion of men who are landless or who have very small holdings, inequality is far more pronounced in Dorayi than in Batagarawa as Table VI.7 shows – roughly a third of all Dorayi holdings are shown to be under one acre, compared with only 12% in Batagarawa. However, it has to be admitted that the Dorayi percentage for small holdings under one acre may be somewhat exaggerated if there are significant numbers of farmers whose holdings consist of considerable numbers of very small plots which were too small to be mapped, see Appendix vii(1).

Table vi.6   *Estimated proportion of manured farmland in holdings of largest farmers*

	Dorayi		Batagarawa	
	Average holdings in brackets			
'Top 5%'	23%	(11 acres)	20%	(23 acres)
'Top 15%'	47%	(7 acres)	43%	(16 acres)

Notes:
 (i) See Notes on Table vi.4 (A); the estimates for Dorayi are necessarily rough.
(ii) The statistics for Batagarawa relate to manured farmland only as bush farms could not be mapped.

While enquiries in other areas in rural Hausaland have revealed no case where the proportion of holdings under one acre was more than 7% (see *R. H.*, p. 238), men who owned no land were probably omitted from most surveys.

Table vi.7   *The sizes of farm-holdings in Dorayi and Batagarawa*

Acreage of holding	Dorayi	Batagarawa	Dorayi	Batagarawa
	Percentages of married men		*Percentages of farmland*	
Nil or under 0.3	19 ⎱ 36	8 ⎱ 12	⎱ 4	⎱ neg.
0.3 to 0.9	17 ⎰	4 ⎰	⎰	⎰
1.0 to 1.9	23	13	14	4
2.0 to 2.9	15		16	
3.0 to 3.9	11 ⎱ 32	⎱ 33	17 ⎱ 44	⎱ 20
4.0 to 4.9	6 ⎰		11 ⎰	
5.0 to 9.9	7	27	24	34
10 acres and over	2	15	14	41
Total	100%	100%	100%	100%

Notes:
 (i) See Notes on Table vi.4 (A).
(ii) See Note (ii) on Table vi.6.

APPENDIX VI(2)
Grain yields per acre

Grain yields are so greatly dependent on the quantity and quality of manure that is applied to particular plots that one can do no more than work on the conventional assumptions (see FAO, 1966, pp. 176, 177) that average yields of guinea corn and bulrush millet are of the order of 600 and 400 lb. respectively.

However, in the Zaria area surveyed by D. W. Norman (Norman, 1973, pp. 131, 136), sole crops were grown on only 17% of the total cultivated area, two-crop mixtures accounting for 42% and three-crop mixtures for 24%. As yields per acre for guinea corn and millet grown as two-crop mixtures were recorded as 648 lb and 330 lb. respectively, it may be that the FAO figures are too low.

VII

The attitude to farmland

As there are no corporate land-holding lineages in rural Hausaland and no 'traditional rules' which govern such matters as land-selling, and as the attitude to the division of land between sons and daughters on inheritance is very flexible (particularly in Dorayi, where division is often long delayed), so it seems that there is a sense in which there is no such subject as 'land tenure', in the ordinary understanding of that term in West Africa, neither 'local custom' nor 'Muslim law' providing a formal framework within which actual practice may be understood. Accordingly I have entitled this chapter 'The attitude to farmland' in order to emphasise that in a constantly changing situation it is the aggregate of present-day attitudes and responses which determines the nature of transactions in farmland.

Perhaps the only general statements worth making about Hausa 'land tenure' are: first, that permanently cultivated manured farmland is effectively owned by private farmers who have long been accustomed to selling it for cash and who are *directly* compensated by State governments if compulsory requisition occurs; second, that temporary rights over bush land are established by actual cultivation but lapse during the subsequent fallowing – accordingly bush farms are seldom sold; third, that there are no land-renting systems proper nor, as a corollary, any classes of absentee landlord – the matter of *galla* in Zaria Emirate (see p. 211 below) is another case; fourth, that the only vestiges of community control of cultivated farmland which exist in some areas, though not in Dorayi, involve restrictions on selling land on migration (see *R. H.*, p. 85) or to non-resident strangers; and fifth, that the very occasional reference of inheritance cases to alkali's courts has made rural communities embarrassedly aware that the strict letter of the law, as understood by Muslim jurists, demands that farmland should be much more rigidly divided between sons and daughters on death than is convenient, practicable or acceptable.

INHERITANCE

As in rural Hausaland generally, no formality attends the division of Dorayi farmland between sons on inheritance; such division as occurs is nearly always amicably arranged by those concerned, and it is only in the unlikely event of a dispute, or of grave irresolution, that the matter is referred upwards to the District Head or the Alkali's court. However, informants in Dorayi (as in Batagarawa) are so embarrassed by their failure to conform, unavoidable though this is, that they are always apt to insist that court officials (if not the court in session) are invariably involved – though it is evident that officialdom could not possibly find the time to handle more than a tiny proportion of the huge volume of intricate cases (which often involve numerous farm-plots) and that inheritors have an interest in avoiding the heavy court charges. (This rural taciturnity is effective: educated townsmen who are aware that countrymen want to be regarded as conforming Muslims do not realise that general adherence to the rigours of Muslim law on such matters as inheritance and usury (see *R. H.*, p. 330) would be wholly impracticable.) I stand by my previous contention (*R.H.*, p. 183) that rural Hausa communities lack a systematic attitude towards inheritance despite (or even because of) the formalism of the official Muslim attitude – and I would add that they are pathetically ashamed about this.

The inheritance of farmland by daughters is dealt with separately below: I now discuss the effect of the intensifying population pressure on inheritance practices and attitudes so far as inheriting sons are concerned.

In the early years of the century farmland was not necessarily divided between the sons on the father's death: the brothers (or the eldest brother) often decided to form a fraternal *gandu* and if there were any among them who objected to this they might have had no alternative but to migrate. As the institution of fraternal *gandu* weakened, and as elderly retired fathers increasingly felt it their duty to sub-divide a large part of their farmland between their sons during their lifetimes, so the general idea that each son was invariably entitled to a share of his father's farmland developed, with the result, as we have seen, that average farm size constantly diminished over time, and that many tiny farms were created (see Table VII.1 below). However, in Dorayi (though less often than in Batagarawa) many of the smallest farms were created by other processes: often they had been farm-portions which had been given to sons or farm-slaves as private *gayauni*, or portions which had been sold, pledged, or hedged off as cassava farms.

Unfortunately in Dorayi we found it impracticable to map all the diminutive farms, especially those around the homesteads – see Appendix VII(1) – with the result, incidentally, that some of the farms bordering on tiny plots have had their areas inflated. So it is impossible to assess the full extent to which tiny farms have been divided on inheritance. However, such division occurs much less often than the principle of 'equal division among sons' would lead one to expect. This is firstly because (as in Batagarawa) some of the separate plots are often shared out (like a pack of cards) in a rough and ready way between the sons; and secondly because brothers (especially those who have inherited little land) often postpone division and/or sharing indefinitely, re-allocating the land between themselves from time to time. Although in this latter case no henna boundaries are planted, the temporary allocations are often clearly visible on the aerial photograph since brothers tend to cultivate their ridges perpendicularly to each other – they are, of course, wholly averse to joint cultivation. This 'failure to divide', which hardly ever occurred in Batagarawa, is a direct result of land shortage, for it facilitates the re-allocation of land, according to need, as individual circumstances change.

There is also another consideration, which I had overlooked in Batagarawa: namely the need to make future allocations of land to brothers who were unmarried at the time of their father's death. Our farm maps show that division between married sons (not between all sons) is the practice at the time of death, even though the widow, who will usually soon remarry, seldom claims the share of the farmland to which she is legally entitled, to assist in the maintenance of her unmarried sons: it is entirely clear that unmarried sons never get a share on death unless they have no married brother. When this question is discussed with informants, varying views are (embarrassedly) expressed as to when an unmarried youth becomes entitled to his share of the inheritance; however this may be, our statistics indicate that if farmland is divided on inheritance all resident married sons sooner or later get a share – although, of course, they may happen to sell it to their brothers or anyone else.

Despite all the practical obstacles, I had always assumed that equal division (or sharing) between sons was the general aim and I was, therefore, surprised to discover that eldest sons in Dorayi actually tend to inherit considerably more than their brothers. For a sample of twenty-seven sets of brothers for whom the statistics appeared to be reasonably reliable, the average area inherited and retained by eldest brothers was 2.7 acres, against 1.4 acres for all other brothers – and in only five cases had the eldest brother not inherited (and retained) most land. Such findings clearly illustrate the danger of relying solely on informants' testimony, especially on a delicate subject like inheritance, for no one ever mentioned that eldest brothers tend to claim the largest share. Perhaps the discrepancy is partly due to a tendency for brothers who had been unmarried when their father had died to receive less than their fair share on marriage. But however this may be, it is certainly clear that the eldest brothers are apt to receive more than their fair share at the time of the father's death.

In a sample of thirty sets of brothers who had divided their farmland there were no cases where each separate plot had been divided: in most cases a minority of farms had been divided; thus, in each of three cases where the sons had together inherited eight plots, only two plots had been divided. The total number of plots known to have been inherited by the thirty sets of brothers was 144, a figure which had risen by only about one-third after sub-division – viz. to 194. Certainly, and contrary to superficial appearances, inheritors are doing a great deal to resist the pressures leading to fragmentation by quietly refusing to conform to the rigours of the 'law'. However, small plots under one acre are more often divided on death in Dorayi than in Batagarawa (see *R. H.*, p. 185 and Table VII.1 below).

FARM-SELLING AND FARM-PRICES

As memories are short and inaccurate, as plots are subject to division, and as there have never been any documents recording land transactions (such as were common in southern Ghana as long ago as 1900), so it is very difficult to study trends in the price of farmland. It seems likely that in 1900 prices of farmland in Dorayi were very low relatively, say, to prices of cattle or farm-slaves, even though there was an absolute shortage of land, and a large external demand for it from city-dwellers desirous of establishing slave-estates. When prices in former times were reported in cowries, sums never ran higher than several thousand shells as against, say, 200 000 for a farm-slave. Considering that in 1900 farm-selling was an ancient practice (see *R. H.*, p. 240), which was especially common in overcrowded localities like Dorayi, why did land not have a realistic market value, as it had had, say, in parts of southern Ghana in the last decades of the nineteenth century?

One obvious explanation is that there was no possibility of planting such perennial crops as oil palms or cocoa – of *investing* in land the value of which was bound to rise as these crops developed. Then, the marked inequality of wealth in this slave-owning society meant that the land-sellers, who were the poorest (free) farmers, were at the mercy of richer men and lacked bargaining strength. There was also the matter of the persistence of the regressive pre-colonial taxation system with its flat rates of taxation per farm – see Appendix II(1) – which sometimes bore so harshly on poor farmers, who could apply little manure, that farming was scarcely profitable.

The likelihood is that prices remained very low, at several £s an acre, until the 1950s, when a persistent rise developed. It may be that by the mid-1960s (cf. Mortimore 1965, p. 52, on prices in Ungogo District) prices had risen to around £10 to £20 per acre, but the bargaining position of sellers remained so weak that there was much price variation. Thereafter a rapid rise developed: Mai Unguwa Cikin Gari (Ciranci) considered that a plot which would have fetched £50 in 1971 had been worth no more than £2 to £3 some fifty years earlier, and he said that a particular small plot which was sold for £25 in 1971 had been bought for only 17s some twenty years before. Although higher prices were paid by city buyers for land near a road, it may be that the general level of prices in 1971 was of the order of £60 an acre (exclusive of the value of henna bushes), which was the official rate of compensation for land which was being compulsorily acquired for road-building in the Dorayi area – I cannot be more precise since it seemed that the rise in prices had greatly reduced the number of transactions involving local buyers. Nor was I able to obtain comparable prices for neighbouring places, such as Kirimbo – see Appendix iv(5) – where farm-mapping was impossible owing to the lack both of a suitable aerial photograph and of henna boundaries.

On the basis of enquiries I made about the means by which each mapped farm had been acquired, I estimate that at least a quarter of all the farm-land had been bought by the present owner, compared with about 18% in Batagarawa, where similar enquiries were made. Rich men had bought at least 44% of their farmland, against 12% for those 'neither rich nor poor' and a negligible proportion for poor men. A remarkably close relationship was found between the size of a farmer's holding and the proportion which had been bought: this proportion rose steadily from 7% for holdings under one acre; to 9%, 11% and 13% for holdings of 1.0 to 1.9 acres, of 2.0 to 2.9 acres and of 3.0 to 4.9 acres respectively; and to 36% and 41% for holdings of between 5.0 and 7.5 acres and over 7.5 acres.

About four-fifths of all rich men were recorded as having bought some farmland, and about four-fifths of all buyers of two acres or more were rich men. In a community where so few of the richer men inherit as much land as they would wish to cultivate, there is no need to examine the various reasons that were given for buying particular farms. However, it is interesting to note that a very small number of local men have recently become land speculators, hoping that the land they had acquired would be compulsorily acquired by the State government or re-sold to a rich buyer: an example was a farmer who bought land for £130 in 1970, re-selling it to a city buyer for £220 a few months later.

As for the resident farm-sellers, they are mostly 'neither rich nor poor', for the rich have little need to sell (except for special purposes such as a pilgrimage to Mecca) and most of the poor have little that is worth selling. Nowadays little selling is prompted by extreme poverty, and the fact that the bargaining position of sellers has consequently greatly improved may largely account for rising prices. However, small plots are still sometimes sold to meet marriage expenses: an example being a man who sold a farm for £19 to finance his daughter's (not his son's) marriage.

Perhaps the most common single cause of selling has been outward migration; but as most present-day migrants own little land, as men who go to Kano city often retain some, or all, of their farmland, and as the number of migrants to other destinations is currently so small, migration is not, at present, accounting for much selling. That the volume of selling is falling fast is indicated by the fact that only one-fifth of the sellers of a sample of 231 purchased farm-plots are now living in Dorayi, the majority of the sellers having since died.

The general effect of local farm-selling is, of course, to transfer land from the 'not so rich' to the rich. But the rate of transfer has not kept pace with the rate of expansion of the population descended from rich men (who have more dependants than poor men), so that the holdings of the rich have been constantly declining in size.

Owing to the recent steep rise in the price of land, to the arrival of city-buyers and to speculative buying, future trends regarding land-selling are unpredictable. Thirty years ago land prices were unrealistically low in relation to the value of the potential net yield of basic crops; now they are so preposterously high that purchase cannot be justified except in terms of speculation, the planting of trees (such as mangoes), or the cultivation of special crops such as cassava, onions (on irrigated farms in the dry season) or other vegetables for sale in the city.

SIZES AND NUMBERS OF FARM-PLOTS

The following Table VII.1, relating to the areas of farm-plots in Dorayi and Batagarawa, has been discussed on pp. 98 and 99 above. It only remains to add that as Dorayi farmers seldom give away farm portions to sons-in-*gandu* a lower proportion of plots is created by this process than in Batagarawa.

The idea that the extent of sub-division of plots is a function of the length of time the farmers have been settled on the land as well as of population density receives some confirmation from Table VII.2 which shows that the proportion of farmers in the older-established sections of Dorayi (namely Cikin Gari (Ciranci), Tudun Mazadu and Gwazaye) who own six or more plots (20%) is far higher than in Dorayi Karama and

Ja'en Yamma (8% and nil), this probably reflecting the higher average population density in the former areas before, say, 1900 (see p. 216).

Table VII.1 *Areas of farm-plots*

Acreages	Dorayi	Batagarawa
	Percentages of plots	
Under 0.5	26 } 61	} 23
0.5 to 0.9	35	
1.0 to 0.9	28	38
2.0 to 2.9	7	17
3.0 to 3.9	2	9
4.0 to 4.9	0.6	} 11
5.0 to 9.9	0.6	
10 and over	neg.	2
	100%	100%

Notes:

(i) The Emir's large *gandu* is excluded from the Dorayi figures.

(ii) The Batagarawa figures excluded forty-nine tiny plots of less than about 0.2 acres which were abandoned house-plots.

(iii) As noted elsewhere (p. 78), considerable numbers of tiny plots in Dorayi could not be mapped so that the proportion of plots smaller than 0.5 acres is actually considerably higher than 26%.

Table VII.2 *Number of plots per farm-holding*

	1	2	3	4	5	6 and over	Total
	Percentages of holdings						
'Old-established areas'	22	25	18	9	6	20	100%
Dorayi Karama	36	23	17	8	9	8	100%
Ja'en Yamma	43	19	29	4	4	–	100%
Total Dorayi	32	23	21	7	7	10	100%
Batagarawa	27	28	23	9	8	6	100%

Notes:

(i) The Dorayi figures relate to all farmers (exclusive of married sons) for whom reliable figures were available.

(ii) To ensure as much comparability as possible, the Batagarawa figures relate to those denoted 'heads of farming-units'.

LAND BORROWING (*aro*)

The incidence of land-borrowing (*aro*) in Dorayi is much higher than in Batagarawa and borrowers are more often non-kin. Whether or not it is correct (as I was constantly assured) that any reliable man who wishes to expand the scale of his farming can always find someone willing to lend land to him, it is certain that this system of temporary land transfer, which usually involves borrowing for one season only, is of crucial significance in overcrowded Dorayi where richer farmers often feel an obligation to lend land to those who are in need.

Aro should not be confused with a renting system: it is the temporary loan of something (more often a gown than a piece of land) which is shortly to be returned. The notion of hiring the longer term use of property such as a house or an animal is quite distinct being known as *sufuri* or *haya*. Cash payments for the use of farmland for one season bear little relationship to the size of the plot (£1 per plot seemed to be a common sum) and are sometimes delayed until after harvest; payment in kind, e.g. a bundle of grain after harvest, may also be expected or voluntarily offered – it is the lender's commission (*la'adan mai gona*). While lenders often confer farms on others as an act of assistance or ingratiation, there are times when it suits their practical convenience to do so, perhaps because of their failure to plant the land or to obtain sufficient manure, in which case *aro* is a means of keeping the land in condition until the next season. The advantage of *aro* to the granter is that it involves no long-term obligations such as may be created when a wife allows her husband the use of a plot or when a father grants a son a *gayauna*. As much *aro* involves portions of farms, and as the pattern of borrowing changes every year, so its incidence cannot be studied with the aid of our farm maps; however, on the basis of numerous enquiries, I judge that less than 10% of the Dorayi farmland is on *aro* at any time.

While *aro* is an important safety valve, which operates much more commonly than in former times, it does less than might be expected to relieve the poverty of the poorest men, many of whom have been obliged to contract out of farming (see Chapter XI). In a sample of fifty-three cases of lending, only nine of the borrowers were classified as poor, against thirty-four who were 'neither rich nor poor' and ten who were rich. Although lenders derive kudos from helping poorer men (such assistance is entirely public, whereas cash lending is covert), they select their borrowers carefully and (as I suppose) receive proportionately no more applications from the most impoverished than from other men.

For a long time I was puzzled by the casual way in which much *aro* is granted and by the low charges in relation to the price of land. But the fact is that the attitude to farmland on the part of those who still possess it in quantity remains remarkably unchanged despite the persistent and intensifying pressure. Farmland has suddenly become worth £60 an acre or more: but this has little effect on the use men make of it.

Riko

When men or women migrate, or wish for some other reason to avoid selling or pledging farmland which they do not cultivate themselves, they sometimes place it 'on trust' (*riko* or *amana*) with a relative or friend for an indefinite period, who will then proceed to farm it as though it were his own. The system works well and is much more common in Dorayi than in Batagarawa, presumably because of the higher value of land; in some cases money and/or grain may be paid to the owner, but more commonly the land is free. The tenacity of the system is well illustrated by the following case.

> Alhaji Abubakar placed a farm on *amana* with Saidu when he left for Mecca; the Alhaji died 'in the east' and Saidu also died, the farm passing to the latter's son Husaini. Three successive *dagatai* tried unsuccessfully to seize the farm from Husaini on the grounds that it had belonged to a deceased traveller – but many years later it is still with him. The actual ownership of the farm rests with Marka, the daughter of the late Alhaji, even though she now lives far away at Fort Lamy having married a Dorayi man whom she happened to meet at Mecca. (Alhaji Abubakar had pledged (*jingina*) a portion of the farm to a man who has since died, and his son is still farming there.)

PLEDGING (*jingina*)

It seems that the high population density has little affected the attitude to pledging (*jingina*), which is less common than formerly and is usually regarded as a prelude to selling. Since creditors to whom farms have been pledged sometimes refuse to return the farm unless the loan is quickly repaid, this type of transfer is less reliable than *riko*, especially as no documents record the transaction. There appear to be no important creditors to whom many men have pledged farms. Pledging, like *aro*, often involves farm portions, and we recorded only twenty-one cases in which whole plots had been pledged.

WOMEN'S FARMLAND

Whereas in former times women sometimes owned slaves who cultivated their farmland, nowadays hardly any women employ farm-labourers, such land as they own being usually either put out on *riko* or cultivated by others as though it were their own. Curiously, the proprietary attitude of husbands to their wives' land is partly justifiable for it is said (at least by men) that a wife ought to obtain her husband's permission before selling her farmland, on the grounds that he would be entitled to inherit part of it if she died. Most land-ownership by women is, therefore, concealed: they certainly owned much more than the total of thirty-five acres which was reported to us in the course of the farm-mapping.

Under Muslim law daughters are entitled to inherit farmland from their fathers, their shares being half as large as their brothers'. In rural Hausa-land generally women seldom claim their shares, unless they have no brothers, and the general attitude is that brothers should compensate their sisters if they complain; it may be, also, that sisters sometimes sell their shares to their brothers. In Dorayi, on the other hand, the attitude has recently become highly confused, partly as a result of a number of court cases instigated by women, and there is no doubt that men more often go through the motion of allocating shares to their sisters and that this tends to aggravate the fragmentation of land, whatever may subsequently happen to those plots.

After Emir Sanusi (1953–63) ordered the courts to enforce the law on inheritance by women, some preposterous retrospective claims have been granted. In one case the adult sons of five sisters who claimed that many years previously their mothers, the daughters of the slave-owner Mazadu, had been deprived of their rightful shares: Mai Unguwa Cikin Gari (Ciranci) said that he had been surprised by the success of their claim, con-sidering that brothers had often formerly given grain to their sisters in lieu of the land to which they had strictly been entitled. Such claims have made some farmers so scared of the legal demands that might be made on them by their sisters that they have refrained from selling inherited land.

THE MEN FROM THE CITY

In 1972 about eighty-six acres of Dorayi farmland were owned by sixty-four men who had migrated from Dorayi to Kano city retaining part (or all) of their farmland, a further sixty-five acres having been acquired quite recently by thirty-one city men who were not known to have had any previous connection with Dorayi. (These figures exclude the land owned by the Emir of Kano and the Chief Blacksmith (see pp. 214–5).)

The attitude of Dorayi residents to these farm-buyers tends to be either favourable or resigned. The Village Heads are the chief beneficiaries, some of them receiving large commissions from the buyers; the sellers, who are seldom poor men, are satisfied with the high prices that are negotiated; and the farm-labourers and local overseers appreciate the additional employment opportunities, and the superior food that is provided. The ordinary farmer when questioned about the rich absentees, shruggingly replies that '*they* can do anything because they are rich'; he does not see how such selling could possibly be prevented.

The commission of some 10% on the selling price of the land which is claimed by some of the Village Heads is payable by the Kano buyer, who often refuses to pay in full. However, with prices for accessible land near a road of up to £100 an acre (or more) in 1972 – one buyer is believed to have paid £600, after three months of protracted bargaining, for a farm of 2.2 acres – certain Village Heads were benefiting greatly. In keeping with the Hausa tradition of negotiating through impartial intermediaries, both buyer and seller have their local representatives for bargaining purposes – though on one occasion an intermediary, who was well known to me, claimed to have represented both parties! Considering the large sums that may be involved, it is surprising that the traditional lack of documentation persists, the transaction merely being witnessed by several people who receive small commissions. Indeed, the whole system of absentee farming is dependent on 'trusting people', for the local foremen who are responsible for the day-to-day management of the farms keep no accounts, but verbally report sums spent on wages and food.

Most absentee owners resemble local farmers in having no permanent labourers, and even the trusted foreman who recruits the labourers is engaged for the farming season only. Those with the largest holdings employ gangs of daily-labourers, hiring perhaps forty to fifty men for several days on their various farms in Dorayi and elsewhere; the foremen report that, given one to two days' notice, they have no difficulty in recruiting the labour required. In 1971 the wage for a long-morning's work was usually about 5s, together with food sent to the farm; the city men sometimes provide cassava meal (*garin rogo*) and pounded groundnut cake (*kulikuli*), which is considered superior to the *kunu* (a kind of gruel) provided by local farmers. One alhaji who owns a farm of five acres (which he had bought from about ten different men) is unusual in employing four permanent labourers during the farming-season, and in having sunk two deep, concrete wells at considerable expense. Only one of the Kano owners has built a house on his farm; he has planted many fruit trees, keeps cattle on his land (the only herd in Dorayi) and has dug a water hole.

It is too early to say whether many of the absentee owners propose to improve their land – for instance, by planting fruit trees; but most of the smallest city farmers concentrate on growing grain. The largest farmer, a Kano businessman who since about 1969 had bought some eleven acres of land near the road from a number of farmers owning contiguous plots, had lost much money in 1971 in an unsuccessful attempt to cultivate cotton – a crop which local farmers had abandoned long ago. Like certain other newcomers he proposes to plant many trees – lime, guava and mango.

In 1972, when absentee city-owners held a far lower proportion of the Dorayi farmland than had their predecessors the city slave-owners (see Chapter xiii), it was too early to judge whether the sale of road-side land to non-residents was a disastrous trend which could not be checked.

IRRIGATED FARMING

The recent introduction of small-scale irrigated farming was discussed on pp. 101–2 above. A great deal of skill is required to construct the carefully levelled irrigated plots, which are similar to those which have long existed on river banks in Hausaland, except that no pulley or beam (*jigo*) is utilised, the water being hauled up by hand from wells sunk on the farmland.

The irrigated beds (*rafi*) are not constructed until after the millet has been harvested from the farmland. The soil is then very carefully cleared and levelled so that water drawn from the well and poured into the main channel (*babban doki*) will flow through the entire plot, which is usually, though not always, quite small – a tenth of an acre or less. From the banked up main channel, a network of smaller leats carries the water to each of the tiny banked in squares (*komaye*, sing. *komi*) where crops such as onions, peppers and tomatoes are grown. The *komaye* are watered one by one by breaking the surrounding earth bank and then setting it up again. Two men are required for watering; one of them hauling the water and the other directing its flow.

For onions, which are much the most popular crop, three types of manure should be used in appropriate proportions: sheep and goat droppings from house compounds; pigeon droppings from birds reared in Dorayi and elsewhere – a pannier of such manure was worth 8s in 1971; and latrine manure (*takin masai*) (see p. 102 above). Onion seed comes from various sources, including Zaria Emirate and Ungogo District. Usually only one crop is grown: it is said that the soil becomes too dry for a second planting.

In Tudun Mazadu, where the system was first introduced, at least one man from every house had an irrigated plot in 1971, a total of eighty plots having been listed; in neighbouring Gwazaye there were at least fifty-five plots. A total of at least 150 wells had been sunk. Although it is generally recognised that the greater prosperity of Tudun Mazadu (where nearly a quarter of all married men were regarded as rich) is partly due to this type of farming, little effort has so far been made to introduce it in Cikin Gari (Ciranci), Dorayi Karama and Ja'en Yamma – it was difficult to believe the common excuse that the water table there was everywhere too low. In Tudun Mazadu sons-in-*gandu* commonly own or borrow (*aro*) small plots as do some poor men. Richer farmers often employ labourers during the short stretch of time after the millet harvest when the beds are being prepared; then, and then only, shortage of skilled labour may be a major restraint.

In late 1971 onions were fetching as much as £7 per donkey-pannier in Sabon Gari market (Kano), and young men were buying bicycles on the proceeds of working small plots. While most growers produced a few panniers only, there were some larger farmers, one of whom produced as many as forty panniers.

APPENDIX VII(1)
The farm-mapping

The farms were mapped with the aid of part of a very clear aerial photograph of Kano city and its surrounding countryside, dated December 1969 and on the scale of 1 to 10 000, which was kindly provided by the Survey Division of the Ministry of Works and Survey, Kano State. Although this photograph was more up-to-date and clearer than that used in Batagarawa, and although henna bushes – see Appendix iv(4) – provided a much more conspicuous farm-boundary plant than the *gamba* grass of Batagarawa, yet the task of mapping the farms was unexpectedly difficult, mainly because of the large number of tiny farms, the existence of henna hedges which were erstwhile (false) boundaries, and the delayed division of farms following a father's death. The first and second problems remained severe even when enlargements of the original photograph had been obtained, and the existence of shade trees round houses which obscured ground details made it impossible to map some of the smallest farms.

My assistant, Malam Musa Ibrahim Bagudu, to whom I am most grateful, spent many weeks walking around all the farms and discussing ownership details with the local men who accompanied him. I then proceeded to discuss his sketch map, based on tracings, with one or more of my special informants who showed a remarkable capacity for locating themselves in their imaginations on the ground and then proceeding, by reference to the points of the compass and to natural features such as large trees, to walk (still in their imaginations) around the farms, expatiating on the means by which the present farm-owner had acquired the land. (We used the term 'farm-genealogy' to denote those of our enquiries on changes in ownership which had much time depth.) The work was very laborious for all concerned and no great accuracy is claimed for all the detail. But I think that the general picture of farm-ownership which emerged has proved sufficiently reliable for present purposes.

We had not originally expected to be able to map so much land. Starting in Cikin Gari (Ciranci), we gradually spread to other areas, ending with Dorayi Karama and Ja'en Yamma. Had we not incorporated the latter two sections it happens that the analysis of the transition from farm-slavery to freedom (see Chapter XIII) would have been altogether impossible. As numerous other advantages were derived from mapping (and studying the population of) an area as large as some $2\frac{1}{2}$ sq. miles – it is necessary to study a substantial population for the number of rich men, for example, to be sufficient for analytical purposes – I am sure that the loss of accuracy resulting from our methods, compared with a meticulous survey of a much smaller area, was a small price to pay for an extensive survey which proved to be so much more enlightening than had been expected.

VIII

The married son

Where land is plentiful, as in Batagarawa, a son (like a farm-slave in former times) may flourish greatly under the umbrella of security provided by the system of paternal *gandu* (see *R. H.*), especially when his father is relatively rich. He will receive a farm plot (*gayauna*) for his own use, he may acquire farms for himself by purchase or otherwise, he may sometimes employ farm-labourers and he will be free to pursue remunerative non-farming occupations during his free time. It is true that (to quote one of the most perceptive, and relevant, analyses of the relationship between fathers and sons, even though it relates to China), 'The relation between father and son was overtly one of severe dominance and submission; a son owed obedience and deference; and a distance was called for between the two men which would allow them to maintain a common front to the world without their entering into great intimacy.' (Freedman, 1966, p. 45.) But alongside his obligations as his father's son the Hausa adult commonly asserts his own separate economic identity – his semi-autonomy. And unless his father is poor, and consequently sells his farmland, he will often be able to count on the reversal of their roles when his father retires.

In overcrowded Dorayi, on the other hand, fathers seldom grant their sons *gayauni*, and few sons-in-*gandu* (as distinct from sons of retired fathers) flourish as independent farmers. The fortunes of fathers and sons are consequently closely bound together, especially as fathers expect their sons to hand over part of their earnings from non-farming occupations. The fathers do not react to the land shortage by showing a willingness to release some of their sons on condition that others remain with them; rather do they persist in clinging on to all their sons even when they themselves are landless and unable to provide them with farming work. As we know (see p. 99), virtually all fathers and sons are co-resident and very few sons (of living fathers) migrate.

In China 'the filial relation was in a sense self-defeating' (*ibid.*, p. 45) for as soon as the son assumed a role which made his position ambiguous – the role of father to his own children – he might seek to supersede his father or to break away from him. But as it was legally forbidden for the son to break away if the father was unwilling and as fierce competition between the brothers checked any urge for one of them to predominate, the joint family often remained in existence until the father's death. In Dorayi, where fathers lack legal powers over their sons, the joint family is just as stable. The son's marriage cements the relationship of father and son and there is nothing destabilising about the son's own promotion to the role of fatherhood – indeed, rather the contrary.

The unmarried son occupies a familiar limbo, having few strict rights and duties and being a kind of household anomaly, hanging about and having no proper place to sleep or eat. In many societies, including rural Fanteland in Ghana – see Appendix ix(1) – the unmarried son commonly establishes his identity by migrating; however, in densely populated Dorayi he seldom seeks his fortune elsewhere, but works spasmodically on his father's farmland or as a farm labourer or in other odd jobs, waiting for the day when sufficient money has been accumulated by his father, other relatives and/or himself, to meet his marriage expenses.

When a son marries for the first time he always builds a sleeping hut (*daki*) in his father's house where his wife, however young she may be, invariably joins him. A young wife has few domestic duties; her secluded life is tedious, the other women in the house treating her almost as though she were an invalid, so that she is likely to spend a large part of the day lying on her bed. Such a state of affairs may continue for some years until the wife is old enough to give birth, and as a young mother she will continue to have few duties. But gradually her position begins to resemble that of her husband's father's younger wives, for she starts to take her turn with the household cooking and to participate in the arduous work of winnowing, pounding and grinding, in which all the adult women in the house co-operate. She will also endeavour to achieve a certain degree of economic independence by means of house-trading or processing foodstuffs for sale.

Most married sons remain in *gandu* (whether or not the father has sufficient farmland to set them to work with any regularity), in the sense that, in principle at least, it is the father's responsibility to provide them (and their dependants) with their basic food requirements in return for any work they may do on his farmland and/or a share of their cash earnings. However, poverty induces much departure from principle, so that sons will often find it necessary to buy grain and their wives will be obliged to fend for themselves. Also, many wives expect to provide their own midday meals and to supplement the ingredients in the common pot. Especially when the father owns little land, the distinction between sons who are in and out of *gandu* may become blurred.

Accordingly, Table VIII.1, which relates to the position of married sons, has to be interpreted with some caution. It suggests that about one in five (twenty out of ninety-five) of the sons of fathers who had not reached retiring age were not in *gandu*, but it attempts no such distinction in the cases of sons of retired fathers – who numbered as many as eighty-six. If a father retires and divides his farmland between his sons, then there is no doubt but that the *gandu* relationship still persists; but in cases where there was little farmland to divide, the sons (who may never have been in *gandu*) may find themselves under no formal obligation to their fathers. Although in the former case retirement is a definite status, men being commonly referred to, for example, as 'Yusufu retire' – using the English verb – in the latter case it was sometimes difficult to determine whether a man was retired or not, so that the only course was to put all very old men into that category. Such formal retirement is very much commoner than it was formerly: the promise of retirement is a sop offered to the sons to dissuade them from migrating from this overcrowded locality where their prospects are so poor.

Table VIII.1   *The position of married sons*

	No.	%
Sons of retired fathers	86	41
Other sons in *gandu*[i]	75	36
Sons not in *gandu*	20	9
'Labourers'[ii]	25	12
Not well (*ba lafiya*)	3	(1)
Not known	2	(1)
	211	100%

Notes:
  (i) Including a few men, such as brother's sons, who worked and lived with the *gandu* head as though he were their father.
  (ii) Men who worked for regular wages in Kano city and else-where – see Appendix XI (1) – some of whom were effectively in *gandu*.

Relatively few impoverished men are active *gandu* heads. Table VIII.2 shows that whereas over one-third (35%) of all older rich men (younger men are excluded from the table as they have few married sons) are *gandu* heads, the corresponding proportion for poor men is only 7%. However, this does not mean that many sons of poor fathers had either left *gandu*, taken up work as 'labourers', or migrated. In fact the most notable distinction between rich and poor men of these age groups is that more of the latter have no married sons, 51% against 39%.

Sons whose fathers own significant areas of farmland seldom formally leave *gandu* or work as 'labourers'. The twenty-five sons who were 'labourers' were the sons of twenty-one fathers, only four of whom were known to own more than two acres. Of the sixteen fathers whose sons had definitely left *gandu*, only one owned more than two acres.

Table VIII.2 *The married sons of rich and poor fathers*

Position of fathers	Rich fathers		Poor fathers	
	No.	%	No.	%
Retired	9	21	10	23
Gandu heads	15	35	3	7
Sons have all left *gandu*	2	5	3	7
Sons are all 'labourers'	–	–	4	9
No married sons	17	39	23	51
Sons have all migrated	–	–	1	(2)
	43	100%	44	100%

Notes:
(i) The table relates to old and elderly fathers only.
(ii) See Notes on Table VIII.1.

The wealth classification demonstrates conclusively that only the sons of elderly rich men stand any significant chance of prospering during their father's lifetime. Of the total of 106 (classifiable) married sons (they were neither in *gandu*, nor working as 'labourers'), only twelve were classified as rich: nine of them were the sons of rich fathers (of whom eight were retired), and none of them was the son of a poor father.

Table VIII.3, which relates only to the sons of retired fathers, demonstrates the close relationship between the wealth of fathers and their sons with great clarity. It shows that only one of the twenty-seven sons of rich retired fathers was classified as poor, as against seventeen of the twenty-three sons of poor retired fathers. Of the eleven rich sons of retired fathers, as many as eight had fathers who were rich and none had fathers who were poor; of the twenty-three impoverished sons of retired fathers, as many as seventeen had fathers in similar plight. (It should be borne in mind that there is not likely to be a close relationship between the wealth of fathers and sons in cases where fathers had died before their sons were married.)

About half of the twelve rich sons (one had a father who was not retired) owed their position to trading. One was a sheep and goat trader who

Table VIII.3   *The relative wealth of fathers and sons*

Fathers' wealth	Sons' wealth			
	Rich	Neither	Poor	Total
	No. of married sons			
Rich	8	18	1	27
Neither	3	28	5	36
Poor	–	6	17	23
Total	11	52	23	86

Note: The table relates only to the married sons of retired fathers.

bought in markets and sold in the city – he was also a mango trader; another bought locust beans (*kalwa*) and other produce at rural markets for resale; a third was a successful 'table seller' – the nearest equivalent to a shop keeper in Dorayi; a fourth travelled long distances to sell henna. A summary of the fifth man's multifarious activities follows:

> He bought grain in Hadejia, more than a hundred miles distant, where he went every week, and sold it in Sabon Gari market and from his house; he also sold henna at Hadejia. He bought rice, grain and cassava meal (*garin rogo*) at different places and sold it to people in his house (where 106 people resided), who did not need to buy from anyone else. He supplied a commercial pig farm with *garin dorowa* (a powder derived from the mealy pulp in the locust bean pod), many sacks having been stored in his shed. He was a firewood cutter, even working in the evenings after he had finished farming.

The other (non-trading) occupations of the rich married sons included machine tailoring (there are very few sewing machines in Dorayi), watch repairing at a town some distance away, the buying of trees for firewood cutting, and Koranic teaching – one son had many pupils who provided him with all the grain he required. Most sons lack the finance, or the Koranic learning, to follow such lucrative occupations.

Finally, it should be noted that only three of the twelve rich sons owed their position to being their rich father's only married son; all but one of the remainder had three or more married brothers.

In Batagarawa the sons of poor fathers had a much higher propensity to migrate than the sons of rich fathers (*R. H.*, p. 98). But in Dorayi, where sons are more severely trapped by their father's poverty than they are in

Batagarawa, there is no such relationship, rates of outward migration of sons being very low for all categories of father. In Batagarawa at least a fifth (probably considerably more) of all married sons (with living, resident fathers) had migrated; and about 45% of a sample of 175 ex-schoolboys, of varying ages, had left their village (see *R. H.*, p. 100). But in over-crowded Dorayi, as we know, only 20 out of a total of 231 married sons were recorded as having migrated. That the failure of sons to migrate is due to the very high population density is suggested by the fact that in Kirimbo – see Appendix IV(5) – where the population density is about half that in Dorayi, as many as a quarter of all married sons had removed.

A total of 239 men were recorded as having migrated from Dorayi during the past few decades (see p. 146), forty-one of whom were said to have had living fathers at the time of their departure. As many as fifteen of these forty-one men were reported to have vanished overnight, never to be seen again – an incidence of 37%. The incidence of 'vanishing' among the total population of migrants (see Table IX.1) was 24%. As such a manner of migration was very rare indeed in Batagarawa, where the destination of nearly all migrants was well known, its high incidence in Dorayi should be attributed to the insecurity resulting from high popula-tion density and the consequent unwillingness of fathers and other kin to agree to the departure of sons. Since this category of migration has particularly strong reference to sons, I deal with it in this chapter.

The young men who disappear under cover of night, usually leaving their wives and all their possessions behind them, are commonly known as *'yan duniya* (lit. 'children of the world', though not in the sense of the English idiom) and are spoken of as having adopted the world as their mother (*ya tafi uwa duniya*). Another, less commonly used, term is *dan Dendi* (*ya tafi Dendi* – lit. 'he went to *Dendi*') – meaning, according to one informant, 'going to a place like a barracks, where there are prosti-tutes, food, etc. where people get lost and forget to go home, where there are people from many different places'. No one defined *Dendi* (or *Dandi*) in the manner of Bargery's dictionary as countries to the south and south-west of Kano, or as 'places south of Zaria' (Abraham's dictionary – see also, p. 145 below). But, as Abraham noted, *Dandi* might be applied in Dorayi to anyone presumed to be living a profligate life in Kano city or elsewhere; and those whose whereabouts are unknown are presumed to be wrong-doers. (Men who roam about the world with no fixed jobs or intentions are commonly known as *'yan iska – iska* being air or wind.)

The *dan duniya* may threaten departure (a case in point is a man who threatened to flee if his mother remarried) but more often no prior hint is given of an act which might even be unpremeditated. The relatives are aghast and humiliated: 'If a boy becomes *dan duniya* they do not tell their neighbours; if the neighbours ask where he is they evade the question; it may be a long time before the truth leaks; if it is the wife who reveals the truth, and if he has no parents or brothers who will help her, then she may suffer seriously.' A deserted wife will usually wait for several months before returning to her parental home, and occasionally her patience will be rewarded by a summons from her husband or by his return. Sometimes brothers depart simultaneously, or in quick succession; usually men travel alone. Great efforts are sometimes made to trace the migrant, and it is not unknown for his sons or brothers to vanish likewise in the course of their search.

The hostile act of vanishing may be directed against the community at large rather than close kin, for young solitary men are quite apt to depart in this way, especially when death, or someone else's migration, starts to destabilise a house. In a particular case a household head went to Mecca and never returned: his maternal brother remained in the house, but after he had died his four sons vanished one by one.

So much shame and misery attaches to these sudden departures, which are often seen as inexplicable in terms of what is known of the humdrum circumstances of the case, that witchcraft is sometimes invoked as an explanation. Some people believe that a man may be driven away by tying a charm to the leg of a Senegal blue-winged or laughing dove (*ḳurciya*), whose flight the victim is obliged to follow. But even the staunchest believers in the efficacy of 'bad medicine' may also offer straightforward explanations, as in the case of a son who was believed to have vanished because his cruel father inveighed against him for disobedience and for spending too much time on Koranic studies, thus becoming more learned than he himself.

The migration of sons is seldom deliberately planned, and it is unlikely that brothers ever agree that one of their number may be, as it were, released. As many as seven of the seventeen surviving fathers of the twenty migrant sons are left with no other married son. It seems that impoverished fathers never urge their sons to migrate, and informants commonly attribute other men's poverty to 'too many sons'. However, as younger men are usually able to sustain themselves (however meagrely) by means of farm-labouring and non-farming occupations (see Chapter XI), it is doubtful whether married sons who are of good health are ever a burden on their father. Thus each of the five married sons of a certain impoverished landless man (a farm-seller) manages to provide him with a daily food bowl. The presence of sons does ensure a father's maintenance during his final decrepitude.

Whether or not a man has personally suffered the disgrace of 'son-migration', the subject is virtually taboo: even trusted third-party informants, who are quite prepared to name the migrants, seldom expatiate on the ignominies involved. Emotions resembling mourning are indeed partly justified for most migrants elsewhere than to Kano city are 'lost' in the sense that they retain few, if any, links with their homeland.

POSTSCRIPT

Since this chapter was written an interesting article entitled '*Yawon Dandi*: a Hausa category of migration' by H. Olofson has appeared. It is mainly concerned with the reasons why the name Dandi or Dendi, a district situated south-west of Birnin Kebbi towards the Niger river, should be employed in the manner related on p. 143 above. The author accepts that the origin of the expression *dan Dandi* is unknown to nearly everyone employing it.

IX

The failure to migrate

Detailed enquiries on migration which were made in connection with the compilation of the house genealogies (see p. 109 above), indicate that the Dorayi population might have been of the order of 25% higher in 1972 had it not been for the outward migration (*ƙaura*) of married men (together with their dependants) during a period which can only be denoted as 'the past few decades'. (It is assumed that the inward and outward flows of women on marriage, divorce and widowhood, roughly balance.) Urged to recollect all those men who had ever lived as adults in any house and who had subsequently left Dorayi, informants mentioned a total of 239 men who had removed either from existing houses or (in a few cases) from houses which had recently been abandoned, of whom some sixty-three are known, or are presumed, to be dead; this total would have been somewhat higher had not informants found difficulty in remembering 'vanished houses' – as we always called them, for abandoned houses soon crumble away. It is therefore possible that in 1972 there were some 200 Dorayi men living elsewhere, compared with the 717 who were at home. (I omit seasonal migration (*cin rani*) which is, in any case, very rare in Dorayi.)

Such strong emotions of shame, conflict and embarrassment are aroused by migration that (as we know) it cannot be generally studied with the help of migrants' kin. However, I think that my list of migrants is reasonably complete, both because the details were checked on numerous occasions with various people and because it was gratifying to find that a subsequently compiled list, based on our farm maps, of Dorayi migrants in Kano city who had retained farmland, included very few additional names. If our statistics are conservatively presumed to relate to migration during the past twenty-five years only, so that an average of about ten men left annually during that period, then the annual rate of migration was between 1% and 2% compared with the very tentatively estimated population growth rate (net of migration) of some ½% to 1%. (Whatever the defects in our figures, their time depth is such as to make them greatly superior to any other comparable published statistics relating to rural Hausaland.)

The main features of the migration, some of which have already been discussed, are easily summarised: (1) Much the most important single destination is Kano city, which received about two-fifths of all the migrants and the proportion of men who migrate outside the Hausa Emirates is very small; (2) Men seldom migrate during their father's lifetime – or before they have married (see Chapter VIII); (3) A considerable proportion of migrants departed soon after their father's death; (4) Such is the shame attached to migration that many men vanish overnight and are never seen again (see Chapter VIII); (5) There is no migration at all for the purpose of taking up land in less densely populated farming localities; (6) A fair proportion of those who migrate to Kano city continue to cultivate some, or all, of their Dorayi farmland; (7) The rate of migration from big houses is no more than about half that for the community as a whole (see Chapter XII); (8) Nearly all migration (except, occasionally, for Koranic studies) is not only intended to be permanent, but is so in fact; (9) Most migrants, at least in the early stages, follow unskilled, ill-paid, irregular occupations – much as they did at home; and (10) While an extremely small number of migrants to Kano become rich businessmen or traders who help their Dorayi kin, the total value of remittances from other migrants, most of whom retain few links with their homeland, is certainly very low.

The destinations of migrants are given in Table XI.1, which speaks for itself.

MIGRATION TO KANO CITY

As Table IX.1 shows, ninety-seven Dorayi men are known to have migrated to live in Kano city during the past few decades. As the list is thought to be reasonably complete, this means that no more than, say, four men migrate to the city annually, compared with the fifty-one 'labourers' who commute there daily and the sixty, or so, men who work there spasmodically as traders, earth-carriers, etc. Considering that many of those who migrate continue to cultivate their Dorayi farmland, why do not more men seek to have the best of both worlds by removing to the metropolis?

To pose such a question is to presume that men better themselves by migration – but of this there is little evidence. So far as is known only one Dorayi migrant, who became a school teacher, was literate in English at the time of his departure and most of the migrants, who are unskilled, join the great pool of partially occupied men who constantly compete for

Table IX.1 *The destinations of migrants*

	Dorayi		Kirimbo[1]	
	No.	%	No.	%
Kano city	97	41	8	16
Nearby countryside	17[ii]	7	2	(4)
Elsewhere in Kano Emirate	10	4	3	6
For Koranic studies – elsewhere than Kano city	11	5	7	14
Soldiers	8	3	4	8
Other Hausa Emirates	24[iv]	10	12	24
Elsewhere	10	4	7	14
'Vanished' (*'yan duniya*)	57[v]	24	6	12
Not known, other	5	2	1	(2)
Total	239	100%	50	100%

Notes:

(i) See Appendix IV (5); these figures relate to a shorter period than those for Dorayi.

(ii) Most of those who removed to the nearby countryside joined relatives or affines.

(iii) These men mainly went to cities: eight to Zaria, four to Katsina and three to Kaduna; other destinations included Funtua – five men.

(iv) Two men went to Ibadan, the same number to Jos and one to Lagos; only one man went outside Nigeria – to the Niger Republic.

(v) See p. 143 above.

irregular, part-time work. Even if their earnings are somewhat higher than at home, their housing costs are likely to be much higher; and housing conditions in Dorayi, where there is a good water supply (such as is so often lacking in the West African countryside) and where many house compounds are large and airy, compare very favourably, especially so far as secluded women are concerned, with the squalid, hot, overcrowded rooms in the city, with their tiny interior courtyards, for which migrants are obliged to pay very high rents. Even if a man is able to build a house, or to join relatives, it does not follow that he and his dependants will be better off than at home.

In the longer run the lot of some migrants may improve: they may be more fully occupied than was ever possible in Dorayi, find a rich patron, become skilled craftsmen or building workers, or discover new opportunities of enlarging their minds through Koranic studies. But the number of Dorayi migrants who enjoy real economic success as traders, contractors or transporters, is diminutive, the list including only five men who have made the pilgrimage to Mecca, compared with ten *alhajai* in Dorayi – and most of these men had initially migrated elsewhere than to the city. Although about a third of the migrants retain some farmland in Dorayi which they may continue to cultivate, occasionally with the help of labourers, most of their holdings are under two acres, the largest being only 3.8 acres.

MIGRATION FOLLOWING THE FATHER'S DEATH

When a father dies the moral pressure on his sons to remain resident is suddenly lifted or reduced and the sons' ability to finance their migration is sometimes enhanced by the opportunity of selling inherited farmland. While most fatherless brothers remain co-resident in Dorayi, there is a fairly strong tendency for two or more brothers to migrate simultaneously, or in quick succession, following their father's death; as many as one-third of all migrants had one or more brothers who also removed, though usually not to the same destination unless it were Kano city.

NO MIGRATION FOR FARMING

Whereas Batagarawa men commonly migrate to less densely populated localities some distance away, where they can establish large farms around their houses (see *R. H.*, Chapter VII), there is no such migration from Dorayi; and enquiries elsewhere in the Kano Close Settled Zone suggest that Dorayi is not a special case – thus, none of the fifty migrants from Kirimbo (see Table IX.1) had removed for farming. Considering that there is much unoccupied, fertile, land in Hausaland within a radius of, say, sixty miles of Dorayi, in localities where migrants would be welcome, why should men fail to relieve the persistent and intensifying pressure on the land by removing there?

Obviously direct questioning – 'Why do you not migrate for farming?' – would elicit no satisfactory response in a community where such action is never contemplated. The only relevant reply I ever received from indirect questioning was that if a man had money it would make more sense to buy additional manure than to remove elsewhere. The core of the matter is, indeed, money. Unless a migrant joins relatives who can assist him when he first arrives (and I doubt whether Dorayi men have any relatives in developing farming areas), he would need considerable capital, say £100 to £200, to tide him over until his crops are harvested and to meet his transport, building and other costs.

In Batagarawa it had been found that no young men migrated for farming: nearly all migrants were moderately prosperous younger middle-aged men with working sons who accompanied them. Why do such men not migrate from Dorayi? The facts of the matter are that there are few Dorayi men of that age who have sufficient means to migrate for farming, and that those who have the money usually lack the incentive. Of the total of 265 younger middle-aged men (*matsakanci*), only those who are rich would conceivably be able to finance their migration, and there are only twenty-four of them. Eight of these men would be reluctant to remove as they have living fathers; two are handicapped by having no working sons; and most of the remaining fourteen men are sufficiently secure to lack the incentive to migrate – one of them is a well known Koranic teacher with many pupils who assist him with his farming, three are successful traders who buy farm produce for resale in local markets, and another man travels widely as a henna trader.

If Dorayi (like Batagarawa) men had earlier established the practice of migrating to certain areas for farming, then there would certainly have been others who had followed them. Considering the entire lack of such migration during the past few decades, the likelihood is that there has been no tendency for free men to remove for farming away from the core of the Kano Close Settled Zone during a much longer period – though whether the exodus of farm-slaves and their descendants during the early years of the century sometimes involved removal to other rural areas is not known.

Although it is very well known that a great variety of modes of migration have been evolved by different West African ethnic groups (see Hill, 1970), it is yet difficult to escape from such stereotyped notions as that migrants in general tend to join their 'brothers', to return home regularly on ceremonial or other occasions, and to resume farming (if they have abandoned it) in later life – none of which applies to Dorayi. Most Dorayi migrants resemble the *'yan duniya* in seeking their fortunes as individuals and do not join others who have preceded them, except sometimes in Kano city; few men return home on ceremonial occasions unless they have joined relatives in the neighbouring countryside; and most migration is permanent – such few migrants as return home do so abjectly as failures. Dorayi people resemble the rural Hausa generally in the latter regard: this means that the crucial factor determining the permanency of migration is not land shortage but the lack of lineage land, the existence of which would automatically entitle men to resume rights of cultivation on their return. The permanency of Hausa migration has often been observed in the receiving areas – see also Olofson (1976).

But the most common and dangerous of all misbeliefs is that there is necessarily a close relationship between population density and the incidence of migration. Our findings in Dorayi show that such a mechanistic approach is unjustified: social factors, such as the cohesiveness of kin groups, may operate more strongly than crude economic incentives and men may be too poor to migrate for farming. The demographic factor is at times profoundly unimportant. In parts of rural Fanteland in southern Ghana where land is very plentiful, fathers actively encourage all their sons to migrate when they are young – some of whom return in their middle years. The contrast between these Fante villages and Dorayi so well illustrates the significance of social factors that I provide brief particulars of the Fante migration in Appendix ix (1).

APPENDIX IX(1)
Migration from rural Fanteland

In 1975, in connection with work on women food farmers, I studied two Fante villages, Taido and Kwaman, which are situated some four and fifteen miles inland from the Ghanaian coastal town of Anomabu. Although these two villages were surrounded by oceans of uncultivated forest, which could be freely cleared and cultivated, and although there was a ready demand in the markets for any foodstuffs which could be produced, yet the rate of outward migration of young men and women (some half of whom had never regularly attended school) was nearly 100%. In one of these villages there were no fathers or mother's brothers (the Fante are matrilineal) who had resident married sons or sister's sons: they had all migrated. In the other village, with its population of sixty-two 'ever-married men', there were only three fathers with sons who had not migrated.

In extraordinary contrast to Dorayi, there was no clash between the generations, for all the fathers, mothers, maternal uncles and other kin agreed with the young people themselves that migration was necessary 'because there is no work here'. In a strange way these farming communities, in which every able-bodied man and woman is a farmer, do not regard farming as *work* (*edwuma*) and the compulsion to migrate is regarded (though this is never overtly stated) as a function of the poor organisation of food-farming. There are no farming-groups resembling *gandu* in Fanteland, and young men are disinclined to work with either their fathers or their mother's brothers. Apart from the clearing of the forest and bush, most of the cultivation and harvesting of food crops is done by women. The wives of newly married young men are inexperienced, lacking in stamina to pursue day-to-day farming on their own, and especially apt to be involved in child-bearing: they, like their husbands, hate the very idea of farming. Although Fante (unlike Dorayi) fathers often pay for their sons to be apprenticed, it is well known that the Fante migrants, who mainly go to towns and cities in southern Ghana, and often hold skilled jobs, may suffer more hardship than at home; but they are prepared to take this risk in the full knowledge that they can exert their rights over lineage land whenever they may choose to return home, as do a fair proportion of people in their middle years, so that the villages do not become depopulated.

X

The rich men

Although the rich men of Dorayi are becoming steadily poorer over the decades – their farm-holdings constantly diminishing in size and their incomes from non-farming occupations declining – they still remain economically viable, possessing some power of manoeuvre in unfavourable circumstances and able to render some help to others. While such farmers store much less grain for the purposes of selling it for a seasonal price-rise than do Batagarawa farmers (see *R. H.*, p. 162) and thus make less profit from selling grain to poorer farmers, this *laissez faire* economic system naturally operates to favour the rich and disfavour the poor. For all kinds of reasons, including the fact that they apply more manure, the rich get greater returns per unit of effort than the poor: although their farming techniques are similar, their yields are higher and their non-farming occupations tend (as we have seen) to be more remunerative. Also, of course, their labour is more fully utilised than that of the poor – though they, too, often have considerable difficulty in setting themselves to work.

In Chapter VI it was established that whereas nearly a quarter of all old and elderly men were rich, the incidence of wealth in the two youngest age groups was but 11% and 4%; that rich elderly men had significantly more wives and other dependants than other men; that rich men had farm-holdings which averaged 6.1 acres, against 2.2 acres for all married men; that only 6% of rich men had holdings of under three acres compared with 74% of all men; and that rich men tended to have much more remunerative types of non-farming occupation than other men. I now turn to consider certain other aspects of the situation of rich men.

Rich men have much more often enjoyed favourable inheritance situations than other men. As Table x.1 shows, about two-thirds (thirty-four out of fifty-four) of the rich fatherless men for whom this information was available are believed to have had rich forebears – this being a far higher proportion than for married men in general. It is also interesting to note that about half of all the fifty-four men happened to have been their father's sole inheritor: it is clear that the accident of either having no brothers, or of having brothers who migrated or were sonless, is a chance circumstance which accounts for some men's wealth. As for the rich sons with living retired fathers, two-thirds (eight out of twelve) of them had benefited from having rich fathers.

Table x.1   *Inheritance and wealth*

Numbers of rich men		
(1) Rich fatherless men		
(a) Favourable inheritance situation:		
rich slave-owning ancestry	9	
other rich male forebears	22	34
'helped by mothers'	3	
(b) Other:		
free-origin	15	
slave-origin	5	20
(2) Rich sons with living retired fathers		
Rich fathers		8
Other fathers		4

Notes:
  (i) Information on inheritance situations was mainly obtained from the five special informants: in the case of slave-owning ancestry, the father or the paternal grandfather, or in a few cases a woman forebear, had been a slave-owner; in three cases special emphasis was laid on the help that a man had received from his mother.
  (ii) Six cases of fatherless men for whom the information was not available are omitted.

As we know (see Table vi.3), rich men are far more apt to be traders than poorer men. However, Table x.2 makes it quite clear that farming remains the preferred occupation of those whose land-holding position enables them to pursue it on a reasonable scale. Only two of the fifteen rich men who cultivate more than ten acres are traders compared with ten of the twenty men who cultivate less than five acres. Many rich men whose inheritance situations had been unfavourable owe their present position mainly to trading. Another notable point emerging from Table x.2 is that those with land-holdings of five acres and over are much more apt to be Koranic specialists than men with smaller holdings. But in this connection it has to be pointed out that over a half of the farmers with the smallest acreages are younger men, none of whom are Koranic specialists, six of whom are traders. Table x.2 relates to fatherless men only, since few men with living fathers own much land and it is, therefore, necessary to add that as many as eight of the twenty rich married sons are traders.

Although there are as many as twenty fatherless rich men whose holdings are thought to be under five acres, there are probably only four rich men (one of whom has retired from farming) whose holdings are less than three acres. Rich men nearly always farm on a scale which accounts for a significant proportion of their incomes. At the same time the relationship between the scale of farming and wealth is less marked than in Batagarawa, where only one of the seventeen rich farmers owned less than five acres.

Table x.2   *Principal non-farming occupations of rich (fatherless) men*

Occupation	10 acres or more	5 to 9.9 acres	Under 5 acres	Total
	Number of men			
Traders	2	11	10	23
Koranic specialists (*karatu*)	6	6	3	15
Wood-cutters (*faskare*)	3	–	1	4
Earth-carriers in city	–	3	1	4
Other	1	2	1	4
'No occupation':				
retired	1	1	2	4
other	1	2	1	4
Not known	1	–	1	2
Total	15 (4)	25 (5)	20 (11)	60 (20)

Notes:
  (i) Farm acreages have been partly estimated in a few cases.
  (ii) Koranic specialists include imams, teachers and students who had no other important non-farming occupation.
  (iii) 'Other occupations' include two tailors and one blacksmith.
  (iv) Those whose sole occupation is making cornstalk beds are included under 'no occupation'.
  (v) The figures in parentheses relate to the number of men in the two younger age groups.

There being no exceptions to the rule that to be rich and respected it is necessary to be a farmer, it may well be asked whether men may not sometimes persist as farmers owing to the prestige this bestows rather than because of its profitability. I think that the profitability of farming (provided sufficient manure is applied) should not normally be called in question in a community where the degree of under-utilisation of labour is so great that the time spent in cultivating the soil scarcely affects the level of other activities. Farmers with substantial acreages always have sons-in-*gandu* and/or labourers to work on their farms and if, owing to their lack of sons, it is necessary for them to supervise the farm work themselves, then they are able to reduce the number of days involved by hiring groups of labourers rather than individual men.

Nowadays the scale of operation of most Dorayi traders is severely limited not only by shortage of capital, but also by serious restrictions on demand and/or supply. As many as eleven of the twenty-three rich men who are traders are concerned with selling goods to local people only, and in the field of produce trading there are only three men whose operations are wholly unlimited by demand because they supply a much wider market than Dorayi and its neighbourhood. Of the six rich men who trade mainly in the city, most sell local goods such as henna and sheep and goats, which are severely limited in supply. In fact most Dorayi men who trade in the city are classified as 'neither rich nor poor', many of them being part-time vegetable sellers (*'yan gwari*).

While men with favourable inheritance situations are more apt to prosper than other men, there have been many who have overcome the poverty of their earlier years: as Table x.1 showed, over a third of all fatherless rich men had not had rich forebears. In former times, before the price of farmland had risen so steeply, impoverished men of slave-descent (see Chapter xiii) or others who had inherited little farmland were sometimes able to build up their economic strength to the point that they became sustantial farmers. It will be remembered (see p. 128 above) that at least 44% of the farmland owned by rich men had been bought and all but three of the seventeen rich men for whom brief particulars are provided in Appendix x (1) had been farm-buyers – the exceptions being cases A(3), A(4) and G. Before turning to consider the consequences of the great rise in farm-prices, which has occurred too recently to be reflected in the statistics and case studies, I must examine the Hausa concept of *arziki*, a word with the double sense of prosperity and good fortune.

According to the philosophy of *arziki* (see also *R. H.*, pp. 185–7) wealth, which comes to few men, is a mysterious personal attribute necessary for success in this world. In other words, *arziki* is a gift which cannot be rationally explained in terms of inheritance, hard work, many sons, intelligence, religious piety or learning, relationships with rich or influential outsiders, political position – or by a conjunction of such circumstances or attributes. A man may appear to possess every advantage in life, but unless he happens to be endowed with *arziki* he cannot succeed; on the other hand, a man's prospects may appear hopeless and yet, magically, as a *mai arziki*, he successfully overcomes all difficulties. (A pronounced lack of *arziki* is, also, a personal attribute: there are men who are born to lose.) *Arziki* is not a reward for virtue: although those who possess it are admired and envied, they are always seen as the predestined winners of a game of chance.

Such a philosophy fitted the realities of the economic situation in Batagarawa – which is probably reasonably representative of Hausa rural communities outside the inner ring of the Kano Close Settled Zone. It reflected the existence of an open society, such that no man, however ill-endowed, was *necessarily* precluded from becoming rich during the course of his life. It incorporated the observation that certain men had a strong tendency to get steadily richer as they got older. In a community which held a very moral attitude towards such virtues as hard work, it was an expression of the bewilderment men feel when faced with the fact that the deserving often fail – though the undeserving may succeed. It represented a realisation that wealth was poorly transmitted between the generations – that the society was not class stratified. As rich men had more wives and accordingly more sons to share their inherited property than poor men; as 'farming businesses' (*gandaye*) usually collapsed on death; as certain other types of business, such as trading, tended to collapse, or to be abandoned, in the prime of life; as the hiatus which occurred on the death of a *gandu*-head was a period of disarray rather than of reorganisation according to accepted procedures – so it was that death was the great leveller (*R. H.*, Chapter xiii).

The philosophy of *arziki* remains strong in Dorayi today, this being to some extent justified by the realities of the situation. Some men are inexplicably successful, whereas others strangely lose all that they possess. Rich men sometimes have very poor brothers. The steady progress some men make as they get older is not always comprehensible in terms of the economic benefits derived from having more working sons, especially as richer men often own insufficient farmland to provide their sons with regular work. The society is open in that authority systems fail to bolster the rich: rich middle-aged men are uninterested in seeking office as Village Head, Village Heads are not notably prosperous, and many rich men are not household heads.

But the philosophy of *arziki* naturally takes insufficient account of one most important recent change. Formerly it had been possible for men who owned little land gradually to accumulate sufficient capital to purchase it; cases B(1), B(2), C(2) and E in Appendix x (1) illustrate the process by which poor men slowly established themselves as substantial farmers by means of odd jobs such as farm-labouring and the making of cornstalk beds, as well as by working on borrowed land. But nowadays owing to the steep rise in the price of land and to the low earnings derived from most non-farming occupations, it would be very difficult indeed for poor men to become notable farmers. Insofar as land ownership continues to be a necessary condition for prosperity, upward mobility will become more severely restricted, for land buyers are necessarily rich men. While in the short run the only foreseeable change which might enable poorer men with very little farmland to break this barrier would be the further development of irrigated vegetable farming in the dry season, in the longer run this would be bound to raise the price of land and to enhance the inequality of land-holding.

However, this conclusion regarding upward mobility does not imply that the proportion of land in the hands of the largest land-holders will necessarily increase. Owing (as we know) to the increasing pressure of population on the land and the nature of the polygynous system, the holdings of the largest farmers have been constantly diminishing in size and there is no reason to believe – see Appendix vi(1) – that the 'top 15%' of all farmers have necessarily managed to increase their share of the farm-land during the past decades despite much land buying. If the low rates of outward migration continue, it is likely that the proportion of land owned by the richest farmers will diminish in future, for the willingness of smaller land-owners (most of whom are not impoverished) to part with their land will probably be reduced. Nor do most richer farmers stand much chance of increasing their bargaining power as land buyers by means of developing their non-farming activities, the scale of which is nearly always severely restricted by limitations of demand and supply.

In Batagarawa where fathers were often in a position to take up more land as their number of working sons increased, and where few sons left *gandu*, it was easy to discern and comprehend a general tendency (which did not necessarily apply to the most impoverished) for wealth to increase with age. (See the discussion of the developmental cycle in *R. H.*, pp. 165 *et seq.*, which is not repeated here.) Since the wealth and age groupings used in Dorayi were not identical with those in Batagarawa, precise statistical comparisons of the relationship between age and wealth cannot be made, but the general pattern would appear to be remarkably similar: thus, in Batagarawa 19% of all those aged fifty or over were rich, compared with 23% of the two oldest age groups in Dorayi, and the corresponding percentages for lower age groups were very similar in both places.

Given the lack of bush farms, Dorayi fathers have had more difficulty than Batagarawa fathers in matching their supplies of land and labour as their family work forces have expanded, and it is therefore likely that an important determinant of the link between age and wealth has been the greater contribution that older sons make to the household finances by means of non-farming work. In Dorayi, but not in Batagarawa, married sons are expected to hand over part of their non-farming earnings to their fathers or to contribute in some other way to the expenses of their fathers' households (of which they are nearly always members), and more elderly (retired) fathers are largely maintained by their sons in Dorayi than in Batagarawa. For this reason it is likely that even if the relationship between wealth and age becomes less pronounced as the incidence of farm-selling diminishes, it will still remain quite marked.

Then there is the question of the contribution made to household expenses by wives. The Hausa system of marriage expenses, which often involves numerous large payments and counter-payments (see *R. H.*, pp. 150–2), operates to increase the supply of wives to the rich at the expense of the poor (as well as to the old at the expense of the young); it also effects considerable redistribution in favour of the younger generation, at the expense of their parents, for the chief beneficiaries are the spouses themselves rather than their parents, and not only because wives often receive large dowries. But in a society where secluded wives do no farming it should not be lightly assumed that the general wish to have more than one wife is explicable largely in economic terms, for the status derived from having two (or better still three or four) wives coupled with men's desire to have large numbers of children would be sufficient explanations. Nevertheless – see p. 173 below and Appendix xi(3) – many wives who are active house-traders do make significant contributions to household expenses, especially when they are middle-aged, and the wives of richer husbands more often receive financial assistance from their husbands than other women. Accordingly rich husbands are particularly apt to benefit from the increased earning power of their growing number of wives as they get older. And the same general point may apply to the married sons of rich men, who tend to get richer as they get older, and who are seldom a burden on their fathers.

So the forecast that upward mobility will become more severely restricted in future does not mean that younger men, who own several acres, will no longer tend to get richer as they get older. There are eighteen men in the two younger age-groups who were classified as 'neither rich nor poor' and who own four acres or more of farmland; even if they buy no more land, most of these men stand quite a good chance of flourishing in later life.

For a long time now the dice have been heavily weighted against men who own little land. However, since a few of them flourished with advancing years the system could have been described as very sticky but not set. Now the door of advancement towards the position of *mai arziki* has been firmly closed against them.

Although in the longer run most rich men will prove to have had rich fathers, yet most of the sons of rich fathers will not become rich. Even in Batagarawa it was found that the average acreage of manured farmland per working son showed little variation with wealth (see *R. H.*, p. 181), so that many of the sons of rich fathers would inherit less farmland than other men. Owing to the declining size of farm-holdings in Dorayi, this conclusion applies with even greater force and most of the sons of the twenty rich men who own under five acres (see Table x.2) will inherit little farmland.

Paradoxically, it is only when one contemplates the plight of rich men, and their descendants, in Dorayi that one comes to a proper understanding of the nature of urban exploitation. In 1900 most of the wealth deriving from *Hausa* long-distance trade and from manufactures accrued to countrymen; even had there been no sizeable cities, the prosperity of many rural communities (especially in the Kano Close Settled Zone) would have been assured by their integral role in the wider economy of the W. African savannah. The inegalitarianism of such slave-owning rural communities had three special features: first, most rich men were not dependent on patrons in the cities, but merely seized the opportunities which were open to them; second, rich polygynous men were enabled to transmit their wealth to some of their sons; third, poor men (in many areas) were assured of a minimum (though low) income from weaving, dyeing and other crafts. Although the rich men's wealth consisted mainly of farm-slaves, cattle and grain stocks, for 'trading-businesses' usually (though not always) collapsed on death, it was because trading and agriculture went hand-in-hand that large scale capital accumulation was possible. Now that countrymen have had their trading and manufacturing functions usurped by city dwellers the rich, as well as the poor, stand economically disenfranchised and few of them are rich enough to interest wealthy patrons in the city. Their physical capital stocks consist only of farmland and (possibly) of grain: the latter are still very apt to be dissipated on death and the former are rapidly shrinking in size over the generations in overcrowded areas such as Dorayi. As for the poor men, who no longer have a guaranteed minimum livelihood from weaving, their plight will be dealt with in the following chapter.

APPENDIX X(1)
Notes on seventeen rich men

N.B. Using the abbreviations defined on p. 110, the age-group of each man follows his number. (Five of the men are TSO, nine DAT and three MAT.)

A. *Koranic specialists*

A(1) – TSO.   The youngest of six sons of a member of a rich slave-owning family, this old man had benefited from being the only son who had stayed in *gandu* with his father; he had also inherited farmland from two of his brothers who had died childless. He is a well-known imam and Koranic teacher and has been to Mecca. Now retired, another local alhaji buys locust beans and grain on his behalf, and he also sends some of his four sons on buying expeditions during the dry season; he sells the locust beans mainly to local women, the grain in the city, and is also a local trader in cassava, groundnuts and henna.

A(2) – DAT.   As a Koranic teacher whose students and sons-in-*gandu* do all his farm work, he probably owes his prosperity largely to the fact that four of his five brothers migrated, abandoning their farmland which he appropriated, so that he effectively inherited over ten acres. He is probably the only remaining man weaver in Dorayi and makes gowns for sale in the countryside. He is the head of a house which was once big and is now dilapidated.

A(3) – DAT.   The head of one of the largest houses in Dorayi, he is an important imam whose father (also an imam) had had six sons, a second house in the city and a mother who had been a slave-owner. He bought or inherited farms from certain of his brothers (three of whom had died sonless) and mainly relies on some $7\frac{1}{2}$ acres of farmland which had formerly been owned by his father, though he also has *aro* farms. Two of his resident brothers are also rich and a third is an alhaji who removed to his father's house in the city. With no occupation other than Koranic work, he is not considered very rich pecuniarily – but his position is secure and he is 'rich with friends'.

A(4) – MAT.   He was his father's only son and owes his wealth to farming on his inherited farmland as well as to the labour and other support received from numerous Koranic students, some of whom are young strangers subsisting mainly on alms, others being local boys. He travelled widely for Koranic studies and made the pilgrimage in 1972. He recently refused an offer of £700 from a city man for a farm of some two acres near a road. He has three wives and eleven dependants.

A(5) – TSO.   This old man and his two brothers are the sons of a rich and well-remembered slave- and cattle-owner. He bought inherited farmland from his brothers and, most exceptionally for a junior brother, is the household head 'because he is richer than his older brother and everybody knows this'. He has nine married daughters and one son, who is likewise considered rich, having bought more than five acres of farmland. He refused (unlike his brothers) to sell his inherited sugar cane farm – for a sum of £260. Both he and his son are Koranic teachers, and he still does some farming.

B. *Slave-descendants*

B(1) – TSO.   A man of some eighty years whose parents were farm-slaves, he inherited no farmland. Remembered as having been 'very poor and wearing wrappers' when he was young, he worked as a farm-labourer and on *aro* farms and also made many cornstalk beds until, by 1962, he was able to buy a portion of farmland formerly owned by his father's owner. He somehow continued buying farms and gradually became rich, cultivating much henna which he stored for a price rise. He bought a house in the city which he sold to finance one of his two pilgrimages to Mecca. Having no son, two young kinsmen help him with his farming, and he also employs labourers. In 1972 he sold a farm for £100 in order to divide the cash between his wives before he died.

b(2) – DAT. The son of a farm-slave who had ransomed himself, he inherited only one small farm, but over the years he managed to buy some ten acres. Starting work as a butcher, he very gradually built up his financial strength by donkey transportation and by cultivating *aro* farms and *rafi* (irrigated onion farms). It was not until recently that he, an elderly man, was able to establish himself as a produce trader, buying grains, rice, etc. in Rimin Gado market and selling from his house – since when he has come to be regarded as one of the richest men in Dorayi. Two of his three wives are prominent house-traders.

c. *Men who became rich through farming and trading*

c(1) – DAT. The only surviving son of a slave-owner and of a mother who went to Mecca, he cultivates about twelve farms (some fifteen acres), many of which had been bought or inherited from deceased brothers (or their sons) or placed on trust (*riko*) with him. Formerly a skin-trader, he is now retired. He owns many sheep and guinea fowl and is noted for buying rams for resale to traders before the Muslim festivals (*salla*). Through an intermediary he grants loans, at high interest, to city wage-earners. In 1972 he discovered that large quantities of grain which he had stored for some three years, without using Gammalin, had deteriorated to the point of being inedible by goats! He has no working sons and employs farm-labourers.

c(2) – TSO. He was one of eight brothers who reached maturity, and he probably inherited little farmland. When he died in 1972 he left a large farm for which he had rejected an offer of £700 and other purchased farms; his large stocks of groundnuts were divided between his two wives; and he also left a large sum of money in his hut (*turaka*) which his son deposited for safe-keeping with another alhaji. He became rich through farming and trading and was also a Koranic teacher. He had sold farmland for £110 to finance his pilgrimage. Although, as an old man, he had stopped farming himself, he had not transferred responsibility to his son, who is a successful farmer in his own right. As a produce trader he never went to market, but commissioned others to buy on his behalf; he was well known for granting credit to women buyers of locust beans and groundnuts and for storing produce for a price rise.

d. *A rich farmer whose brothers had remained subordinate to him*

DAT. Having financed his pilgrimage by selling a sugar cane farm for £300 (a farm which he had bought some ten years earlier for £17), he died in

Mecca in 1972. Although his father had died ten to twenty years earlier, his farmland had never been divided between his five sons, two of whom had vanished, the other two having been in fraternal *gandu*. With no non-farming occupation other than Koranic reading, he had become rich through farming, and had bought or otherwise acquired some ten acres. He had a very large irrigated onion farm and owned a horse.

E. *A rich man, who is not a trader, who bought nearly all of his farmland*

DAT.   An elderly man, who owns the largest acreage in Dorayi, he was one of five brothers who had probably inherited little farmland. However, starting as a young man in *gandu* and gradually extending his acreage, he finally managed to buy nearly twenty acres from the proceeds of farming. He has been twice to Mecca; he is a prominent local creditor; he grants loans, at high interest, to wage-earners in the city; he stores large quantities of grains and groundnuts (which he has grown himself) for sale when seasonal prices have risen – in March 1972 his stocks from his 1971 crop remained untouched. Although not the head of the big and prosperous house where he lives, eighteen people, including his three wives and three sons-in-*gandu*, live in his house-section.

F. *Notable traders*

F(1) – DAT.   The owner of at least fifteen acres, perhaps a third of it inherited, he is said to have owed his good start in life to his mother, who was a rich village cloth-trader who gave him a farm. He has prospered as a farmer and also as a produce trader – he is the only man described as being 'just like a *madugu*', an old-style caravan leader. He buys produce in Katsina and Bauchi Emirates and also in nearby markets and undertakes much storage for a price-rise; he sells both locally (from his house) and in the city. Unlike other Dorayi produce buyers he has several business associates. He is particularly noted for buying great quantities of locust beans, and three of his four wives make and sell locust bean cakes from beans which they buy from him. He grants loans, at high interest, to wage-earners in the city and is a local creditor.

F(2) – MAT.   One of the best-known traders in Dorayi, he resells much grain from his house which he buys weekly at Rimin Gado market and elsewhere, and he also trades in rice and locust beans, sometimes selling in the city. He sometimes works as a tailor in the city, owning a machine. His father (who had been one of ten brothers) had become rich through farming, but neither of his other two sons is at all well off as they sold their inherited farmland.

G. *An old man who has only recently become rich with the aid of his six married sons*

TSO. Born about 1898, the present prosperity of this alhaji, who was one of the six sons of a farm-slave of Nupe origin, is attributable entirely to his six married sons, five of whom live in his house, the other being a successful cloth wholesaler who lives (and was born) in Kano – it was he who recently financed his father's pilgrimage. While he had had some help from his rich mother, who had become a prosperous trader in henna, grains and groundnuts after being freed from slavery, his success in raising such a large family was largely attributed to the making of cornstalk beds. One of his brothers is very poor, although he, too, has five resident sons.

H. *Sometimes, as in this case, several brothers flourish*

2 DAT, 1 MAT. In a big house (the home of sixty-eight people) there are four brothers, three of them rich, the other very poor; their father had been a rich cattle-owner and their paternal grandfather a wealthy slave-owner who, together with his farm-slaves, had lived in their present house, from which no man, apart from a school teacher, is ever known to have migrated. None of the three brothers have sons-in-*gandu* and all of them employ many labourers from time to time. Their wealth (they all became rich through farming and from storing produce for a price-rise) is partly attributable to their favourable inheritance situation, but two of them had also benefited from having a mother who had prospered as a house-trader after her husband's death; she had been especially notable for storing locust beans, groundnuts and grains for a price rise – there had been no one like her in her hamlet, and there is no one like her in Dorayi today.

XI

Extreme poverty

Extreme poverty of the type that is experienced in rural Hausaland is not in itself calamitous: it is a severe non-fatal, though debilitating, condition (rather than a progressive illness) which presumably greatly enhances the risk of death from other causes, but which is not to be confused with starvation or famine. It does not affect whole communities, but individual conjugal or extended families, or (much less frequently) isolated individuals. Having many different causes, some of which operate in all communities, it is ubiquitous, though variable in incidence.

In Batagarawa (*R. H.*, Chapter x) it was clear that the victims of extreme poverty were not a separate group of under-privileged men whose circumstances had necessarily been hopeless from the start. Many of them had reasonably well-off brothers; some of them had inherited large acreages; several of them had once been prosperous. In terms of their origin the very poor were a fairly representative cross-section of the population.

Economic conditions are so harsh and risky in rural Hausaland that it is in a sense ridiculous to analyse the causes of poverty in individual cases: rather should one ask how it can be that some people emerge from the morass. In Batagarawa it became clear that the condition of *individual impasse* was largely explicable in terms of the general workings of the rural economic system. Poor men applied less manure to their farms and obtained lower yields per unit of effort; poor men were those who sold their grain immediately after harvest when prices were lowest; poor men had unremunerative types of non-farming occupation; poor men often had 'no time to farm' – their granaries being empty soon after harvest, they were obliged to pick up a living from day-to-day by working in odd jobs for others or by collecting 'free goods' such as grass or firewood; poor men (being farm-sellers) often owned insufficient manured farmland to set their sons to work; poor men could seldom borrow money, being considered bad risks. In short the odds were set to such a degree against poor men that they stood little chance of benefiting from the general tendency for wealth to increase with age – a conclusion which received some confirmation from the finding that the incidence of poverty was unrelated to age. If it happened that a man was poor (and there were numerous accidental reasons why this might be so), then a concatenation or conspiracy of circumstances necessarily operated against him and there was much truth in the philosophical attitude (of *arziki*) that declared that however energetic or intelligent he might be, it was only if he also had luck on his side that he could fight back successfully.

Perhaps the most important finding in Batagarawa was that men do not necessarily flourish in circumstances where land is plentiful: a high incidence of extreme poverty was compatible with the existence of much uncultivated fertile land, within one to three miles of the village, which could be freely taken up by any farmer. So strong is the mechanistic belief that farmers live by land alone, that my insistence in *Rural Hausa* that men might be 'too poor to farm' has met with a hostile reception, the politest of my critics merely insisting that population densities are necessarily very high within a radius of, say, ten miles of Katsina city – whereas they actually vary greatly according to direction as the population density map for 1952 shows. By no means all the uncultivated fertile land to the west and south-west of Batagarawa lies within a forest reserve (as some have insisted) and nearly two-thirds of all farmers actually cultivated one or more bush farms, most of them nearby. It is true that some of the extensive farmland that had recently been acquired by members of the ruling class in Batagarawa lay further away from the village than ordinary farmers would care to go; but there were many cases of ordinary farmers who had built up their position by means of cultivating nearby bush farms the most striking of which related to a young man – see *R. H.*, p. 156, F(2) – who was the largest employer of farm-labourers in Batagarawa although he had received little farmland from his (living) father. When he had left *gandu*, this young man was already a produce trader – he would not otherwise have started to flourish as a farmer; but many of the poorest farmers who owned little manured farmland actually cultivated no bush farms, having been prevented by their poverty from so doing.

So the discussion in this chapter is based on the belief that in rural Hausaland there is not necessarily a close relationship between population density and the incidence of severe impoverishment: this is partly because rural communities are innately strongly inegalitarian, a fairly high incidence of individual poverty being found in all old-established areas, but also because incomes from non-farming occupations still vary considerably from place to place, even though the decline of craftwork and long-distance trade has reduced the discrepancies. As informants in different localities have different standards by which they assess poverty, it is obviously important not to attach too much significance to the fact that the incidences of extreme poverty in Dorayi and Batagarawa were almost equal (27% of all classified married men, exclusive of sons-in-*gandu*, against 24% in Batagarawa). But I do claim that poor men in Dorayi are not necessarily worse off than their counterparts in Batagarawa owing to the wider range of non-farming occupations.

Given the situation in Batagarawa, there proved to be nothing particularly surprising about the condition of *individual impasse* in Dorayi, where poor men are, again, a reasonably representative cross-section of the population and where the economic system constantly militates against the poor. (On the former point, it is worth noting that statistics show that poor men have about as great a chance of having brothers who are rich or 'neither rich nor poor' as have men in general.) In Dorayi, as in Batagarawa, the incidence of poverty does not vary with age, and it seems reasonable to postulate the existence of a kind of threshold which has to be overcome before the general tendency for wealth to increase with age operates in particular cases. Once over this threshold, a very small number of poor men formerly proceeded from strength to strength – see Appendix x(1) – and became quite prosperous, and there were others whose position showed some improvement. But the likelihood is that most poor men remained, as it were, impacted in society as they got older. (Of course the fact that the incidence of poverty does not diminish with age does not, in itself, prove that few poor men prosper as they get older, for there are always some whose circumstances worsen with age.) Such findings mainly reflected conditions before the recent steep rise in the price of land which now precludes the great majority of Dorayi men from buying it.

In Dorayi the poverty-stricken are not a class apart: in English parlance they would be considered as indigent or penurious, i.e. lacking or needing, rather than destitute, meaning forsaken or abandoned. The two most common Hausa words for a poor man both derive from *talauta* which, according to Bargery's dictionary, means to 'become poor, but not destitute': they are *matalauci* and *talaka*. And reference to extreme poverty often involves the use of *wahala* (suffering) – *sha wahala* being to suffer (trouble). (The word for peasantry, or subjects, in the political sense, is *talakawa*, the plural of *talaka*; it is, of course, used condescendingly by townsmen to refer to the presumed backwardness of countrymen in general, although it strictly relates to the entire population other than the diminutive number of *masu sarauta*, viz. the Emir, other office-holders in the capital and the twenty-five Kano District Heads. It is interesting that *talaka* has travelled widely in West Africa, being (Lloyd, 1974, p. 168) the standard term for a poor man in Yorubaland.)

Before I proceed to argue that most poor men in Dorayi are, in fact, indigent or penurious but not destitute, it is necessary to examine the means by which poor men earn their living.

Few severely impoverished men derive more than a small proportion of their income from farming on their own account. As we know – see Table vi.4(A) – 93% of all poor men are estimated to own under three acres of farmland (many of them being landless) and many poor men find it difficult to borrow land (*aro*). The principal non-farming occupations of poor men were summarised in Table vi.5, which records that about a third of them make cornstalk beds; that nearly a half have no occupation other than farm (or general) labouring or transportation (by head or by donkey); and that few such men are traders or work in Kano city. As the problem of defining the principal occupation presented particular difficulty with impoverished men, many of whom pursue a variety of odd jobs, this type of classification is of limited value and I now turn to examine the various types of occupation which are open to the impecunious, most of which fall into the following seven categories.

1. *Working with other local men for wages or the equivalent*
    (a) farm-labouring;
    (b) assisting local craftsmen, such as builders or well-diggers, who (in Dorayi) often build structures for their own use;
    (c) firewood cutting – *faskare*; and,
    (d) the picking of fruit or other tree crops.
2. *Transportation for payment* by headload or donkey
    (a) transportation of locally grown produce or craft goods for sale; and,
    (b) transportation of manure from the city.
3. *Collecting* (and maybe transporting and selling) certain types of grass, honey, leaves and other fodder, earth, laterite, etc.
4. Simple types of *craftwork* or repair
    (a) cornstalk beds for sale in the city; and,
    (b) other types of work such as small-scale carpentry, for which demand is mainly local.
5. Small-scale *trading*, including trading on behalf of others.
6. Casual *Koranic teaching* or the giving of charms.
7. *Serving* other people
    (a) 'beggar-minstrels' (*maroka*) – very uncommon;
    (b) washermen – likewise uncommon;
    (c) working as servants (*barori*) – all of them young kinsmen or newly arrived strangers;

(d) running errands, going to places with messages, buying trade wares – especially on behalf of secluded women; and,

(e) odd jobs such as trapping guinea fowl.

It is to be noted that none of these occupations provides poor men with full-time work; that, with the notable exceptions of the making of corn-stalk beds and the transportation of manure, few of these occupations depend on the nearness of Kano city – however, some of the sixty weekly paid 'labourers' – see Appendix xi(1) – are undoubtedly very poor; that most poor men depend on the local demand for their services which (as we know) is severely limited; that few of these occupations necessitate the ownership of any capital, not even trading capital for poor men usually obtain goods on credit which they repay after selling; and, that opportunities of employment as specialised craftsmen are rare owing to the 'do-it-yourself' attitude towards house-building and repair.

I now examine some of these occupations, additional material being provided in Appendix xi (2).

FARM-LABOURING

The great majority of poor men under the age of, say, fifty work as farm-labourers (*'yan kwadago*) from time to time, and it may be that about a third of elderly men (*dattijai*) also do this. The supply of labour vastly exceeds the local demand and some men work on the farms of city-owners in other localities. As in Batagarawa, there are a few young men who work fairly regularly throughout the farming-season, but most men work sporadically or occasionally and there are no local farmers in a position to offer full-time work to a labourer during the farming season. Rough statistics suggest that only about a third of all farm-labourers are poor, the remainder being 'neither rich nor poor'. It should be unnecessary to emphasise that men do not abandon farming *because* they take up labouring: as in India (see Myrdal, 1968, pp. 2214 *et seq.*), many labourers are also farmers, and labouring is often undertaken for the purposes of financing farming – e.g. for the purchase of onion seed. In 1971 the usual wage-rate for a long-morning's work of about six hours was 6s with food served on the farm – see Appendix xi(2).

FIREWOOD CUTTING (*faskare*)

Those richer men who buy trees for the purpose of firewood cutting are apt to employ others to fell the trees and to cut, split and bundle the wood for sale. One of the most remunerative occupations open to young and vigorous men is provided by the system known as *kashin maraba*, which entitles the fiewood cutter to sell half of the bundles on his own behalf. If a man were to cut twelve bundles daily worth 2s 6d each at 1971 prices, he would have earned 10s, even if he had paid 5s to a transporter to take the bundles to the city for sale. (A much more humble job is the cutting out of tree roots as an inferior form of firewood.) The demand for firewood from the city is insatiable; but the supply of suitable trees for felling is very tight – these include Egyptian mimosa (*gaburuwa*), tamarind (*tsamiya*), ebony (*kanya*) and locust bean (*dorowa*) – and some Dorayi men travel some distance to find them.

TRANSPORTATION OF PRODUCE OR CRAFT GOODS

While most crop transportation from farmland to homestead is probably undertaken by the crop-owner (or his dependants), richer men often pay others to transport produce or craft goods to Kano city for sale there. Earnings vary according to the type and size of load (see Appendix XI (2) for a scale of charges) and the time of year, but in January 1972 they may have averaged about 3s to 4s per donkey trip – or some 10s per trip if the transporter drove two donkeys and brought back manure on the return journey. (As donkeys – which are all males – are bought and never reared and as they require fodder (which has a saleable value) and natron (*kanwa*), considerable costs have to be deducted in computing net earnings.) About two-thirds of all poor men own no donkey (compared with only a tenth of all rich men); such transporters are either obliged to resort to head-loading (which is suitable only for certain types of load, notably grass and *zana* matting) for which they are unlikely to be paid more than 2s per trip, or have to hire donkeys at the rate of about 2s to 3s – which many owners are reluctant to permit.

MANURE TRANSPORTATION

Poor men would earn considerably more from transporting organic manure (*taki*) from the city, were it not that many richer men (even 'very rich men'), and their sons, do this humble work for themselves, owing partly to their reluctance to allow others to use their donkeys, but also because they (like everyone else) usually suffer much compulsory idleness in the dry season. However, the opportunities of transporting manure for others provide large numbers of poor men who own, hire, or borrow donkeys, with a small income. In 1971–2 the manure, being of very low quality, was worth no more than 1s to 1s 6d per pannier in Dorayi (according to season); the buying price in Kano city was about 6d per pannier unless the rubbish were freely collected from ditches or dumps. The charge for donkey-hire was often one-half of the manure collected. Poor men may stockpile manure in the hope of reselling it when the price has risen.

COLLECTING 'FREE GOODS'

In Batagarawa poor men had considerable opportunities of collecting 'free goods' – including grass, palm fronds, firewood etc. (see *R. H.*, p. 247) – but this is not so in Dorayi owing to the lack of uncultivated bush. Grass for thatching (when dry it is known as *shuci* or *cibci*) may not be freely collected – it is deliberately cultivated as a crop by some farmers, particularly by those who lack manure – nor may *gamba* grass which is used for *zana* matting; but other grasses suitable for fodder are laboriously collected by poor men – this being considered the lowliest of all occupations. (Weeds are collected by children after hoeing.) Poor men sometimes dig earth or laterite for sale to local builders, but earth is not transported from this locality for sale in the city. (Perhaps honey collection ought not to be included under this heading since the hives (*amya*), which are placed in trees, require baiting with expensive ingredients.)

CORNSTALK BEDS

Although any man may happen to make cornstalk beds for sale in Kano city – just as, in former times, any woman might happen to spin cotton thread – poorer men, especially if they are too old to be employed as farm-labourers, may derive a large part of their income from this humble craft-work, though cornstalk is very scarce during the farming season. Transport costs represent such a high proportion of the value of these beds, that Dorayi people can undercut those living further away from the city, and it is doubtful whether any communities living more than, say, five miles from the city sell beds there. These so-called beds (*gado* – or more specifically *karaga*) resemble flat mats – see Appendix xi(2); too brittle to be floor coverings, they are used as couches or seats or for displaying wares, such as meat, for sale. In December 1971 I estimated that a man's profit from making cornstalk beds during a long-morning might have been 3s 6d – his total receipts might have been about 4s 9d if he owned a donkey and transported the beds himself at some other time; however, poor men who bought cornstalk on credit, might have had higher costs. It is possible that this humble craft had been relatively more profitable in former times.

OTHER CRAFTS

In Dorayi, where most men (as already noted) are their own house-builders and repairers and even their own latrine diggers, there are far fewer specialised craftsmen than in Batagarawa, but whether this is mainly a function of poverty or of dispersed settlement I am unable to judge. However this may be, the proportion of craftworkers is very small; the range of specialisms very narrow; the types of goods made for 'export' very few – little other than cornstalk beds and blacksmiths' wares; and (cornstalk beds apart) the opportunities for poor men very scanty. It is to some slight extent accidental that the range of craft occupations should be so small: thus, it happens that there is no clay fit for potting and that (in contrast to some areas) there is only one male weaver. I do not know why in this locality few men make panniers (*mangaloli*) from imported palm fronds – as many do in nearby Kirimbo – this occupation, as well as mat-making, being reserved for women. In fact very few poor men in Dorayi possess any real skills other than house-building (many of the small, self-built, mud houses are among those most aesthetically satisfying) and well-digging, and the quality of the odd jobs that they undertake, such as carpentry, is nearly always very poor. Probably because the work is so arduous and unpleasant, three of the five specialist well- (and latrine-) diggers are poor. Insofar as poor men are engaged in craftwork this is usually in the capacity of assistants: they are earth collectors, earth-puddlers and block makers for builders, and general fetchers and carriers.

SMALL-SCALE TRADING

Any man may happen to engage in casual, small-scale trading, involving local produce, if he is considered sufficiently reliable to receive credit; any man, also, may happen to work as a small-scale intermediary (commission-seller, or *dillali*). But poorer men are comparatively handicapped in a situation where even richer traders often suffer from severe limitations of demand and supply, as we have seen. In West African rural communities butchering is an occupation especially associated with poverty; this is not so in Dorayi, where so little meat is eaten that the butchers, none of whom is poor, are mere retailers of meat bought in Kano.

Poor men waste much time looking for work, contacting people, inefficiently collecting crop residues and so forth; but the multiplicity of ill-paid, part-time occupations, most of them of a petty nature, which are open to them, ensures (I think) that few become a burden on the community as a whole, unless they are ill or old and lack close relatives who are able to help them. Richer men do not give Muslim alms to ordinary able-bodied poor men (except to some malams) and the sheer numbers of the indigent (about a quarter of all married men exclusive of dependent sons) precludes the offering of much support by the few men who have anything significant to offer. The general situation is (appallingly) stagnant, but not disastrous. This miserably inefficient, competitive, ill-equipped, rural economy, where most men work far less hard than they would wish, shuffles along much as it did forty years ago – only relieved by the migration of some married men and their dependants.

Such stagnating stability is, of course, associated with the high degree of co-residence of kin. Of the forty-four indigent men who are elderly or old, only nine have no younger co-resident, married brother or son, and I think that the wider community regards only about six of them as being in serious plight. As for younger indigent men (of whom there are 102), as many as 68 reside with one or more brothers and/or their father. Of course impoverished kinsmen may drag each other down, but it is important to note that (other things equal) the larger the group of co-resident brothers or of fathers and sons, the greater the chance that some of them will find remunerative work on any particular day: there are in fact only eight sets of brothers all of whom are poor. While the extent to which brothers assist each other financially is probably very limited (at least this is what men always say in Dorayi), all members of a group of brothers who regularly take their evening meal together can usually rely on receiving cooked food (see Table xii.4 on wealth and poverty in big houses).

In Dorayi (as in Batagarawa) an inability to borrow cash (as such), except in very small sums, is one of the hall-marks of severe impoverishment. In fact the main way in which richer men (and women) help poorer people is by granting them non-cash credit which enables them to set themselves to work – to engage in a particular economic activity. Poor men often receive saleable local produce, such as henna, on credit and pay for it after resale: donkeys are borrowed on credit, maybe in return for half the manure that is fetched; payment for cornstalk is delayed until the beds have been sold; grain is granted to farm-labourers who repay in terms of work; payment for the use of a borrowed farm is made after harvest. When cash loans are made, these are usually very small and very short term, and related to particular activities; thus, small bridging-loans granted for no more than a day, or even for a few hours, to enable particular transactions to be completed, are quite common.

So poor men who are in need of 'lumps of cash' (for instance to meet the marriage expenses of their sons, the dowries of their daughters, or the costs of a naming ceremony) will usually be in great difficulty unless their close kin are prepared to help them. Their ability to mortgage their future is very limited; and they seldom own any physical assets which might be sold or pledged. Many sons of impoverished men are obliged to meet their own marriage expenses (maybe with their mother's help) or to marry women (the so-called 'second-hand wives') who have been married before.

No animal, not even a goat, may be sacrificed at their naming ceremonies (see *R. H.*, pp. 299–300). Whereas in rural Hausaland generally there is a flourishing institution, known as *biki*, such that individuals form part-nerships (reciprocal exchange relationships), which chiefly operate in con-nection with ceremonial expenditure (see *R. H.*, p. 211), I was told that formal *biki* relationships in Dorayi seldom involve poor men. Nor do men (unlike women) ever form rotating credit associations known as *adashi* (see *R. H.*, p. 203).

In Batagarawa men commonly borrowed bundles of unthreshed grain before harvest in return for the promise to repay double the amount after harvest (*R. H.*, p. 223); but although I made dozens of enquiries about this *dauke* system in Dorayi, I was always told that the practice was un-known. While it is possible that the fear that *dauke* is usurious may have led to its concealment, I am sure that the formal practice is far less common in Dorayi than in Batagarawa and seldom involves bundles of grain. In Dorayi poor men sometimes sell their crops before harvest, but no one is prepared to discuss the details of such transactions.

As I have constantly emphasised, the ability of men in general (not only of poor men) to set themselves to work is severely restricted by limitations of demand and supply. It is, therefore, important to consider the implica-tions of the interesting and strange fact that such restrictions do not affect the considerable number of women who produce groundnut oil, ground-nut cake and locust bean cakes for sale in Kano city, for they are not only able to buy their full requirements of groundnuts and locust beans from produce traders who obtain their supplies from outside Dorayi but may also readily sell however much they produce. As secluded women also engage in house-trading – see Appendix xi(3) – and produce a fair quantity of craft goods, notably mats and panniers, from raw materials which are not necessarily in short supply, it follows that their contribution towards household expenses may be far greater than convention demands and that they may be in a position to give direct financial assistance to their hus-bands. Indeed, an interesting parallel may be drawn between the position of secluded women today and of farm-slaves in former times: despite their inherent lack of freedom, both wives and slaves might achieve a consider-able degree of financial independence by means of their non-farming occu-pations.

While the wives of rich men, like the slaves of rich slave-owners, are those most likely to flourish, any energetic wife with luck on her side may gradually build up her financial position, and some wives with poor hus-bands derive financial support from their kin. Thus, one of the best known women traders in Dorayi has an impoverished husband, but is assisted by her mother who is a trader in the city; she pays men to buy grain and groundnuts on her behalf and also stores sacks of locust beans for sale when seasonal prices have risen. Women are not precluded by their own or their husband's poverty from obtaining supplies of groundnuts for processing into oil and cake, for short-term credit is commonly granted; thus, in big houses which specialise in such production, nearly all wives (other than the very young) are apt to be producers on their own account – and the poorer wives may also work for payment for others. Ironically, it may be positively advantageous for a woman house-trader to have a poor husband if, as a result, he has time on his hands which he can devote to obtaining supplies of trade goods in Kano city.

Even if it is elderly impoverished men, in particular, who are apt to benefit from assistance from their wives, many of whom are considerably younger than themselves – only one of the forty-four oldest poor men had no wife and about a third had two wives or more – it is necessary to add that many wives are undoubted financial liabilities to their husbands. Because Dorayi still possesses the ethos of a farming community, the economic norms of the rich often wrongly appear to be those of the community as a whole; when the poor emulate the rich by seeking to increase the number of their dependants, they may find themselves dragged down further into the abyss as a result. There are many women who undertake little processing of groundnuts and locust beans, maybe because they lack the necessary equipment, cannot get produce on credit, or are too tired or weak to undertake this heavy work single-handedly, there being no nearby grinding mill. (The capabilities and interests of women are commonly overlooked by planners, who do not realise that rural Hausaland is exceptionally ill-equipped, by West African standards, with diesel-operated grinding mills or that general living standards might be enormously improved if financial assistance for their acquisition were granted.)

LANDLESSNESS

Since most sons (with living fathers) own no land, the proportion of landlessness should be related to other men – 12% of whom (sixty-two out of 506) are thought to own little or no land – see Appendix xi(4). About 15% of these sixty-two men are strangers (themselves or their fathers); about a quarter are known to have been farm-sellers; and most of the remainder had probably never owned much land.

Whereas in Batagarawa landlessness invariably implied extreme poverty, this is not so in Dorayi where as many as a third of the landless were classified as 'neither rich nor poor' – fifteen sons and sixteen other men. While most of these men had borrowed (*aro*) farms, a small proportion appeared to have lost all interest in farming, being mainly dependent on occupations not open to the poorest men in this community, these including butchering, administration (*dagaci*), praise singing (a stranger), certain types of trading, *bori* (spirit possession, mainly strangers), smithing and the purchase of trees for firewood cutting (*faskare*).

Poor men in Dorayi (like the unemployed in Britain today) inhabit a looking glass world of contrareity, their interests often (though not necessarily) standing opposed to those of the rest of their community. They are the men who make the worst use of available natural resources, who 'import' more than they 'export', who hardly ever have influential friends in the city. I had hoped to obtain a better understanding of their relationship to other members of the community from comparative material. It would be tempting to draw analogies with indigent populations in West African cities did these not usually contain so large an element of (younger) strangers; were the opportunities of picking up a living there less variegated; and were the contrasting situation of rich men not so marked. (Besides the anatomy of city poverty remains ill-explored.) As for comparative literature on West African rural societies, south of the sahel, this is so scanty as to force those with theoretical interests in inegalitarianism to look elsewhere, which is a pity. (Most of the standard ethnographies, all of which pre-date the new theoretical approach, relate to lineage-organised societies, which (in principle at least) assure all lineage members the right of access to land – but whether in practice anything approaching an 'equal right' either within or as between lineages has seldom been explored.) While 'social security' aspects of village communities have received much attention, the gravely impoverished tend to be regarded as unfortunate, weak, decrepit or feckless individuals rather than as the fortuitous victims of the rural socio-economic systems as such – an attitude which resembles the misconceptions about the unemployed in Western societies which prevailed until about forty years ago. (Maybe the fatalistic determinism of social demographers is a natural reaction to this indolence of thought?)

The nature of the land tenure situation in rural Hausaland precludes an analysis of *individual impasse* in terms of developing landlordism or the creation of a farm-labouring class: as already noted, most farm-labourers are also farmers or their sons, and no landless man derives more than a small proportion of his income from working on the farms of others. For these and other reasons I have found comparisons with South Asia to be of little help. Besides, in South Asia, as in West Africa, the lack of reliable statistical material prevents the study of the plight of the ultra-poor. According to Myrdal, an accurate statistical picture of the numerical strength of the main 'social groups' in farming communities cannot be produced for any South Asian country; there, as in West Africa, 'the fact that rigorous enquiries. . .have not been sponsored officially must be partly ascribed to the vested interests in concealment among the upper strata' (Myrdal, 1968, p. 1056).

At this point I think that readers of this book will not need to be reminded that there are other important reasons why the study of *individual impasse* in rural West Africa is so unfashionable – and so difficult. I will only abruptly reiterate that in this particular case it was also very painful.

APPENDIX XI(1)
The 'labourers' in the city

In 1972 about fifty-one Dorayi men commuted, often by bicycle, to Kano city or environs to work for regular weekly or monthly wages and another nine men were in regular paid work outside Dorayi, four of them being road-workers. (Numbers fluctuated as jobs were often held for short periods only.) These men, who are always called *lebura* (from 'labourer'), worked mainly in humble capacities at Bayero University College or other nearby institutions, or had such jobs as gardeners or watchmen in Kano city – as already noted (see p. 85) only a very small number of Dorayi men are able to secure jobs in factories or on construction work. In 1972 monthly wages, which were often for part-time work, may have been of the order of £10 (less tax) or up to £13 or £14 if overtime was worked. (I was reliably informed that most factory workers got less than the legal minimum.) Especially as many of the labourers did some farming in their spare time, it is probable that most of them were better off than those mainly dependent on casual work in Dorayi: assuming that they worked a six-day week their daily earnings might have been of the order of 8s – somewhat higher than the maximum daily proceeds from making cornstalk beds. However, such men as had living fathers (and there were twenty-five of them) probably handed over part of their earnings to them.

Most of the labourers lived very near to the city, mainly in Dorayi Karama, and enquiries made elsewhere showed that very few men living more than a few miles south of the city were commuters. Although about 13% of all members of the youngest age group (*magidanci*) were labourers, few younger men in southern Dorayi sought, or found, such work. Only seven elderly men (*dattijai*) were labourers.

At least fourteen of the thirty fatherless labourers in Kano city would probably have been classified as poor had they not had labouring work – eight of them were probably landless and six probably owned less than one acre. Men with substantial acreages never work as labourers: there were probably only eight labourers who owned more than 2½ acres of land.

APPENDIX XI(2)
Notes on various occupations

Farm-labouring ('kwadago')

In 1971 the usual wage-rate for a long-morning's work of about six hours was 6s with food served on the farm; the rate for evening work was 3s 6d. The rate nearer to the city was somewhat higher. Poor men who were employed for compassionate reasons – they tended to be older or weaker than most labourers – sometimes received lower rates. The only farmers who employed large numbers of labourers on any occasion were city men, whose foremen reported that they had no difficulty in recruiting gangs of thirty or more labourers for about two days' work. (Short-term work with large gangs is preferred.) Certain prominent local farmers were well known for paying wages in advance to trusted labourers. Surprisingly (for this had not been recorded elsewhere), Dorayi men sometimes worked for their brothers as paid labourers. In Batagarawa (see *R. H.*, Chapter XIII) the demand for labour was so spasmodic that it was most unusual for any labourer to work more than three days weekly during the farming-season; applying these figures to Dorayi, it is unlikely that many labourers there earned more than about £1 weekly.

Donkey transportation charges

Transportation charges are subject to seasonal variation, but in January 1972 they were as follows. It will be noted that there are two systems of remuneration – either per unit (pannier, bundle or sack) or a proportion of the selling value of the produce.

Wares	Payment per donkey load
1. Onions	6s to 7s per pannier (*mangala*)
2. Henna leaves	2s per load of 6 sacks
3. Henna powder (*gari*)	4s per load of 2 sacks
4. *Zana* matting	3s 9d per load of 5 mats
5. Mangoes	4s per pannier (*mangala*)
6. Cornstalk (*kara*)	One-third of the selling value of three bundles
7. Cornstalk beds	A quarter or a third of the selling value of some 10 to 12 beds
8. Firewood	A third of the value of 3 bundles – say, 2s 6d

Notes: 1. Based on a very high price of about £9 10s per pannier.
2 and 3. The weight of 6 sacks of leaves roughly equals that of 2 sacks of powder, but the value of the 2 sacks of powder was greater.
4. A mat or screen made of reeds or coarse grass.

7. At a quarter of the selling value of 1s 6d per bed, the charge might be nearly 4s.

Cornstalk beds

These beds are made by binding together lengths of guinea corn stalk (*kara*) with locally made string and sticks from the *zamarke* tree. While I sometimes heard that a man with a small family might wholly maintain himself by making these beds, I am somewhat sceptical owing to the difficulty of obtaining supplies of cornstalk during the farming season. As beds are of variable sizes and as prices and raw material costs fluctuate, net income can only be roughly estimated. The estimate of 3s 6d per long-morning (see p. 170 above) is based on the estimated production of five small beds worth 1s 6d, assuming costs of raw material and transport to have been about 7d and 3d per bed respectively. Richer (unlike poorer) makers may store beds for a price rise.

APPENDIX XI(3)
Women's house trade

Few Dorayi men go regularly to market to buy the day-to-day requirements of their households, finding it more convenient to purchase grain, beans (*wake*) and other farm produce, groundnut oil, palm oil, cassava meal (*garin rogo*), locust bean cakes, vegetables, kola nuts, salt, natron, pepper, local soap, sugar, matches, cigarettes, kerosene and many other wares from other houses – only meat being obtained from specialised retailers (see also p. 188 below). Although grain, other farm produce and kola nuts may be sold by men, most household transactions involve secluded women traders, who are linked with their suppliers and customers by their husbands, unmarried daughters and other children. I think that such house trade flourishes throughout Hausaland – though in present-day Dorayi there are few women traders who compare in importance with a number of famous (unsecluded) women traders of former times, one of whom sold huge quantities of cassava to men who came out from the city to buy from her. (See *R.H.*, where I discuss what I term the 'honeycomb market' – each woman sitting in her own 'cell', prices being uniform on any day as though the market were an open one – and also Hill, 1969 and 1971).

The general rule in Dorayi, as elsewhere, is that each woman trades on her own behalf, independently of her co-wives. However, in the making of groundnut oil (and cake) and locust bean cakes (*daddawa*) women in the same house often co-operate over the heaviest tasks, such as pounding, so that there is a tendency for women in big houses to specialise in certain work. Thus as many as nineteen of the twenty-one wives in one big house sometimes make groundnut oil for sale, buying groundnuts at the prevailing market price either from their husbands or from other sources. In that house women sell few other wares, but in another house, where eleven out of twenty-one wives sometimes make locust bean cakes (buying most of the locust beans from a rich man trader in the house), other occupations included the weaving of blankets or cloths for carrying babies (*majayai*), grain-selling (the grain being bought in bulk by the woman's husband with her capital), the making of donkey harnesses, the selling of cigarettes, matches, etc.

A few prominent women traders store produce for a price rise, as they did much more commonly in former times. I think that in areas of dispersed settlement house trade is less flourishing than in compact villages like Batagarawa; and it is partly owing to the lack of school children that there is such a small demand for cooked snacks in Dorayi. Whereas in Batagarawa many women served complete meals for consumption out-of-doors, there is no such trade in Dorayi, and no millet porridge (*fura*) is made for selling or for serving to farm labourers.

APPENDIX XI(4)
Landlessness

Owing to the difficulty of mapping very small plots, the number of men who owned little or no land is necessarily an estimate – it was put at ninety-nine, of whom at least nine were strangers. However, as many as thirty-three of these men were not strictly landless because they had borrowed farms (*aro*), which in some cases provided holdings of several acres. The following crude analysis of the causes of landlessness (in its loose sense) relates to the sixty-two fatherless men.

Table XI.I   *The causes of landlessness**

	Total number of men	Number of slave-descent†
Farm-sellers	16	3
Pledged farms	3	1
'Never had a farm'	9	4
Fathers were farm-sellers	4	–
Father a slave with 7 sons	1	1
Father a slave with 9 sons	3	3
Father migrated and had no farms	2	–
Father died when he was a child	2	2
Father probably had no land	6	5
Strangers – themselves or their fathers	9	n.a.
Other, or not known	7	1
	62	20

* Many of these men had borrowed farms (*aro*).
† See Chapter XIII.

XII

The big house

The evidence is that in rural Hausaland generally most sons hive off from the parental home fairly soon after marriage so that most houses are inhabited by no more than two or three married men and their dependants. But in Dorayi, as we have seen, not only do nearly all married men remain in their parental home indefinitely, but brothers, also, stay together after their father's death, to the point that only eighteen of the total of 298 married men who have deceased fathers and one or more married brothers are living in a separate house from their brother(s). Given the expanding population, the consequence of this cohesiveness of both fathers and sons and sets of brothers is that houses tend to grow over the decades. Not only this, but they also tend to go on expanding quite indefinitely, first because members of the second and subsequent descendant generations have no greater an inclination to hive off than their forebears and second because of the exceptionally low rate of migration out of Dorayi from big houses.

The consequence of these various factors is the surprising phenomenon of the really big house – surprising in the West African, not merely the Hausa, context. In Dorayi there are twenty-four big houses inhabited by seven or more married men and their dependants, the largest of which is the home of twenty-two married men – or 106 people. (The biggest house that I visited is the home of at least forty-one married men – probably more; although situated very close to Dorayi, it had to be excluded from my lists as no one, least of all the inhabitants themselves, could provide reliable genealogical material.) In Batagarawa there were no big houses, as thus defined, the largest house having been occupied by five married men only. The existence of big Muslim houses (as distinct from big houses inhabited by the pagan Maguzawa) has been reported from nowhere else in rural Hausaland: it is, I am sure, a direct consequence of the persistent and intensifying pressure on the land.

For the purposes of this analysis it is most convenient, and at times even essential, to regard the married man, rather than the person or adult, as the basic unit. As has been emphasised elsewhere, the composition of the female population undergoes continuous change, and males are the constant element. So it is best to assess house-size in terms of the number of married men, as in Table XII.1. (The average number of dependants per married man in the big houses is 4.1 and for seventeen, out of twenty-four, such houses the figure lies between 3.5 and 4.5.)

Table XII.1   The 'size' of houses

Number of married men	Percentage of houses		Percentage of all married men	
	Dorayi	Batagarawa	Dorayi	Batagarawa
1	34 ⎫	67 ⎫	10 ⎫	45 ⎫
2	22 ⎬ 77	23 ⎬ 98	13 ⎬ 45	31 ⎬ 92*
3	9 ⎪	6 ⎪	8 ⎪	12 ⎪
4	12 ⎭	2 ⎭	14 ⎭	5 ⎭
5	6	2	8	8
6	5	–	8	–
7–10 ⎫	6 ⎫	–	13 ⎫	–
11–15 ⎬	4 ⎬ 12	–	15 ⎬ 38	–
16–22 ⎭	2 ⎭	–	11 ⎭	–
	100%	100%	100%*	100%

* The apparent error in this figure results from rounding.

As Table XII.1 shows, nearly two-fifths (38%) of all married men live in big houses. Whereas in Batagarawa 76% of all married men lived in houses including no more than two married men, the corresponding proportion for Dorayi was only 23%. However, about a third of all Dorayi houses are inhabited by one married man only.

THE HAUSA HOUSE

In some regions of West Africa a firm distinction has to be made between house-groupings, often confusingly known as compounds (a word which also denotes the interior 'yard' of a Hausa house), and the component separate dwellings or houses. Thus in Gonja, in northern Ghana, where compounds are named units, the component households are basically conjugal families 'whose food is grown by a single farming group and prepared by the members of a single cooking group' (E. N. Goody, 1973, p. 52). In Yorubaland, where traditional compounds were often very large since they housed all the male members of an agnatic lineage, the separate dwelling-units formed 'a series of linked rectangular courtyards', each with a definite identity (Lloyd, 1974, p. 33). But in rural Hausaland it is not necessarily possible to distinguish the constituent parts of the entire dwelling (which is always known as *gida*) either in structural (architectural) terms, or sociologically, particularly as the composition of cooking groups may undergo seasonal change. It is true that large houses may be regarded by their inhabitants as divided into 'sections', which may or may not be structurally walled off (see below); but such sections often house groups which are larger than conjugal families and which may comprise more than one cooking group.

The Hausa house consists of a walled, fenced, or hedged yard, in which various structures including thatched sleeping-huts (one for each married woman), granaries, wells, screened latrines and somewhat make-shift kitchens (most cooking and food preparation being done in the open) are set, and in which small livestock, as well as people, live. In Dorayi most married men, other than a few rich men, have no interior room (*turaka*) which they may call their own. In any case, men nearly always meet or entertain their men friends (who cannot enter the house owing to wife seclusion) outside the house or in the entrance-hut (*zaure*), a square and mud-roofed (or round and thatched) room, with non-opposite entrances – this is sometimes detached from the house. While very large houses may have a separate sleeping-room for unmarried males (young men, youths (*samari*, sing. *saurayi*) and boys who are too old to sleep in their mother's huts), they more often sleep in the entrance-hut – or even outside the house as though partially ejected from it. Most houses have one entrance-hut, but a few very big houses have several; however, this presented no definitional difficulty, a house being defined as a residential unit such that all of its sections are accessible to any resident without going outside.

THE HOUSEHOLD HEAD (*mai gida*)

Every house, big or small, has a recognised head, a *mai gida* – translatable in this context (though the term has many other levels of meaning) as 'the man in charge of' or 'the embodiment of' the house, for a long-established house has no individual owner. The *mai gida* is nearly always, in some sense, the senior man in the house, being, for example, the oldest in years or the senior son of a late senior brother – if a junior man in a house is a Village Head (*dagaci*) he may or may not be *mai gida*. The functions of the *mai gida* resemble those of their counterparts in rural Ashanti which have been so carefully described by Fortes (1970): 'the head's position is primarily a status in relation to which co-operation, harmony and cohesion are maintained in the group' (1970, p. 12). Members of the dwelling-group do not have to seek the head's permission to erect new structures within the house, and married men are responsible for their own maintenance and repairs. In extreme circumstances (such as persistent thieving, or misbehaviour with other men's wives), a *mai gida*, in response to pressure from the dwelling-group, may expel a member, who will then be obliged to erect a new house or to migrate; but more often he is concerned to persuade members to remain in the house. The *mai gida* has to give permission for the holding of naming or marriage ceremonies at the house, which all married men will attend. He is the man who should receive visiting strangers. Although the functions of decrepit or senile heads gradually pass to others, heads are never formally deposed – as are Village Heads. One of the most flourishing big houses has a notorious elderly, cantankerous *mai gida* ('he behaves like a madman, although he is not') who once pushed his father down a well; yet during his prolonged headship no man has ever left the house – all having learnt how to tolerate or avoid him.

In the Ashanti towns, where few dwelling-houses were more than thirty years old, every man or woman 'aspires to have his or her own house' (*ibid.*, p. 14). In Dorayi, on the other hand, no women aspire to be household heads. As for middle-aged Dorayi men, far from regarding it as 'unbecoming' not to live in their own house, as their counterparts do in Ashanti, they are no more inclined to set up their own houses than anyone else. While most of the heads of 27 big houses (3 big houses which are just outside Dorayi are included to increase the size of the sample) are either old (*tsoho*) – 12 men – or elderly (*dattijo*) – 10 men, there are as many as 5 old men and 45 elderly men in these houses who are not heads.

The status of the *mai gida* of a big house to some degree resembles that of a lineage head in a lineage-organised society, the house itself bearing some resemblance to lineage land. Perhaps it is reasonable to regard the big house as according a minimum of security to individuals who would otherwise lack corporate support owing to the lack of lineage land? Female, as well as male, members of the 'kin-group' (see below) have the right of taking up residence in a big house – a right which (in this overcrowded area) husbandless women, and/or their sons, often exert. Consequently, an appreciable proportion of maternally related kin reside in big houses, especially as older sons who have removed there with their mothers often remain in the house after her departure on remarriage, and as young maternally related men sometimes remove there alone on their father's death. That a Dorayi house, unlike a habitation in a compact *gari*, is a concept or organisational principle, as much as a physical structure, is shown by the fact that the actual building is never sold: while a man who migrates may sell the farmland on which his habitation stands, the actual structure is seldom, if ever, reoccupied but quickly crumbles away.

KIN STRUCTURE

As in Ashanti, 'the norm is for the dwelling group to be a single kin group; that is, one in which the members are all connected with one another by kinship or marriage' (*ibid.*, p. 10) – though, as will be seen, the matter of slave-descent somewhat complicates the position in Dorayi. The relationship of the *mai gida* to the married men in 26 big houses is shown in Table XII.2. The *mai gida* together with paternal kin comprise

Table XII.2   *Big houses: relationship to 'mai gida'*

	Married men		Number of houses including each category of kin
	No.	%	
Mai gida himself	26[i]	9	26
Sons	49[ii]	16	19
Brothers	40[iii]	13	16
Brothers' sons	43[iv]	14	13
Father's brothers' sons	47[v]	16	11
Father's brothers' sons' sons	18	6	6
Other paternal kin	17[vi]	6	5
Related through women	26[vii]	9	8
Descended from co-slaves	10[viii]	3	2
Non-kin	22[ix]	7	7
Not known	3	[1]	2
	301	100%	

Brothers through Other paternal kin bracketed = 71

Notes:

(i)   The largest of all the 27 big houses is omitted: its members are the descendants of 4 co-slaves and of their owner.

(ii)   Two houses each have as many as 6 married sons.

(iii)   One house has as many as 7 married brothers, another having 6.

(iv)   One house includes as many as 11 brothers' sons.

(v)   One house includes as many as 10 father's brothers' sons.

(vi)   As many as 9 of these men are brothers' sons' sons, all living in one house.

(vii)   Three houses each include 5 maternally related kin, all of whom are sisters' descendants.

(viii)   These men are descended from a co-slave of the forebear of the *mai gida*.

(ix)   Seven of these men are the descendants of one slave who joined a 'free house' (not his former owner's house); another 7 belong to one of the few houses for which accurate genealogies could not be compiled – so a few of them may be paternal kin.

at least four-fifths (80%) of all married men; and as many as 9% of men are maternally related to the head. Most houses (19 out of 26) include sons of the *mai gida* and/or married brothers (16 out of 26) and half of them (13) include brothers' sons.

The kin structure of the twenty-four big Dorayi houses is compared with that of all other houses (exclusive, of course, of 'one-man' houses) in Table XII.3. As would be expected, the smaller houses include a much lower proportion of paternal kin who are more distant than sons and brothers than do the larger houses.

Table XII.3 *Big houses: number of married men per 'mai gida'*

	Number of married men per 'mai gida'	
	Big houses	Other houses
Sons	2.0	0.9
Brothers	1.5	0.7
All other paternal kin	4.6	0.4
Related through women	0.9	0.1
Other	1.3	0.1
	11.4	3.2

Most of the big houses have remained on the same site for half a century or more, though many of them have had to expand onto adjacent farmland. There has been no tendency whatsoever, as with the pagan Maguzawa (information from Dr Murray Last), for houses to remove every few decades to a new site: whatever the sociological considerations, high population densities would sufficiently account for this. Furthermore, houses hardly ever break up into separate segments, as they do with the Maguzawa, it being most unusual for more than one married man to remove to a separate house, though his example sometimes stimulates others to follow suit, and there have been a few instances (as will be seen) of big houses 'exploding outwards' into sets of related houses. The twenty-four big houses are, indeed, astonishingly stable. It is possible that from as many as sixteen of them no man has hived off into a new house during the past thirty or forty years or more, and the largest number of men to have removed from any one house is only three.

HOUSE-SECTIONS

Some big houses include a network of mud-walled paths leading to architecturally distinct 'sections', the whole having the air of a tiny compact village (*gari*); at the other extreme the separate sections (where they exist) may be structurally invisible, the whole interior yard consisting of a conglomeration of huts, granaries, open working-places, and so forth, as though all the residents were members of one two-generational house-hold – though all big houses in fact include at least one kinsman who is not a brother of the *mai gida*. (Fig. 7 relates to a house which is an intermediate case.) When houses are compartmentalised the term 'section' is more likely to correspond with sociological and economic realities than when they are not – in the latter case opinion may differ as to whether a married son (for instance) is in the same section as his father or not. This

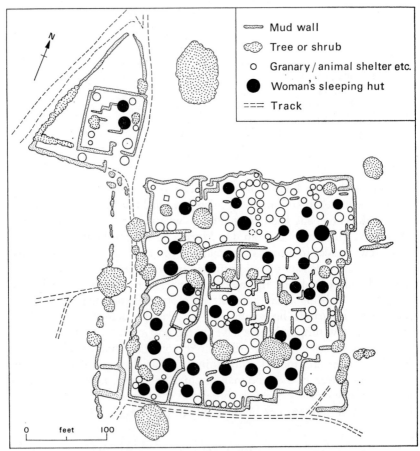

Fig. 7. Gidan Sambo, a big house very close to Dorayi – see Appendix XII(1), House 1. The main entrance is to the south-east and there is another entrance to the north.

uncertainty as to what co-residence in a section involves is reflected in vague terminology: two words for house-section are *shiyya* and *waje* – nouns with the general meaning of 'place' or 'direction'.

The general rules, to which there are exceptions, are that the following groups of married men tend to comprise separate sections: fathers and married sons (other than sons who themselves have married sons); and sets of brothers none of whom have married sons – if there are many brothers, the sons of each mother occasionally occupy separate sections. If these rules are presumed to apply in all instances (as they may not, for instance, in the case of sons who have left *gandu*), then it is found that about one-third (36%) of all sections are occupied by one married man (and his dependants), that the corresponding proportions for two, three and four married men respectively are 36%, 14% and 7% and that the two largest sections include seven and eight married men. (The corresponding number of wives per section varies between one and nine; only about one-fifth of all wives are alone in a section.) Nearly three-quarters of all big houses (again on the above assumptions) have between four and seven sections.

Members of the same house-section are no exception to the rule that married men, other than those in *gandu*, never farm jointly; accordingly, the wives of a set of fatherless brothers in any section do not form a single cooking-group, except in the rare event of the brothers forming a fraternal *gandu* – but they may work together in such pre-cooking, heavy, food-preparation tasks as pounding, as indeed may wives in different house-sections. But as brothers are apt to partake of their food together, or in two or more groups, food-sharing may well occur, especially if one brother has insufficient to eat. The wives, also, form a potentially food-sharing group.

On the other hand, the wives of fathers and of their married sons, usually do comprise one cooking-group, at least for the main meal of the day, which is in the evening, all the food for which is (or ought to be) provided by the father. If one woman is in charge of the cooking on any day then the rotational system usually involves son's wives, on an equal basis with father's wives, unless they are very young or newly married. However, when an elderly father retires from farming, and hands over responsibility to his sons (maybe dividing his farmland), his wives also retire from cooking, and the wives of each son will then cook separately, each providing their husband's father and his wives with plates of food.

NODES ON THE ECONOMIC LANDSCAPE

In an area of dispersed settlement where, as we know, there is a singular lack of nodes on the economic landscape so far as the community as a whole is concerned, a really big house may provide such a node for its members and maybe, also, to some degree for the population generally. The best example is a house in Dorayi Karama which is the home of fourteen married men and seventy-one people, where virtually all requirements of foodstuffs, except meat, may be bought from one or other member of the house, and which also attracts many ambulant traders, selling cloth, clothing, shoes and sundry items for personal use. Such a house is, in itself, a species of market-place, serving outsiders as well as its own members. Two or three rich men (*masu arziki*) in the house buy and resell all the grain that is required by the household (additional to 'own production'); at least eight wives make groundnut oil cake for sale and two others make locust bean cakes; numerous snacks are on sale; groundnuts, vegetables, palm oil, kerosene, kola nuts (in quantity), cigarettes, sugar, salt, natron and other wares are usually available. A grinding-mill has been installed, women members of the household paying the same fees as any outsider; and one room is reserved as a mosque. However, some big houses are far from being 'self-sufficient' – thus, the notably prosperous house (House 2, p. 196), for which a genealogy is provided in Appendix xii (1), buys most of its grain requirements from grain-traders in other houses.

THE FARMLAND

It is unusual for most of the farmland owned by the members of big houses to lie near the house – indeed, farmers resident in smaller houses are often better situated so far as the location of their farmland is concerned. As a house grows in size the farmland which originally surrounded it becomes increasingly inadequate and farmers seek to buy land elsewhere. Also, some of the members of big houses are apt to be farm-sellers, so that much of the land around a house may come, in course of time, to be owned by farmers in other houses. In fact only six of the twenty-four big houses are mainly surrounded by their own inherited land and a fair number have all their farms elsewhere. So there is no reason to suppose that a farmer's efficiency is enhanced by residence in a big house. Nor do the members of big houses tend to own more land than other farmers. If the five notably impoverished big houses (see p. 189 below) are excluded, then it is found that the members of big houses own, on average, about as much farmland per head (half an acre) as the Dorayi population generally.

ECONOMIC SECURITY

Membership of a big house is no guarantee of economic security, for some of the big houses are notably impoverished (see Table XII.4), so that their members may even be regarded as dragging each other down. However, if the five impoverished big houses are omitted, it is found that (see column 5 Table XII.4) there are fewer poor men in the remaining nineteen houses (8%) than in houses which are not big (32%). As this low incidence of poverty is not to be explained by the age-structure of these nineteen dwelling-groups, which is similar to that of the population as a whole, it seems likely that economically insecure men benefit from living in big houses – unless there are too many of them in any particular house. On the other hand the proportion of rich men in the nineteen houses is not notably high – 17% against 13% for smaller houses (see column 6, Table XII.4). However, it is worth noting that nearly a third of all the men in the six notably rich houses are wealthy (see column 1, Table XII.4).

Table XII.4   *Wealth and poverty in big houses*

Classifi-cation of married men	Big houses				Total big houses excluding poor houses	Total houses 'not-big'	One-man houses
	Rich houses	Houses neither rich nor poor	Poor houses	Total big houses			
	(1)	(2)	(3)	(4)	(5)	(6)	(7)
	Percentages of married men						
Rich	29	9	5	14	17	13	7
Neither	65	82	50	69	75	55	51
Poor	6	8	45	18	8	32	41
	100	100	100	100	100	100	100

Notes:

(i) A 'rich house' (column 1) is defined as a big house in which two or more rich men live – there are six such houses; a 'poor house' (column 3) is a big house where four or more poor men live – there are five of them. (There was only one house which fell into both categories, as thus defined: it was classed as 'poor' as eight poor men, compared with two rich men, resided there.)

(ii) Column 6 relates to all houses where fewer than seven married men reside. Column 7 relates to all houses where one married man only resides.

FARM SLAVERY

When I first noticed the existence of big houses in Dorayi and in other sections of the KCSZ, I naturally wondered whether many of them had originally been houses where large numbers of ex-slaves had lived. But I found that this was not so. As many as 19 of the 27 big houses are inhabited by men who are all of free-descent (in the male line), compared with 5 dwelling groups which are of slave-descent and with 3 of mixed origin – like House 3, p. 197. Very few of the present-day big houses were formerly big slave-houses (see Chapter XIII).

In terms of descent those who live in big houses are a typical cross-section of the population of Dorayi Karama and Ja'en Yamma where (see Chapter XIII) most of those of slave-descent reside; the proportion of married men who are of slave-descent in these two localities is 37% both for the population as a whole and for the big houses.

THE GROWTH OF BIG HOUSES

Given the various factors conducive to the growth of big houses which have so far been discussed, there might be thought to be a strong case for regarding smaller houses (in particular one-man houses), rather than big houses, as anomalous. As sons and fathers, as well as sets of resident brothers, cling together; as the rate of outward migration from bigger houses is very low; as house-segments do not hive off; as the population of the big houses is certainly increasing; as big houses occupy smaller sites per head than smaller houses; as most big houses appear to provide a measure of security to their members; as there are numerous socio-economic advantages, especially for secluded wives, of residence in big houses, some of which resemble small market-places – so it might seem that the phenomenon of the big house requires no explanation, but that it is the continued existence of so many smaller houses which is surprising.

Why, then, does one man in ten (see Table XII.1) live alone (with his dependants) in a house? About a third (twenty-four men) of the sixty-two men, for whom information is available, find themselves alone in their houses, not because they had chosen to live in this way, but because everyone else in the house had died or migrated (in some cases they had fled from a house in process of disintegration) or because for some reason, such an insanity or thieving, they had been obliged to leave their former house. As many as 8 of the 62 men live alone because they (or their fathers) were strangers who had built houses; and 4 men had removed from their former houses because they were non-kin, another 2 because they were maternally related kin. Of the remaining 24 men, as many as 10 had belonged to houses (none of which were big) which had broken up into several adjoining one-man houses. Only 14 men who had formerly lived with their paternal kin had deliberately hived off as individuals to set up their own houses, at least 7 of them having removed following their father's death. Accordingly, the existence of so many one-man houses cannot be regarded as basically due to a preference for living alone. And that rich men are the very people who do not tend to hive off is shown by column 7 of Table XII.4, which shows that the proportion of rich men in one-man houses is exceptionally low – 7%.

It seems that in recent years few big houses have diminished significantly in size. One dilapidated house, which will soon fall back to the soil whence it came, is occupied, for the time being, by the only one of a set of eight brothers who has not died or migrated, together with a late brother's son. In another case the sole occupant of a ruined house which had once been very large has had to erect a wall around his room. There are few other similar cases.

So I think that the continued existence of houses of such a wide size-range is best understood in terms of the idea that once a house attains a certain size it tends to grow and flourish, but that there are many reasons why this threshold may never be reached. While none of the twenty-four big Dorayi houses is currently declining in size, and many of them are growing very rapidly, there are smaller houses which lack the stability and capacity for growth of the big houses. Small houses, especially those occupied only by a set of brothers or by a father and his sons, may be seriously destabilized by death or migration: men do not like living alone, except in small houses which they have built for themselves, and they tend to abandon an erstwhile big house where few remain resident.

A further consideration would seem to be that the advantages of living in a large house were formerly not so pronounced. In southern Dorayi, especially in Gwazaye and Tudun Mazadu, there are considerable numbers of 'sets of related houses' with a common named ancestor, very few of the houses being big. Why did the descendants of these well-remembered men not form big houses? Or why, if they did so, did they fall apart? What are the circumstances associated with this different pattern of development?

These problems may be approached in terms of the generational depth of houses. As Table XII.5 shows, the single common ancestor from whom the members of a big house stem (one of his forebears, rather than he himself may have been the actual founder of the house) is seldom further removed than the father's father of the *mai gida*, so that most paternally related, married male members of dwelling-groups belong to categories of kin included in the following simple diagram.

In fact, as the table shows, as many as nine of the twenty-seven big houses stem from men only one generation senior to the present *mai gida*; and one house was founded by the old *mai gida* himself – an ex-slave.

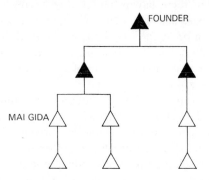

Whereas very nearly all of the big houses stem from a man one or two generations back, the 'sets of related houses' would have been big houses of greater generational depth had individuals not hived off. No statistical comparison with the big houses is possible, both because the numbers of houses in a set tend to be so large and because reliable information on the . identity of those who had earlier hived off (whether father or son for instance) was often unobtainable.

Table XII.5   *Generation of founder of big houses in relation to the 'mai gida'*

| | Number of houses | | | |
	Slave-descent	*Free-descent*	*Mixed-descent*[1]	*Total*
Self	1	–	–	1
One ascendant generation	2	6	1	9
Two ascendant generations	2	11[ii]	2	15
Three ascendant generations	–	1	–	1
Unclear	–	1	–	1
Total	5	19	3	27

Notes:
  (i) As it is not always clear who founded houses of mixed slave- and free-descent, the oldest of any possible alternatives is shown here.
  (ii) In one of these cases the founder is strictly in the third ascendant generation in relation to the young *mai gida* (who is a Village Head), but in the second generation in relation to the latter's father's brother who is living in the house.

Apart from these sets of related houses in the south, it was possible to identify only five existing houses in northern Dorayi which might have developed into big houses during the past fifty years or so, had they not broken up. Most of these houses resembled the big houses in that individuals, not segments, had broken off, though in one exceptional case a house had recently divided into two neighbouring houses owing to a quarrel.

Although the sets of related houses tend to be of greater generational depth than the big houses, all the evidence is that big houses have no tendency to become unstable at some particular stage of their development, such as when their founder is in the third, rather than the second, ascendant generation. As there are no corporate lineages; as everyone, except sons-in-*gandu*, works on his own farmland; and as local removal depends on the initiative of individuals not groups – it would, in fact, be very odd if the death of the last survivor of the senior generation seriously destabilized a house. Why, then, is there only one big house whose founder is known to be in the third ascendant generation?

I am sure that the answer to this question is very simple: namely that most present-day big houses were first established between about sixty and a hundred years ago, by newcomers to the area and by ex-slaves. Many of the houses are in the northerly part of Dorayi, which had presumably been sparsely inhabited before this development, probably because of restrictions imposed for security reasons on building houses within a certain radius of the city wall – a radius which, as elderly informants said, was later reduced. Rich city farmers desirous of establishing slave-estates were naturally attracted to this zone when house-building began to be tolerated there, and rurally based farmers removed there also, some of them from near by, others from further afield – a fair number of the founders of big houses (or their fathers) are recorded as having been strangers 'from the east'. Each house that was established was surrounded by its own farmland onto which it could expand as its population increased.

As already noted, the area of Gwazaye and Tudun Mazadu in southern Dorayi is the old-established locality where most of the 'sets of related houses' are situated; it also lies within the somewhat larger section of Dorayi where very few men are of slave-descent. It therefore seems likely that, at the time when the large houses were first being established in the sparsely populated zone further north, southern Dorayi resembled much the inner ring of the KCSZ in being very densely populated.

How does it come about that, so far as is known, big Muslim houses are so rare in rural Hausaland generally, possibly being confined – see Appendix XII(2) – to certain sections of the KCSZ? I suggest that such houses tend to develop, and to survive, where the following conditions obtain:

first, strangers settle dispersedly in an area where population is (initially) sparse, so that large farms, some of them cultivated by slaves, may be established around the houses; second, population densities subsequently increase very rapidly indeed (this resulting from further immigration, the influx of slaves, natural increase and the seeping in of farmers from nearby) so that the large houses become 'encapsulated', it being difficult to take up more land, or to spare land for erecting more houses; third, large 'slave-houses' provide free men with a demonstration effect; fourth, the very high population densities are not relieved by a strong tendency, on the part of the population generally, to migrate; fifth, the land shortage finally becomes so serious that sons have little economic independence during their fathers' lifetimes, being under severe economic restraint at the very time when they could be expected to contribute most to the general welfare – with the result that when their fathers die they often lack the means to separate, even had they not already become habituated to fraternal co-residence.

APPENDIX XII(1)
Genealogies for three big houses

A few personal details relating to the residents of these three big houses are provided to add to the interest of the genealogies.

Notes on diagrams

1. As it was often difficult to ascertain the birth-order of deceased sons in this polygynous society, no significance attaches to the ordering of sons, other than first-born sons, on the diagrams.
2. Married men only are included.
3. In order to conceal the identity of houses, all names are false.

4. Deceased men are shown thus:

Men who migrated are shown thus:

House 1. Slave-descent (Gidan Sambo) (see Fig. 7)

Twenty-five of the twenty-seven men in this immense and stable house (from which only six men are recorded as ever having migrated) are descended from four brothers, all ex-slaves, whose father (Abdu), who had built the house, had been a slave owned by a titled land-owner (Yahaya) from Kano city. One of Yahaya's sons lived here and when he died his young son was adopted by one of the ex-slaves; this son still lives here, together with his married son –

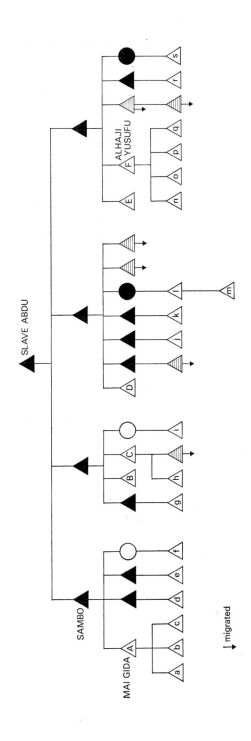

providing a small element of free-descent in a house which is basically of slave-descent.

Unlike most big houses, this house (which is situated just outside Dorayi) has a name – Gidan Sambo. Sambo was Abdu's third son; he was an important malam, owned cattle, and 'became very rich'. He probably started acquiring land some time before 1920, buying some of it from the slave-owning family. Sambo's sole surviving son (A) is the present *mai gida* – 'because his father was so rich'; now old, he has retired from farming, having divided his farmland between his three married sons, (a), (b) and (c). Two other paternal grandsons of Sambo – (d) and (e) – are also in the house, as well as a daughter's son, (f).

The richest man in the house is Alhaji Yusufu (F). Having inherited no land, he bought many farms, reselling one to a city man for £150 to £200, to finance his recent pilgrimage to Mecca. One of his wives (she was Sambo's daughter) is 'very rich': she is a farm-buyer and a storer of produce for a price rise. The Alhaji's four married sons – (n), (o), (p), (q) – are now responsible for his farming; one of his brothers, (E), who, like himself, is a Koranic teacher, lives in the house, as do sons of a deceased brother (r), and of a sister (s). Ten other married men in the house are descended from Sambo's two other brothers: they are (B), (C), (D) in the senior generation, and (g), (h), (i), (j), (k), (l), and (m) in the two junior generations.

House 2. Free-descent

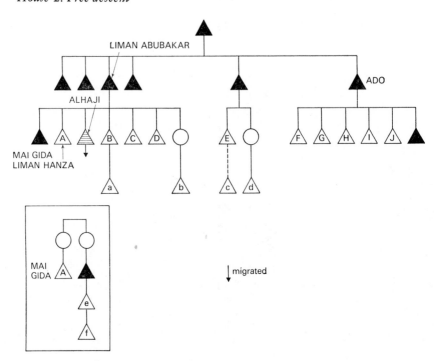

This notably prosperous house, from which no man has ever migrated (except for one who went to live in his father's house in the city), is the home of fifteen married men (eighty-two people) and is expanding rapidly. The house-founder was a rich farmer whose wife had inherited slaves; he had six sons of whom one was Liman Abubakar, who in turn had six sons, of whom one (who subsequently became an Alhaji) was the man who went to the city – he still owns a farm in Dorayi. Another of Liman Abubakar's sons was Liman Hanza, the present *mai gida*. A son of a daughter of Liman Abubakar is also in the house, having come to live there on his father's death. The most prosperous man in the house is Alhaji (E), a well-known Koranic teacher, who has numerous pupils, many of whom come from elsewhere and live at the house; too young to have a married son, he has a servant (*bara*) – (c) – and his sister's son – (d) – is in *gandu* with him. One of the house-founder's sons was Ado, a slave-owner who removed to another house; on his death his sons – (F) to (J) – returned to this house. Finally, a son of Liman Hanza's mother's sister's son is in the house – (e) – together with his son.

House 3. Mixed-descent

(i) Slave-owner's descendants

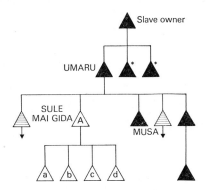

*They established houses of their own

(ii) Slave's descendants

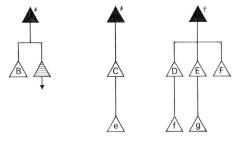

‡Umaru's slaves.
†Umaru's wife's slave.

The fourteen married men in this house, which is the home of about fifty-seven people, are: a son (A) and four grandsons – (a) to (d) – of a rich slave-owner Dagaci Umaru; five sons – (B) to (F) – and three grandsons – (e) to (g) – of three slaves owned by Umaru or his slave-owning wife, Mairo; and one former servant (*bara*), a stranger from Sokoto, who married the widow of one of Dagaci Umaru's sons. Mairo, who was the daughter of Dagaci Umaru's father's sister, came from Kura District, bringing with her at least six inherited slaves, who worked on her husband's farms. The slaves all lived in Dagaci Umaru's large house (surrounded by farmland), in which his slave-owning father had formerly lived. Dagaci Umaru probably died about forty years ago leaving five sons of whom only one (Sule, the *mai gida*) now survives. As Sule's brothers have no surviving married sons, most of his father's farmland passed to him, part of which is considered as held in trust (*riko*) for an unmarried brother's son who has migrated. Sule sold part of his inherited farmland to finance his unsuccessful candidature for *dagaci*, and his large farm of some eight and a half acres, which adjoins the house, is a small part of the original *gandu* owned by his grandfather, whose other two sons (now dead) had also received portions. Mairo, the woman slave-owner, only had one son by Dagaci Umaru. He had a chequered career, being jailed for embezzlement of tax money, while acting as *dagaci* when his father was ill; on his release he refused to live in the house any longer and after selling and pledging farmland to his mother's ex-slaves and others, he set off for Mecca on foot, reportedly dying *en route*.

Sule lives in one section of the house with his four married sons – in 1972 he was in process of dividing his farmland among them. Considered 'rich in sons' but not in worldly possessions, he is a Koranic scholar; he buys grain and cassava in rural markets, which one of his three wives (who provides the capital) sells from his house. None of Sule's four sons (two of whom commute as 'labourers') is in the least prosperous: it remains to be seen whether their position will improve when they become farmers on their own account as it seems that their father had been an inefficient farm manager. This house has been categorised as impoverished (see Table xii.4 above), for one of Sule's sons together with the former servant and four of those of slave-descent are notably poor. One of the latter (D) is an old man, who is nearly blind, who insists on head-loading cornstalk beds to the city; he has never owned a farm, but his son, who looks after him, has farmland on *aro*.

APPENDIX XII(2)
The geographical distribution of big houses

There appears to be no mention in the literature of large Muslim houses comparable to those of Dorayi. The three largest houses found by M. G. Smith in two areas in northern Zaria accommodated only forty-three, thirty-three and twenty-five people (Smith, 1955, pp. 19, 23). Among the rural Hausa in the Maradi area of the Niger Republic, the eleven largest houses (out of a total of

2097) were each the homes of only six married men (Nicolas *et al.*, 1964, p. 135). Insofar as houses including married sons have been reported as existing, emphasis has always been laid on their fragility – on the tendency for them to break up when the grandchildren become at all numerous, if not before.

On the other hand, as noted above, big houses commonly exist among the pagan Hausa (the Maguzawa), with whom 'brothers are expected to live together in the same compound, it being considered disgraceful if they separate' (Greenberg, 1946, p. 17). Dr Murray Last has provided me with particulars of a Maguzawa house in the Malumfashi area (Katsina Emirate) where nineteen married men resided.

The first big house I saw in the KCSZ lay to the east of the city, only about two miles from the Central Hotel, less than a quarter of a mile from the expanding modern suburb Nassarawa which, in 1971, was threatening its existence: called Gidan Madugu (after an ancient, still surviving, caravan leader), it housed 22 married men and some twenty cattle. In Kawo Village Area (east of that house, see p. 85), at least 13 out of 119 houses were the homes of 7 married men or more, and about 30% of all married men resided in them; these proportions were about as large as those in Dorayi, the same applying to Kirimbo Village Area (see Appendix iv.5).

Unfortunately, aerial photographs and maps, however large-scale, are of little assistance in detecting big houses, which tend to be indistinguishable from dense house-clusters. On the basis of such slender evidence as I collected, I think it is possible that significant proportions of big houses are found only in certain areas in the centre of the KCSZ. I neither saw, nor heard of, any large houses to the north of the city and of few to the west, and it is possible that the main concentrations lie east and south. These scanty notes (which are presented in the hope that others may explore further) relate to areas of dispersed settlement only; whether there are big houses in the walled towns of the KCSZ is not known for certain – but I think they are rare.

XIII

From slavery to freedom: farm-slavery in Dorayi

INTRODUCTION

The 1901 Proclamation on Slavery prohibited slave-raiding, abolished the legal status of slavery (which meant that runaway slaves could not be retrieved through the courts) and declared that all those subsequently born of slave parents would be free – but it did not prohibit slave-holding as such. Faced with the existence of ancient and flourishing slavery-systems, which probably involved several million men and women, the Colonial Office and Lugard were agreed that it would have been altogether beyond the power of the understaffed colonial administration to have enforced any policy of immediate emancipation – and this quite apart from the sympathy which Lugard felt for slave-owners as a class. In 1901 Joseph Chamberlain had stated that it had not been intended to interfere at that stage with what he euphemistically termed 'domestic relations' (PRO, CO 446, 76), and this had remained the longer term policy of the British Government. Subsequent Slavery Proclamations (1904 and 1907) prohibited all transactions in slaves and made it clear that the Government was not liable to pay compensation to slave-owners in respect of slaves who were legally freed by the courts, but slave-holding was never legally prohibited. Nor, in the longer run, was there any need for this. While the institution continued to flourish during the first twenty years, or so, of colonial rule, it then rapidly declined, dying a natural death by about 1930, owing both to the diminishing stocks of slaves and to the changed attitudes of the times.

Understandably enough, the colonial administration preserved very great discretion about the persistence of large-scale slavery at so late a date, not only in its general dealings with the Colonial Office (which it could not wholly trust) but also within the Political Department itself, where there was a conspiracy of silence. Nowhere in the elaborate and detailed administrative instructions which Lugard issued to his political officers in his *Political Memoranda* (1906) was there any indication of whether farm-slaves were to be regarded as beyond the pale when it came to such mundane matters as counting the rural population or assessing the capacity of a community to pay tax. On the whole it seems likely that the vast population of farm-slaves in rural Hausaland went uncounted and untaxed – this was one of several reasons for the persistent under-estimation of the population in the early years. (But see Appendix xIII(1), p. 221: is it possible that taxes on specialised farm produce – see Appendix II(1) – were payable by slaves?) Political officers regarded it as highly improper to make any mention of a matter on which (despite the general policy of indirect rule) they found themselves so gravely at variance with the Emirs – except, of course, in relation to ransom through the courts and the establishment of homes for freed slaves. The author of the 1911 Assessment Report on Dan Isa Sub-District – see Appendix IV(1) – was either greatly daring or careless when he mentioned that in assessing the size of the 'permanent population' he had excluded the 'floating element' – which was presumably a euphemism for the slave element. I have found no other such veiled (let alone unveiled) references to contemporary slavery in any of the numerous Assessment Reports I have consulted in the Nigerian National Archives at Kaduna.

But although for day-to-day administrative purposes Lugard must somehow have conveyed (though not in his printed instructions to political officers) that the whole matter of farm-slavery was beyond the pale, he yet expressed himself freely on the subject in certain of his *Political Memoranda* (1906), perhaps hoping to demonstrate that Muslim slavery systems were a special case. *Memorandum* No. 6 ('Slavery Questions') dealt with official policy on slavery on such matters as ransom, the acquisition of concubines and inheritance; and *Memorandum* No. 22, which has seldom, if ever, been cited, was entitled 'The condition of slaves and the native law regarding slavery in Northern Nigeria', having been based on information sent to Lugard by Residents in reply to circular questions – see Appendix xIII(1). The latter is a most useful, uninhibited report which, unlike the former, was omitted from the revised edition of the *Memoranda* published in 1919. (As mentioned by A. H. M. Kirk-Greene in his introduction to the third edition of the *Memoranda* (Kirk-Greene, 1970), Lugard had originally sought to prevent the Colonial Office from seeing the 1906 version, which is consequently very scarce – the copy owned by Lugard's brother Edward is now in the Royal Commonwealth Society's library. The full title of both versions, which are always referred to as *Political Memoranda*, is *Instructions to Political and other Officers, on Subjects chiefly Political and Administrative*.)

Lugard's successor, Governor Girouard, was initially little interested in slavery, though he was much concerned with the allied subject of land tenure. However in 1908, which was a famine year, he was troubled by reports of 'constant desertions of domestic slaves'; unfamiliar with the earlier history, he suggested to the Colonial Office (16 November, 1908, PRO, CO 446, 76) that one remedy would be a decree of general emancipation with compensation to the owners – as 'has been invariably witnessed elsewhere in the Empire'. Perhaps this was the last time that such action was suggested to the Colonial Office, which was very angry. 'No action' commanded Lord Crewe, the Colonial Secretary: the persistence of slavery 'is anomalous and inconvenient, like a thousand other things in an anomalous Empire'. R. L. Antrobus, the Colonial Office official, recorded (27 March 1909): 'I have told Sir P. Girouard that Lord Crewe does not propose to send any answer at present. Put by.' (PRO, CO 446, 82.)

The likelihood is that the survey instigated by Lugard before 1906 was unique – that no additional information on farm-slavery in Northern Nigeria was ever collected. In his later writings Lugard had nothing new to reveal and was mainly concerned to justify the success of his original policy. As early as 1919 he had claimed, in his revised *Memoranda*, that in the Northern Provinces this 'most difficult problem has been solved without any social upheaval' – solved in the sense that in the Muslim states there were, in his opinion, no slaves who were unaware that they could assert their freedom if they chose (Kirk-Greene, 1970, p. 221). (If true, this represented little change since 1900, as will later be seen.) In *The Dual Mandate in British Tropical Africa* (1922), he affirmed (on the basis of what evidence?) that the slaves 'were willing and anxious to pay the ransom money' (p. 376) – complacently adding that the ransom was 'often an equitable return from a household slave for maintenance she has received in her master's house' (p. 378).

In the past few years there has been a great quickening of interest both in African slavery systems and in the transition from slavery to freedom, and it was fortunate that in 1972 it was not too late (though it soon will be) to study the Hausa system of farm-slavery with the help of informants who remembered it for themselves. In the belief that farm-slavery conditions in Dorayi (despite its proximity to Kano city) were reasonably representative of those in the central Hausa Emirates of Kano and Katsina, I here set my Dorayi findings within the general context of a wider discussion, which I have sought to enliven by reference to Lugard's writings which often throw so much light on the false suppositions of his time.

THE HAUSA FARM-SLAVERY SYSTEM

As I have recently noted elsewhere (Hill, 1976), the general incidence of farm-slavery in rural Hausaland must remain for ever unknown. Fortunately, however, Lugard's above mentioned *Memorandum* No. 22 (1906) makes it quite clear (though only implicitly) that incidences were apt to be high, though they were also variable. If – see Appendix 1(1) – one is justified in assuming that the population of Hausaland in 1900 was of the order of eight to ten million, then it is likely that several million people were in servitude, most of them being farm-slaves and their dependants. There is no doubt that in many sections of rural Hausaland, as in ancient Greece, 'there were enough slaves about for them to be, of necessity, an integral factor in the society' (Finley, 1968, p. 60).

Unlike genuine chattel-slaves in the ancient and new worlds, farm-slaves in rural Hausaland normally enjoyed so many rights, including those of self-ransom, that it is reasonable to ask whether the term 'slave' is, in fact, an appropriate rendering of the Hausa *bawa* (f. *baiwa*, pl. *bayi*, *bauta* being slavery)? However, quite apart from the impossibility of finding any alternative English word (as will become apparent, any words involving notions of 'serfdom' or 'labouring' would be even less acceptable), it is clear that present-day definitions are sufficiently commodious to include the Hausa variant. M. I. Finley states (Finley, 1968, p. 307) that the classical Roman definition of slavery as an institution 'whereby someone is subject to the *dominium* of another contrary to nature', may be accepted as 'universally applicable', though without the controversial phrase 'contrary to nature' – and provided the word *dominium* (which can be translated as 'power') is understood to imply 'the idea of property'. But while it is the totality of the slave's powerlessness which justifies the term 'chattel-slave', it is Finley's opinion that in any sociological analysis equal stress must be given to his deracination.

In principle (at least) most Hausa farm-slaves were *deracinés* in that their owners were mostly Muslims while they themselves (at least at the time of capture) were usually unbelievers. But whatever might have been the deviation from official command on this matter, it seems likely that most farm-slaves in the central Emirates of Kano and Katsina were in origin strangers who, themselves, or their forebears, had been uprooted on capture, whether during warfare or in slave-raiding conducted for its own sake. I therefore concentrate attention in this chapter on the very common type of farm-slavery which involved farmers in buying their slaves (if they had not inherited them) either in market-places or (more often) in houses which were owned by slave-dealers or by other farmers. (Only large markets had slave-sections; thus I was told that the nearest slave-market to Kazaure was Kano city – over sixty miles distant.) As slavery was an ancient system and as (presumably) there had been much buying and selling of farm-slaves for many generations, it came about that in 1900 many farm-slaves were unaware of the various places of origin of their forebears. There were other reasons, also, why populations of farm-slaves often constituted settled communities.

In Hausaland farm-slaves were apt to enjoy many rights. The main non-economic right (and this had legal validity) sprung from the prohibition on the sale of women slaves who had borne children by their masters. The main economic right was that which enabled slaves (or those acting on their behalves) to ransom themselves by paying appropriate sums in cash (cowry shells) to their owners – sums which were often regarded as a (somewhat notional) doubling of their market value. Although such rights of redemption were recognised by Muslim law, the alkalis' courts were relatively seldom involved, and not only because the number of courts in relation to the population was so small. The two types of ransom were respectively *pansa* (or *fansa*), which was such that the ransom was paid as a lump sum, the slave being freed immediately, and *murgu*, under which the slave entered into an agreement with his master to cease working for him for a period so that he might earn the whole, or part, of the redemption money. It is important to note that Maliki Law accorded slave-owners no rights whatsoever over their freed slaves and that a ransomed or manumitted slave enjoyed total freedom, being devoid of obligations to his ex-master.

A second economic right related to a slave's freedom to follow remunerative occupations on his own account, when not required to work on his owner's farmland. Slave-owners had a duty to give their farm-slaves plots of land where they could grow crops for sale, or for their own consumption, and some slaves cleared or acquired farmland for themselves, maybe by purchase. Probably most male and female slaves resembled free people in pursuing one or more types of remunerative non-farming occupation, which were similar to those of the free population except that slaves could not be *alkalai* or prayer-leaders (*limamai*); the general principle was that a slave's spare time was at his own disposal. The fact was, of course, that it was in the interests of slave-owners to encourage their slaves to earn money, as their obligations, which were enjoined by the Qur'an, to provide them with all their basic requirements, including food, clothing and housing, were thereby reduced. (See Sanneh (1976) on the unequivocal statements about slavery and slaves made in the Qur'an.)

The idea that slave and free members of a farming-group were to be treated with equal liberality becomes entirely comprehensible when it is realised that a slave-owner's married sons worked alongside his slaves on his farmland, maybe under the authority of a slave foreman (*sarkin gandu*), both sons and slaves having been spoken of as being in *gandu* with their father or master, to whom they were subordinate. In terms of their freedom to cultivate their own farms (or to pursue other occupations) in the afternoon and evening and on specified off-days, as well as in other respects, the rights of slaves closely resembled those of sons-in-*gandu* today (see *R. H.*, Chapter III); and slave-holders had similar obligations to those of present-day *gandu* heads. A slave's right to ransom himself, or to demand manumission if ill-treated, effectively corresponded to a son's freedom to leave *gandu* at any time; and a slave-owner's right to sell a slave (which will be discussed below) essentially corresponded to a father's right to dismiss his son from *gandu*.

For numerous reasons, including the high incidence of slavery, there is no doubt that the vast majority of slave-owners were ordinary private farmers, who literally invested in slaves in the same spirit as that in which they may invest in plough-oxen today. A. G. Hopkins' generalisation that West African slaves were mainly used 'to provide foodstuffs for leading officials, for their immediate circle of dependents, and for the army' (Hopkins, 1973, p. 24) is altogether inapplicable to rural Hausaland – and probably to Northern Nigeria generally. In a part of the world where there were no corporate land-holding lineages, and where (as we have seen) the apparatus of feudalism was lacking, it is hardly necessary to add that farm-slaves were not serfs attached to the farmland: they were not transferred to the buyer if the land on which they worked was sold, their attachment being solely to their owner.

A father's obligation to assist his sons-in-*gandu* to marry, was paralleled by the farm-slave's virtual right to marry and to demand that his owner should help him to obtain a suitable slave-wife. In great contrast to ancient Greece and Rome, where there were few women slaves in the countryside, the numbers of male and female farm-slaves may have been roughly equal, most slaves (whether or not they had the same owner) living *en famille* with their spouses and children, richer slaves tending to be polygynous. Whereas in antiquity there were so few slave children that the stock of farm-slaves in any locality had constantly to be replenished from outside, this was not so in Hausaland, which goes a long way to explain the settled nature of slave communities.

A slave-owner's freedom to sell any slave living *en famille* (like a father's freedom to dismiss a son-in-*gandu*) was severely limited by local public opinion, which (backed up by generalised legal notions) held that children should not be separated from their parents, or spouses wrenched apart, unless the owner had become impoverished (perhaps owing to partial famine conditions as in 1908) or the slaves were unmanageable, troublesome or criminal. Whereas in cases of impoverishment (other than famine) slaves were commonly sold directly to another local owner, maybe of their own choice, when it was the slave who had offended the aim might be to sell him to a dealer for removal elsewhere. Slave-owners encouraged their slaves to marry and settle down, because (among other reasons) this reduced the risk of abscondment. As they enjoyed a measure of social security, the slaves were not 'mere chattels', without qualification.

But in one significant respect slaves were less secure than is nowadays commonly supposed, for it seems that in general there were no special restrictions on the sale of second (and later) generation slaves – such as were first mentioned by the explorer Clapperton – see Appendix XIII(2). This important conclusion, which of course runs counter to M. G. Smith's influential findings in northern Zaria (see in particular Smith, 1955 and 1960) that have been widely understood as applying to rural Hausaland generally, derives partly from my field enquiries (in Kazaure as well as in Kano Emirate) and also from Lugard's *Memorandum* No. 22 (*op. cit.*), which reported that no farm-slave in Kano Province ever enjoyed immunity from sale, however long in the services of his master; more importantly, however, it is a conclusion which is entirely in accordance with commonsense. In societies where it was reprehensible (without good reason) to sell individual slaves living *en famille*, and where slaves, as a class, enjoyed the right of ransom, it was not to be expected that the owner's right to sell would depend on generation – especially as both parties to the transaction were commonly local farmers, as slave-spouses might be of different generations and as it is by no means clear whether the concept of generation had to do with original capture, arrival in the particular locality, or ownership by the particular master. Furthermore, Hausa slaves (other than concubines who had had children by a free man) were not, as will be seen, in process of assimilation into their owner's family, however that term might be defined, so that they required no protection against the interruption of such a process.

At this point it is necessary to examine the Hausa terminology. M. G. Smith reports that in northern Zaria the 'children of slaves' were denoted *dimajai* (sing. *dimajo*). This word is of Fulani, not Hausa, origin, and in my experience is apt to be outside the vocabulary of Kano people, who usually use the word *cucanawa* (sing. *bacucane*) instead. It is significant that in present-day Kano *cucanawa* is commonly employed as a collective to denote the general body of slaves, without regard to generation, and that the singular word *bawa* is used interchangeably with *bacucane* to denote any individual slave – though strictly a slave of the first generation, however that term may be defined. Hausa, as distinct from Fulani, terminology does not in practice support any firm generational distinction.

In fact Smith is rather concerned to stress the higher status of the *dimajai*, in relation to first-generation slaves, than their relative inalienability. Might it not, therefore, be that in Fulani society the *dimajai* were not slaves at all, but members of a class which was intermediate between slavery and freedom? In fact Stenning, in his study of the Wodaabe pastoral Fulani of Northern Nigeria (Stenning, 1959, p. 66), states that *diimaajo* (pl. *rimaibe*) were sons of men (*dimo*, pl. *rimbe*) whose mothers had borne children by their masters so that they had become (at least partially) enfranchised on his death. This clue to the puzzle of the generational distinction in northern Zaria will be pursued further below.

Reverting to the question of slave-owners' rights, all authorities are agreed that the slaves themselves had no formal rights of bequest, and that all their property was in principle transmitted to their owner on their death. This has sometimes led to the conclusion that slaves had no right to hold property of any kind. But such an idea conflicts with the facts that slaves were entirely free to devote their own earnings to any purpose (including self-ransom and the acquisition of their own farm-slaves to work on their personal farms), that their right to accumulate cash was undisputed, and that they might inherit property from their masters. An elderly former slave-owner, Alhaji A'ala of Kazaure, may have solved this conundrum when he told me in 1971 that in actual practice the 'rule' regarding inheritance only applied to slaves without issue. Just as matters of inheritance (see Chapter VII) are seldom referred to the courts by rural people today (actual practice conforming but loosely to the Muslim rules), so slave-owners would have been most unlikely to have taken legal action against slaves on this matter or to have exerted their full legal rights.

The slave-owner's right to bequeath his slaves to his heirs was not qualified by custom to the same degree as his right to dispose of his slaves by sale. However, there was often a considerable hiatus at death, partly owing to the practice of 'posthumous enfranchisement' – a declaration which was binding on the heirs that the slaves were to be freed on their master's death (see Ruxton, 1916, p. 357) – but more importantly because of voluntary (or semi-voluntary) manumission by the sons, and slave-desertion in protest against serving a new master. But as other forms of property, also, were subject to dissipation on death (grain stocks being consumed and plundered before the final decisions on the share-out had been taken), a stock of farm-slaves was as much a form of heritable capital as was a herd of cattle – for the latter might be led away. As for the division of the farm-slaves among the sons (and sometimes the daughters) on death, this in itself did not necessarily lead to the immediate break up of the slave *gandu*: this was partly because sons were more inclined to remain in fraternal *gandu* than they are today, but also because the actual division, as with other forms of property, tended to be rather casual, following no fixed formula, and maybe taking account of individual circumstances including the preferences of the slaves themselves.

As a form of agrarian capital, slaves, like cattle, commanded a price which was determined by supply and demand. Females were valued more highly than males – see Appendix xiii(1) – presumably mainly because they were a superior long-term investment, the children of a slave-couple usually belonging to the mother's owner. Depending on 'quality', sex, age and so forth, prices of adults may commonly have ranged from about 150 000 to 300 000 cowries, or the equivalent of about £3 10s to £7 – sums which have some meaning when compared with the value of an adult's annual grain requirements, which in 1900 was possibly of the order of £1 to £2.

Why were private farmers prepared to invest such large sums? What was the function of agricultural slavery? In asking the same question about ancient Greece, Finley (1960, p. 70) quotes Xenophon who said that 'those who can do so buy slaves so that they may have fellow workers'. The same applied in rural Hausaland where wage-labour (as elsewhere in rural West Africa) was very rare (and was, as I shall argue, less efficient than slave-labour); where land in most localities was plentiful and could be freely appropriated; where many men, as good Muslims, preferred that their wives should not toil, openly, in the fields; where there was a widespread market for grain and other crops produced on the *gandu* farm (it is misleading to suppose that slave-holding was necessarily based on 'production for export', however that term might have been defined in the Central Sudan, which was itself a huge market for agricultural produce – and A. G. Hopkins is at fault in stating (1973, p. 245) that it was not until this century that it became profitable 'to trade staple crops outside the area of production'); where there were many opportunities for slaves, like free men, to earn money for themselves, thus reducing the burden of their maintenance on their masters; where many masters appreciated their freedom to engage in long-distance trade during the farming-season; and where there was a great demand for porterage.

Whatever allowance may be made for variations in the incidence of slavery in different regions of Hausaland, it seems certain that, as a general rule, high proportions of farmers owned no slaves – that economic inequality among free men was even more pronounced than it is today. As this was so; as slave-owners' sons worked alongside the slaves; and as the owners of small numbers of slaves would have been apt to have worked on the farmland themselves – so the farm-slavery system had not developed to the point where free men (unlike free women) disdained agricultural work, as had happened, for instance, in parts of the Sudan (see McLoughlin, 1962). There are no reliable data on the distribution of farm-slaves among slave-owners, and the numbers owned by very rich farmers are always liable to exaggeration, but field enquiries suggest that many private farmers (at least in certain areas) owned no more than, say, two to four (male and female) slaves, and that few private farmers owned more than about ten to twenty. They also reveal that some slave-owners were women.

This brief summary of the farm-slavery system will surprise readers of M. G. Smith's works owing to its omission of any reference to the type of slave estate which was found in northern Zaria – the *rumada* (sing. *rinji*) which were 'hereditary settlements of slaves with some free men, but mostly the former, built by nobles and others enjoying similar means' (Smith, 1955, pp. 102–3). This omission is deliberate (though it will later be repaired) since it is clear that such estates and villages were typically Fulani, not Hausa, institutions. According to Smith's own description, northern Zaria is a peculiar, peripheral area of Hausaland both because Hausa and settled Fulani were found living in close proximity almost everywhere and because many of the 'local chiefs' who belonged to old-established Fulani lineages enjoyed far more political independence in relation to the Emir than their Hausa counterparts in the central Hausa Emirates. The fact that the farm-slavery system in that area basically related to slaves owned by members of a Fulani ruling class accounts (as will be seen) for the peculiar transition from slavery to freedom that occurred there.

THE TRANSITIONAL PERIOD

The foregoing outline of the system of farm-slavery which existed in the early years of colonial rule is based on fieldwork in Dorayi and elsewhere and on literary sources. (A list of the most notable historical sources is provided in Hill (1976); it is not repeated here as similar lists appear in numerous other publications – but see Appendix XIII(2).) In my account of the transitional period from slavery to freedom I lean very heavily on my findings in Dorayi, for this was a subject on which Lugard (almost the sole writer on the subject) was most misleading, mainly owing to his lack of comprehension of the essential nature of land tenure. Lugard also suffered from some remarkable misapprehensions regarding the identity of the slave-holding class.

In his *Political Memoranda* Lugard made no secret of his solicitude for slave-owners as a class. While he hoped that the institution of slavery would die a natural death within a limited number of years, it was his policy 'not to hasten that event unduly, and to secure to the Mohammedan gentry the continued service of their existing household slaves during the period of transition' (*Memorandum* No. 6, 1906, p. 140). (He was happy to note that 'the lack of initiative inherent in the African temperament will induce a slave even to suffer much ill-treatment before he will take the plunge of leaving his master' – *ibid.*, p. 141). Contrary to the evidence provided by *Memorandum* No. 22, the colonial administration usually tended to assume that most slave-owners were, in some undefined sense, 'upper class' – C. W. J. Orr (1911, p. 203) affirmed that they 'belonged for the most part to the more intelligent and influential class of native'. Lugard was necessarily concerned that his policy should not appear to be *direct rule*, that it should not 'result in pauperising and destroying the ruling classes, which it was the object of Government to preserve and strengthen' (*Memorandum* VI, 1919, in Kirk-Greene, 1970, p. 221). On the other hand, there were times when he seemed to assume that a class of 'free peasants' who owned their land came into existence *for the first time* as slavery declined. In his *Memorandum* X on Lands, 1919 (*ibid.*, p. 346), he stated that he had earlier held the view that –

Nothing would so effectively tend to emancipate the peasant class from the servile attitude of mind which long generations of slavery had induced in them, or better promote a sense of individual responsibility, than to become pro-prietors of their own fields; in other words that the slave, or the communal tenants, should be replaced by the individual occupier.

Fortunately (or so he was informed) this desirable state of affairs had already come about by 1918: the former owners of slave-estates having preferred to become salaried officials of the Native Administration, their land had 'lapsed to the peasant cultivators' (*ibid.*, p. 356). 'Everyone (I am informed) now has a farm. The country is a mass of peasant occupiers, who, however, cannot alienate their holdings.' In another *Memorandum* of 1919 (VI on Slavery) he expressed the view that the newly emancipated peasant population would 'take up land for themselves or engage in trade, and neither remain as slaves, nor seek wages for hire' (*ibid.*, p. 224).

   As part of the policy of supporting the aristocratic slave-holder Lugard had earlier hoped to prevent fugitive slaves from occupying land.

Government thus does not interfere with the legal right of the serf [viz. slave] to assert his freedom, but, before granting him permission to acquire land, it may, if the occasion demands it, insist on his showing good cause for his desertion of his former work, and if he fails to do so, it may decline to grant him the new land, the ultimate title to which is now, for the most part, vested in Government. (*Memorandum* No. 6, 1906, p. 142.)

But in fact, as we know, the administration (which would presumably have acted through 'local chiefs') lacked the power to allocate farmland to anybody – let alone fugitive slaves. For this and other reasons, it is doubt-ful whether the official attitude of solicitude towards slave-holders had much effect in slowing down the inexorable progress towards effective abolition, which resulted from the official policy of running down slave-stocks and from the changed attitudes of the times – a process which was completed in about a generation.

In his *Political Memoranda* of 1919 Lugard had been too ready to accept his advisers' statements that slavery was already dead. But his respect for Muslim law was so great that this did not greatly concern him.

Generally speaking, the intention and policy of Government is not to interfere with the relation of master and slave, in the Northern Provinces, so long as the relation is voluntarily maintained by both parties, in districts which recognise Moslem law and are under the jurisdiction of Moslem courts, but to abolish the status of slavery, absolutely and entirely, throughout every other district of Nigeria (*Memorandum* vi, 1919, Kirk-Greene, 1970, pp. 220–1).

In the central Hausa Emirates manured farmland had been commonly sold for cash in the late nineteenth century (and presumably earlier) and the larger slave-owners had often bought their *gandu* lands. Following the *Report of the Northern Nigeria Lands Committee* (HMSO, Cd 5102, 1910), the Land and Native Rights Ordinance of 1910 was introduced: this declared that all lands in the Northern Provinces were 'Native Lands' held in trust for the people by the Governor, who in exercising his powers should have regard to existent native laws and customs. This Report was based on the fallacious idea that 'the English conception of an estate in land is wholly foreign to Nigerian customs and ideas' (*ibid.*, p. xii) and, as we know, the Ordinance had no practical effect on transactions involving individual farmers. (See Bull, 1963, p. 63, for the opinion that the views of the Committee reflected collectivist theories rather than Northern Nigerian experience.) It is true that local regulations in Kano and Katsina might have prohibited farmers from selling land on migration, and that permission to sell land to strangers had usually to be sought (this was generally readily granted at a local, not a District, level), but transactions in farmland involving local buyers and sellers continued to be freely negotiated. As, in addition, there was free access to uncultivated land, such as existed in most areas, and as classes of absentee landlords were lacking, there were no controls over land which prevented ex-slaves from evolving into free farmers immediately after they had gained their freedom.

But in northern Zaria, where Smith concluded that it was 'usual for descendants of slaves to seek relations of clientage with the owners of their parents' (Smith, 1960, p. 260), so that it was 'difficult to appreciate the extent to which servitude continued...fifty years after proclamations intended to eliminate slavery [?]', the special political conditions were, of course, reflected in land tenure. In northern Zaria, according to Smith, the slaves' descendants paid rent, known as *galla*, to the former slave-owner or his successor, as they did not in Kano (see Rowling, 1952) and such was the political dependence of Hausa people on the local Fulani rulers that free men, also, were apt to pay this rent. Furthermore there were so many independent slave-estates (*rumada*) which fell outside the jurisdiction of the District Head (*hakimi*), though enclosed within his territory, that this led to restrictions on the sale of land (see Cole, 1949) such as did not exist elsewhere.

But as there was vacant land in Zaria which could be freely appropriated by ex-slaves, like anyone else, why did the former slaves not escape rent by removing there? The explanation would seem to be that those ex-slaves who paid *galla* had never been formally ransomed or manumitted, but were the *dimajai* who, as already suggested, were (or felt themselves to be) neither slave nor free (Smith's analysis takes little account of the absolute freedom resulting from legal ransom.) Whereas slaves were usually employed in direct labour for their owner as members of his *gandu*, '*dimajai* were the likeliest dependants to be put out of the *gandu* on allotted land to farm separately for their own subsistence, handing over a fixed amount of farm produce to the owner as *murgu* in lieu of direct service' (Smith, 1955, p. 104). Although, as already noted, the legal sources define *murgu* as a payment made for a fixed term, during which the slave could earn money for his redemption, in northern Zaria the payment apparently amounted to a permanent rent for the use of land, additional to *galla*, although at one point (*ibid.*, p. 104) Smith denotes it as a 'declaration of allegiance'. But the position is by no means clear, especially as, according to Bargery's Hausa dictionary, the various meanings of *galla* include 'payment made by a slave in lieu of work' and 'money received as rent or for hire'. And, according to Mr A. H. M. Kirk-Greene (personal information), *galla* derives from the Fulani word *ngalla* which may be defined as 'the usufruct of a slave' (sing.), or 'revenue accruing from land' (pl.).

There is no evidence for the existence of similar rent-paying villages in Kano or Katsina: in those Emirates the ex-slaves owned by private Hausa farmers became wholly detached from their former masters, neither rendering them any special services nor occupying their land. This would, indeed, be consistent with the Islamic legal concept of 'absolute enfranchisement'.

THE DORAYI FIELDWORK

As is well known, it is usually impossible to discuss matters of slave origin with those of slave-descent and in Dorayi there were special reasons, including the genuine ignorance of younger men, why there would have been no possibility of estimating the proportion of men who were descended from slaves (in the male line) by questioning the population at large. Most of my statistical material on slavery was, in fact, an integral part of the genealogical information which, as already related (see p. 109), was gathered with the help of five dependable Dorayi farmers, who had no more difficulty in dealing wtih the origins of houses of slave-, than of free-descent – the principal informant on slavery having been the late Mahamman Lawal, Hamlet Head of Cikin Gari, Ciranci. This material provides an excellent, reliable, and unique framework for examining the processes which converted an African slave-owning rural economy into a community of free farmers, especially as it may be related to our statistics of the present-day distribution of farmland between owners and to our assessments of wealth and age. Fortunately for our purposes, farm-slavery in Dorayi persisted strongly until the early or mid-1920s and for houses of slave-origin informants were usually able to provide the names of the slaves (and of their slave-owners) from whom residents were descended.

THE SLAVE-OWNERS

The slave-owners of Dorayi were both local farmers and rich city men (together with one woman) who had acquired farmland there – the latter including the Emir of Kano and the Kano Chief Blacksmith (Sarkin Makera). Of the thirty-four slave-owners who were identified, twenty-four were probably local people, of whom three were women. As all the non-resident private slave-owners (or their inheritors) disposed of their land when slavery ended, our list may omit a few of the names of owners whose ex-slaves and their descendants all left Dorayi.

It is clear from these figures that most local farmers owned no slaves – and informants constantly emphasised that slave-owners were relatively rich people. Probably most of the local owners possessed no more than about four (male and female) farm-slaves, who were often related to each other; such owners were ordinary farmers, not prominent traders or office-holders, of whom there were hardly any in Dorayi. Two of the women owners had inherited their slaves; the third was an interesting case of a woman who had been a slave herself when she arrived in Dorayi, having then freed herself and acquired two slaves.

There were at least three local men who owned some fifteen or more slaves. First, there was Madaki (or Kaura), who had been Dagaci of Ja'en in the early years of the century, whose father and two brothers had also been wealthy slave-owners. He owned an enormous house in which he lived together with some twenty men and women slaves and their dependants; he also had a house in Kano city, in which he occasionally resided, which provided a useful refuge for members of his Dorayi house in the event of war. As the women slaves were all married or related to men slaves (one of the men had three slave wives), the group as a whole was very stable and it was reassuring that two of the informants should have independently provided remarkably similar lists of the slaves' names. One of Madaki's wives had been a slave; she married a slave following Madaki's death and her descendants by both marriages are still living in Madaki's old house, which is nowadays the home of five married men who are Madaki's descendants together with eight men descended from Madaki's slaves. Madaki (who probably died over fifty years ago) was far wealthier than anyone living in Dorayi today: his position was altogether superior to those of the present *dagatai* and to that of his sole surviving son and his descendants.

The most prominent local slave-owner was the notorious Alhaji Halilu, a Koranic scholar who had no other non-farming occupation. Although he died some sixty years ago, his name is constantly on people's lips. He reportedly owned 'about thirty slaves', who lived in a special house, as well as a large herd of cattle. It is remembered that he sold huge quantities of cornstalk (*kara*) in Kano city; that he bought slaves there with the proceeds; that he had been an unusually cruel master who chained his slaves if they refused to fetch manure from the city; and that he bought many farms 'from those without food'. When he died many of his slaves departed, others having been inherited by his sons.

The nineteen local slave-owners for whom figures are available owned well over a hundred slaves, of whom only one survives to this day. Most of the freed male slaves probably remained in Dorayi until they died; most of their sons and grandsons must have migrated, for only about thirty-four of them (all figures relate to married men only) are resident in Dorayi today – the corresponding figure for the local slave-owners' descendants being about a hundred.

Turning to the slave-owners from the city, much the largest estate was owned by the Emir of Kano. Sarki Aliyu (1895–1903) built a large house there, and in 1972 a son of his slave foreman (*sarkin gandu*) was still living on the land, having been born about 1885. (The *Kano Chronicle* (Palmer, 1908, p. 75) reports the building of an official house at 'Dorai' in the fifteenth century.) He said that in the early days there had been 'about fifty' men and women slaves working on the land; that many of them were strangers who spoke poor Hausa, having presumably been captured in recent raids – they were referred to as *baibayi* (lit. 'pagans') and 'they spoke by gesture as if they were deaf'; that they lived in separate houses which they had built for themselves; that each slave was given a farm plot (*gayauna*) for his own use – a plot which could be inherited by a son or lent (*aro*) to someone else, but which could not be sold; that some slaves became rich enough to ransom themselves; that the slaves were paid for any work (such as thatching) which they did for the Emir in the dry season; that some free men worked alongside the slaves; and that there were some slaves still working there on the accession of Sarki Abdullahi Bayero in 1926. Although a large portion of the original estate is still in the Emir's possession, only about six of the slaves' descendants are still living in Dorayi; much of the farmland that is not required by these men (who pay no rent) is 'lent' (*aro*) to many other Dorayi farmers, the remainder being farmed by prisoners or daily labourers.

As for the slave-estate owned by the Chief Blacksmith, this is a somewhat different case; although it is (and was) much smaller than the Emir's land, as many as twenty slave-descendants (married men) now reside in one large Dorayi house, all of them being the sons or grandsons of one slave. One of these men is responsible for recruiting and supervising the daily labourers who are employed by the present Chief Blacksmith for cultivating part of the land; the rest of the land provides inalienable plots (*gayauni*) for household members.

These two former slave-estates are unique in Dorayi, both because all the other non-resident slave-owners have long since disposed of their land and because they pertained to the continuing *offices* of Emir and Chief Blacksmith and were not personal property. For reasons which have been discussed elsewhere (see p. 9), such estates were relatively very rare within the context of Kano Emirate generally.

As for the nine non-office-holding outsiders who are known to have owned slave-estates in Dorayi, our farm-maps show that all of them ultimately sold, or gave away, all their Dorayi land. Very few, if any, of the present generation of absentee farmers (lists of whom were compiled in connection with the farm-mapping) is the descendant of such a slave-owner and there is only one Dorayi house that is inhabited by a slave-owner's son – he had settled in Dorayi as a local imam.

The ex-slave-owners disposed of their land over several decades. One of the very few Assessment Reports to have mentioned slavery – and then only in retrospect in 1932 – notes that farms on the main route from Kano to Zaria, which ran down the western boundary of Dorayi, had been prized by 'wealthy merchants' who owned farm-slaves:

The abolition of slavery threw these estates. . .out of cultivation. The original owners are dead. . .Yet the estates still remain, owned by aged widows and small traders who exist in the ruined mansions of their husbands and fathers which line the road to Goron Dutse [the westerly of the two Kano hills]. (Report on Kumbotso District by S. A. S. Leslie, NAK, Kano Prof 5/24, No. 764.)

Insofar as these estates were situated in Dorayi, none of them still exists.

So it is that the private absentee slave-owners (with a single exception) have all vanished without trace, merely leaving a few slave-descendants behind them. As many as twenty-six of these descendants (married men) are descended from three (out of four) male slaves who had been owned by a woman salt trader, Mai Beza, who gave, or sold, some of her land (known as Gandun Mai Beza) to them, selling the rest to others. (*Beza* is a kind of salt from Azben and the north.) The most notorious absentee owner was Babali dan Mai Kanwa, a Kano man who reportedly owned 'about 70 farm-slaves and 100 cattle', only some of which were in Dorayi. Originally a butcher, he turned to buying cattle and slaves in Adamawa, ultimately receiving a prison-sentence for slave-dealing – whereat many of his farm-slaves departed. His friend Mazadu in Dorayi had given him a big farm there, and he also reclaimed some swampy land at a stream. His sons gradually sold his farmland over a long period, though a small portion was given to the sole slave-descendant resident in Dorayi – who soon sold it. (Many of the other slave-descendants are butchers in Kano.)

THE SLAVE-DESCENDANTS TODAY

In present-day Dorayi 183 married men (or 26% of the total) were re-corded as being of slave-descent in the male line. These men are descended from fewer than fifty slaves: thus, if fifteen of these men for whom in-sufficient information is available are omitted, 168 men were descended from about forty slaves only, as many as fifty-four of them from three slaves only. It is clear from this and other evidence that most slave-descen-dants migrated from this over-populated locality.

The need to analyse large populations when studying the incidence of slave-descent is illustrated by the fact that this incidence is very much higher in two of the five Dorayi sub-divisions, namely in Dorayi Karama and Ja'en Yamma where the proportion of slave-descendants is over one-third (40% and 35% respectively), than in the other three sub-divisions (only 4%). While this discrepancy may be related to the lower incidences of farm-slavery in the latter three areas, the basic explanation was probably the lower population density in the zone closest to Kano city (see p. 193 above), where more land could be appropriated by ex-slaves.

The 183 slave descendants live in about forty houses. Only one of these houses is inhabited by the descendants of both slaves and their owners for, as a general rule, such slaves as happened to live with their masters built new houses for themselves on attaining their freedom, and there is no known case of 'slave-assimilation' – by which is meant the incorporation into the slave-owner's family of any person of slave-descent. (This matter is, of course, entirely distinct from concubinage, the incidence of which cannot be judged.) Nor, as will be seen, did slaves become regular servants (*barori*) of their masters.

Accordingly, men of slave and free origin are alike in inhabiting houses which vary greatly in size. It happens that about two-fifths of each group live in 'big houses' (see Chapter XII). Most big houses are, therefore, inhabited by men of free-descent and no house is big because it is inhabited by descendants of numerous co-slaves. As there is only one Dorayi house which is occupied by the descendants of as many as three co-slaves, and as about three-quarters of all the houses of slave-descent are inhabited by the sons and/or grandsons of a single slave, so there is no concept of 'slave-descendants' village' in Dorayi. Those of slave-descent live in houses dotted about the countryside, like those of free-descent.

It is impossible to form any idea of whether the slave-descendants tended to depart as soon as they had reached adulthood or whether their migration extended over a long period. Certainly many slave-descendants, like many men of free-origin, removed to nearby Kano city (see Chapter IX), though whether they were apt to remove there with their fathers or to delay their departure until their fathers' death is not known. Although there is no recorded case of a man of slave-descent having migrated in the capacity of a farmer in the past few decades, this conceivably happened in earlier times. But it is very interesting to note that once the slave-descendants had settled down as free farmers their propensity to migrate was no higher than that of other farmers: this conclusion derives both from the house-genealogies and from the fact that the age-structures of the populations of free- and slave-descent are quite similar. The stability during the past few decades of some of the houses of slave-descent is remarkable: thus, only 3 of the 10 married sons of two slaves of the woman slave-owner Mai Beza were recorded as having migrated and all the 20 married grandsons of the 7 sons are resident in Dorayi. In another case 3 out of 8 of a slave's sons were known to have migrated after their father's death, but all the 17 sons and 3 grandsons of the other men remained resident in Dorayi – see also House 1, Appendix XII(1).

A high proportion of the ex-slaves or their sons must either have succeeded in acquiring land for themselves or have retained their private plots (*gayauni*), for over a half of all the farmland owned by men of slave-descent was recorded as having been inherited from their fathers – a proportion which was little lower than for the population as a whole. However, there were many men of slave (as of free) descent who had inherited no land. The incidence of landlessness among fatherless married men is 17% for those of slave origin compared with 11% for those of free origin – see Appendix XI(4).

As for the average acreages owned by individual farmers, here again it was found that descent was not a matter of great significance: thus the average holdings of all married men (for whom reliable figures were available) in the two sub-divisions where most slaves' descendants live is 1.9 acres, against 1.7 for those of slave-descent. The proportion of those who owned five acres or more is roughly equal (about 10%) for the two populations, but the proportion who owned two acres or more is somewhat higher for those of free-descent.

However, there are significantly higher proportions of impoverished men and lower proportions of wealthy men (*masu arziki*) in the population of slave-descent compared with that of free-descent. For the age-group of fifty-five and upwards, the proportions of *masu arziki* are 15% (slave-descent) and 22% (free-descent). That such discrepancies are mainly a function of the extreme land shortage in Dorayi is suggested by corresponding (though less reliable) data for Batagarawa (see *R. H.*, pp. 178–180) which suggested that there was no significant relationship between standard of living and descent.

The price of Dorayi farmland has recently risen so steeply that, as we know, only the most prosperous men can nowadays afford to buy it. But, as we have seen (see cases B (1) and B (2) on p. 161 above) there is no mystery attending the process by which landless men of slave-origin evolved into relatively prosperous members of society in former times, when farm-prices were far lower. Of course there are some sets of brothers of slave-descent who have never emerged from the stranglehold of their father's poverty – just as there are some of free-descent who are in like plight. An example is provided by the five surviving sons and one grandson of an ex-slave who died recently: the sons had inherited only three acres from their father and four of them are now severely impoverished. Given the high price of land, the chance that they will ever emerge from their poverty is now remote.

FARM-LABOURING

As the numbers of slaves declined, so the system of farm-labouring developed, making it possible, for the first time, for richer farmers to expand their labour-forces by means of paid labour. As labourers were employed on a daily basis, as work was spasmodic, and as small work-teams rather than single labourers were preferred, so it was that employers were apt to engage numerous different labourers at different times during the farming season, most labourers working with many different farmers (see *R. H.*, Chapter VIII). There had never been any question of freed slaves, or their dependants, being obliged to render labour-services to their former masters.

In Hausaland, as in West Africa generally (south of the Sahel zone), it is a rule that no *class* of landless, full-time, local labourers ever emerges in rural areas: local labourers are always poorer farmers, or their sons, who supplement their incomes by working, at times, on the farms of others. (The principle is the same in anomalously over-crowded Dorayi where farm-labouring never provides a landless man with an income remotely sufficient to maintain him throughout the year.) Just as slave-owning would not have been generally profitable had the slaves not been to a large extent responsible for maintaining themselves by working on their personal farms and in non-farming occupations, so the labour-employing farmers of Dorayi would not have been able to offer their labourers sufficient work to maintain themselves throughout the farming-season, let alone the long dry-season: those men who derive some income from farm-labouring resemble the slaves in being obliged to supplement this income by farming and/or non-farming work on their own account. While the farm-labouring system must be seen as benefiting both parties, from the angle of the richer farmers it is a less efficient substitute for farm-slavery, especially as the labourers' work always has to be supervised by the farmer, or his son, there being no trusted slave foremen. It is no wonder that several of the local slave-owners, such as Madaki, were far richer than any farmer today.

CLIENTAGE AND STATUS

Nor did ex-slaves work as servants or clients (*barori*, sing, *bara*) with their ex-masters. On the basis of M. G. Smith's findings, it is commonly believed that there are many such *barori* in rural Hausaland, whereas the fact of the matter seems to be that, at least in the central Hausa Emirates, clientage is surprisingly rare and non-institutionalised. According to present-day evidence, few men outside the diminutive ruling-class have full-time *barori* attached to them; most *barori* are mainly occupied as independent farmers; and *barori* are no more apt to be of slave-descent than anyone else – in fact, as in Dorayi (where none is known to be of slave-descent), they are often indigent strangers on whom others have taken pity (see also *R. H.*, p. 207).

But even if those of slave-descent are, in no sense, servile members of society, it might still be that they tend to be of lower status than those of free-descent? Considering that more than half of the Dorayi population was born more than twenty-five years after slavery had ended; that most younger people are entirely uninterested in whether they themselves, or anyone else, is of slave-origin; that those of slave-descent pursue similar non-farming occupations to those of free-descent (with the interesting exception that fewer of them are Koranic teachers or scholars) – considering such points, it would be very odd indeed if there were any significant link between slave-descent and status. In fact all the evidence is that in a society where there are no members of the ruling-class (*masu sarauta*), individual status is mainly a function of age, wealth and religious learning – descent (as such) being an unimportant factor. Mahamman Lawal (the Hamlet Head) was emphatic that whereas he used to look down on the slaves (*cucanawa*), who sat segregatedly in the presence of free men, nowadays 'all are the same'. It is relevant to note that in present-day Bata-garawa (see *R. H.*, pp. 179–80) the question of slave-origin appears to have no significant influence on the choice of marriage partner.

But, of course, there was a long transitional period before the slave-descendants 'became equal', as is illustrated by the case of Dagaci Duma, an ex-slave who became Village Head of Ja'en in 1912, who was reported to have been so rich and powerful that he overcame the (then) disability of his slave-descent. It happens that his case also illustrates the tendency for wealth to become dissipated over the generations. Although Dagaci Duma later became one of the largest farmers in Dorayi ('employing fifty labourers and owning many cattle'), the way of the world is such that his large house is now in process of dissolution, the sole surviving resident having erected a wall to shield himself from the ruins.

CONCLUSION

But, it may be argued, how can findings regarding the process of transition to a free society in so peculiar an area as Dorayi be thought to have any general validity? The reply to this question is twofold: first, that given the conditions of Hausa farm-slavery and of land tenure outlined in the first part of this chapter, such findings do little more than confirm common-sense; second, that the greater the scarcity of farmland the higher the likeli-hood (other things equal) that farm-slavery *would* leave a permanent mark on social organisation, which means that, in these terms, Dorayi is a peculiarly appropriate case. In terms of the organisation of farm-slavery and associated questions of land tenure, northern Zaria has to be con-sidered a Fulani, not a Hausa, case. Within the vast area of rural Hausa-land, especially in other peripheral regions with mixed populations, there are doubtless other important special cases which future fieldwork will reveal; and it may be that further work will show that socio-economic organisation and land tenure systems are not as uniform in central Hausa-land as research has suggested up to date. Meanwhile it seems reasonable to work on the assumption that slavery is stone dead. Such was the peculiar nature of slavery and such the social structure within which slavery functioned, that entirely free rural communities, uncontaminated by remnants of servitude, have evolved in the central Hausa Emirates.

APPENDIX XIII (I)
Lugard's Memorandum *No. 22 of 1906*
(*'The condition of slaves and the native
law regarding slavery in Northern Nigeria'*)

As copies of Lugard's *Political Memoranda* of 1906 are so scarce (see p. 201 above), a few brief notes on *Memorandum* No. 22, additional to those incorporated in Chapter XIII, are given here. Although Lugard regarded the memorandum as relating primarily to 'such rulings by Alkalis of acknowledged authority, as have reached me from Residents of different Provinces in reply to circular questions' (*ibid.*, p. 295), he also included many observations made by Residents themselves. He emphasised not only that conditions varied greatly in different Provinces, but that there were many divergences in the evidence.

Values of slaves

Reporting from Bornu, Hans Fischer stated (*ibid.*, p. 297) that slaves were divided into classes according to length of body, physical ability and sex, the most valuable being eunuchs. Male slaves were measured from the ankle-bone to the shoulder: those measuring from four to six spans were boys; those of seven spans were young men (*samari*); the last two classes being bearded adults and old men. Boys of six spans commanded the highest price; then young men 'but these were not regarded as so safe an investment as boys, as being more liable to run away'. As for females, the most valuable were young women who commanded a higher price than the corresponding young men (*samari*); in general females were priced more highly than male slaves.

Hours and conditions of work

Reporting from Sokoto, Major Burdon wrote (*ibid.*, p. 298) –

The hours of work for a farm slave are supposed to be from daylight till midday, but this depends very largely on the character of the master. A hard man will keep his slaves at work till the afternoon or evening, and will, moreover, neglect to provide them with food whilst working for him. But the slave's remedy and the master's punishment lay in the ease with which an adult slave could desert...The master is supposed to provide food, and good food, for his slaves whilst they are at work on his farm. Sensible men provide such good food that the slaves regard it as a feast, and work with a will. A diet of nothing better than beans is answerable for many a desertion.

Kano Province

From Kano Province it was reported (*ibid.*, p. 300) that farm slaves might buy and hold farms of their own – and that the whole produce of the land was their own, 'provided they pay the tax' (which tax? – see p. 201 above). Trusted slaves were allowed to engage in trade; there was no difficulty in self-redemption; and it was not uncommon for a master to will property to a slave. 'No serf [slave], *or child of a serf* [my italics], ever enjoys immunity from sale, however long in the service of his master' – the only exception being the slave concubine who had borne her master a child.

Bauchi Province

From Bauchi Province it was reported (*ibid.*, p. 302) –

Slaves are kept in every village and town, and their condition differs little from that of their own proprietors...[A farm slave] is allowed to purchase as many wives as his means allow, and is as a rule as well housed as his master...Many farm slaves become rich and own many slaves of their own.

Zaria Province

It is significant that Capt Orr reported from Zaria Province (*ibid.*, p. 308),

that it was especially common for Fulani owners to free their slaves, and in certain parts of the Zaria Province there are whole towns peopled entirely by ex-slaves freed by the Fulani.

APPENDIX XIII (2)
Clapperton's observations on farm-slavery

When in Sokoto in 1826, the explorer Hugh Clapperton made detailed observations on 'domestic slavery'; the following extracts (Clapperton, 1829, pp. 214–15, 216) are included here both because he, as the earliest systematic observer, seems to have been the most reliable of all, and also because the belief that second-generation slaves were never sold may originally have stemmed from him.

The domestic slaves are generally well treated. The males who have arrived at the age of eighteen or nineteen are given a wife, and sent to live at their villages and farms in the country, where they build a hut, and until the harvest are fed by their owners. When the time for cultivating the ground and sowing the seed comes on, the owner points out what he requires, and what is to be sown on it. The slave is then allowed to enclose a part for himself and his family. The hours of labour, for his master, are from daylight till mid-day; the remainder of the day is employed on his own, or in any other way he may think proper. At the time of harvest, when they cut and tie up the grain, each slave gets a bundle of the different sorts of grain, about a bushel of our measure, for himself. The grain on his own ground is entirely left for his own use, and he may dispose of it as he thinks proper. At the vacant seasons of the year he must attend to the calls of his master, whether to accompany him on a journey, or go to war, if so ordered...

The children of slaves, whether dwelling in the house or on the farm, are never sold, unless their behaviour is such that, after repeated punishment, they continue unmanageable, so that the master is compelled to part with them...The children of the slaves are sometimes educated with those of the owner, but this is not generally the case.

References

Note: A very much fuller bibliography relating to rural Hausaland is in R. H. and a list of publications relating to farm-slavery is in Hill (1976). Unpublished, including archival, material (other than theses) is not included here, nor are such official publications as *Colonial Annual Reports*, full references to which are provided in the text.

Abraham, R. C. 1946. *Dictionary of the Hausa Language*. University of London Press.

Ajayi, J. F. A. and Crowder, M. (eds.). 1971 and 1974. *History of West Africa*, I and II. Longman, London.

Anjorin, A. A. 1965. 'The British Occupation and the Development of Northern Nigeria, 1897–1914'. Unpublished Ph.D. thesis, London University.

Baden-Powell, B. H. 1899. *The Origin and Growth of Village Communities in India*. London.

Bargery, G. P. 1934. *A Hausa–English Dictionary and English–Hausa Vocabulary*. Oxford University Press, London.

Barth, H. 1857. *Travels and Discoveries in North and Central Africa, 1849–1855*. Vols. I to v, London; American edition reprinted in 1965 in 3 volumes, Cass, London.

Bell, Sir Hesketh. 1911. 'Recent Progress in Northern Nigeria'. *Journal of the African Society*, x, July.

Bohannan, P. and Dalton, G. (eds.). 1962. *Markets in Africa*. Northwestern University Press.

Bovill, E. W. (ed.). 1966. *Missions to the Niger*, IV, *The Bornu Mission, 1822–1825*, Part 3 (Captain Clapperton's Narrative). Hakluyt Society, Cambridge University Press.

Bull, Mary. 1963. 'Indirect Rule in Northern Nigeria 1906–11', in Robinson *et al.* (eds.) (1963).

Caldwell, J. C. and Igun, A. A. 1971. 'An experiment with census-type age enumeration in Nigeria'. *Population Studies*, July.

Caldwell, J. C. and Okonjo, C. (eds.). 1968. *The Population of Tropical Africa*. Longman, London.

223

Clapperton, H. 1829. *Journal of a Second Expedition into the Interior of Africa from the Bight of Benin to Soccatoo*. Reprinted Cass, London, 1966.

1966. *See* Bovill (ed.).

Cohen, A. 1969. *Custom and Politics in Urban Africa*. Routledge, London.

Cole, C. W. 1949. *Report on Land Tenure, Zaria Province*. Government Printer, Kaduna.

Dalby, D. 1964. 'The noun garii in Hausa: a semantic study'. *Journal of African Languages*, III, 3.

1975. 'The concept of settlement in the West African savannah', in Oliver (ed.) (1975).

Fika, A. M. 1973. 'The political and economic reorientation of Kano Emirate, Northern Nigeria, 1882–1940'. Unpublished Ph.D. thesis, London University.

Finley, M. I. 1968. 'Slavery' in *International Encylopaedia of the Social Sciences*.

Finley, M. I. (ed.). 1960. *Slavery in Classical Antiquity*. Cambridge University Press.

Fisher, A. G. B. and Fisher, H. J. 1970. *Slavery and Muslim Society in Africa: The Institution in Saharan and Sudanic Africa and the Trans-Saharan Trade*. Hurst, London.

Food and Agricultural Organisation (FAO). 1966. *Agricultural Development in Nigeria, 1965–1980*. Rome.

Forde, D. 1946. 'The North: the Hausa', in Perham (ed.) (1946).

1964. *Yakö Studies*. Oxford University Press, London.

Forde, D. 1947. 'The Anthropological Approach in Social Science'. *The Advancement of Science*, IV, Sept.

Forde, D. and Kaberry, Phyllis M. (eds.). 1967. *West African Kingdoms in the Nineteenth Century*. Oxford University Press, London.

Fortes, M. 1970. *Time and Social Structure and Other Essays*. The Athlone Press, London.

Fortes, M. (ed.). 1949. *Social Structure: Studies presented to A. R. Radcliffe-Brown*. The Clarendon Press, Oxford.

Fortes, M. and Evans-Pritchard, E. E. (eds.). 1940. *African Political Systems*. Oxford University Press, London.

Freedman, M. 1966. *Chinese Lineage and Society: Fukien and Kwantung*. The Athlone Press, London.

Girouard, P. 1908. 'The development of Northern Nigeria'. *Journal of the African Society*, VII, July.

Goody, Esther N. 1973. *Contexts of Kinship: An Essay in the Family Sociology of the Gonja of Northern Ghana*. Cambridge University Press.

Goody, J. R. 1971. *Technology, Tradition and the State in Africa*. Oxford University Press, London.

Greenberg, J. H. 1946. *The Influence of Islam on a Sudanese Religion*. Monographs of the American Ethnological Society, New York.

Gutkind, P. C. W. 1975. 'The view from below: political consciousness of the urban poor in Ibadan'. *Cahiers d'Études Africaines*, xv, 1.

Hill, Polly. 1969. 'Hidden trade in Hausaland'. *Man*, September.

1970. *The Occupations of Migrants in Ghana*. Museum of Anthropology, University of Michigan.

1971. 'Two types of West African house trade', in Meillassoux (1971).

1972. *Rural Hausa: A Village and a Setting*. Cambridge University Press.

1974. 'Big houses in Kano Emirate'. *Africa*, xliv, 2.

1975. 'The relationship between the city and countryside in Kano Emirate in 1900'. *West African Journal of Sociology and Political Science*, i, 1.

1976. 'From slavery to freedom: the case of farm slavery in Nigerian Hausaland'. *Comparative Studies in Society and History*, 18, 3.

Hodgkin, T. L. 1960. *Nigerian Perspectives: An Historical Anthology*. Oxford University Press, London. Second revised edition, 1975.

Hopkins, A. G. 1973. *An Economic History of West Africa*. Longman, London.

Horton, R. 1971. 'Stateless societies in the history of West Africa', in Ajayi *et al.*, 1.

Hyam, R. 1968. *Elgin and Churchill at the Colonial Office 1905–1908: the Watershed of the Empire-Commonwealth*. Macmillan, London.

Johnson, Marion. 1970. 'The cowrie currencies of West Africa', Parts i and ii. *Journal of African History*, xi, 1 and 3.

1976. 'Calico caravans: the Tripoli-Kano trade after 1880'. *Journal of African History*, i. 1976.

Kirk-Greene, A. H. M. (ed.). 1968. *Lugard and the Amalgamation of Nigeria: A Documentary Record*, being a reprint of the Report by Sir F. D. Lugard on the Amalgamation of Northern and Southern Nigeria and Administration, 1912–1919. Cass, London.

1970. *Political Memoranda by Lord Lugard*. Third edition, with a new introduction by the editor. Cass, London.

1972. *Gazetteers of the Northern Provinces of Nigeria*, i, *The Hausa Emirates (Bauchi, Sokoto, Zaria, Kano)*. Cass, London.

Kuczynski, R. R. 1948. *Demographic Survey of the British Colonial Empire*, i, *West Africa*. Oxford University Press, London.

Last, M. 1967. *The Sokoto Caliphate*. Longman, London.

Lloyd, P. C. 1974. *Power and Independence: Urban Africans' Perception of Social Inequality*. Routledge and Kegan Paul, London.

Lovejoy, P. E. 1973. 'The Hausa kola trade (1700–1900): a commercial system in the continental exchange of West Africa'. Unpublished Ph.D. thesis, University of Wisconsin.

Low, V. N. 1972. *Three Nigerian Emirates: A Study in Oral History*. Northwestern University Press.

Lugard, F. D. (Lord). 1906. *Political Memoranda*. Waterlow, London.

1907. *Memorandum on the Taxation of Natives in Northern Nigeria*, Colonial Reports – Miscellaneous No. 40, HMSO, Cmd 3309.

1919. *Political Memoranda*. Second version for confidential circulation to colonial officers. *See* Kirk-Greene (ed.) (1970).

1922. *The Dual Mandate in British Tropical Africa*. Allen and Unwin, London. Fifth edition, Cass, London, 1965.

McLoughlin, P. F. M. 1962. 'Economic development and the heritage of slavery in the Sudan Republic'. *Africa*, XXXII, 4.

McPhee, A 1926. *The Economic Revolution in British West Africa*. London. Second edition, Cass, London, 1971.

Meek, C. K. 1925. *The Northern Tribes of Nigeria*, II, containing the report on the 1921 census. Oxford University Press, London.

Meillassoux, C. (ed.). 1971. *The Development of African Trade and Markets in West Africa*. Oxford University Press, London.

Morel, E. D. 1911. *Nigeria: Its Peoples and its Problems*. London. Reprinted Cass, London, 1968.

Mortimore, M. J. 1967. 'Land and population pressure in the Kano Close-Settled Zone, Northern Nigeria'. *The Advancement of Science*, April.

1968. 'Population distribution, settlement and soils in Kano Province, Northern Nigeria, 1931–62', in Caldwell, *et al.* (eds.) (1968).

1970. 'Settlement evolution and land use', in Mortimore (ed.) (1970).

1972. 'Some aspects of rural-urban relations in Kano, Nigeria', *La Croissance Urbaine en Afrique Noire et à Madagascar*, No. 539, Colloques Internationaux du C.N.R.S.

Mortimore, M. J. (ed.). 1970. *Zaria and its Region: A Nigerian Savanna City and its Environs*. Department of Geography, Ahmadu Bello University, Zaria.

Mortimore, M. J. and Wilson, J. 1965. *Land and People in the Kano Close-Settled Zone*. Department of Geography, Ahmadu Bello University, Zaria.

Myrdal, G. 1968. *Asian Drama: An Inquiry into the Poverty of Nations*, I–III, Penguin Books, London.

Nicolas, G. and Mainet, G. 1964. *La vallée du Gulbi de Maradi: Enquête socio-économique*. Documents des Études Nigériennes no. 16, IFAN–CNRS (cyclostyled).

Norman, D. W. 1973. 'Crop mixtures under indigenous conditions in the northern part of Nigeria', in Ofori (1973).

Northern Nigeria Lands Committee. 1910. *Report*. HMSO, Cd 5102.

Minutes of Evidence and Appendices. HMSO, Cd. 5103.

Ofori, E. D. (ed.). 1973. *Factors of Agricultural Growth in West Africa*. Institute of Statistical, Social and Economic Research, University of Ghana, Legon.

Oliver, P. (ed.). 1975. *Shelter, Sign and Symbol*. Barrie and Jenkins, London.

Olofson, H. 1976. '*Yawon Dandi:* a Hausa category of migration'. *Africa,* 46, 1.

Omosini, O. 1968. 'Origins of British methods of tropical development in the West African Dependencies, 1880–1906'. Unpublished Ph.D. thesis, University of Cambridge.

Orr, C. W. J. (Sir Charles). 1911. *The Making of Northern Nigeria.* London. Reprinted, Cass, London, 1965.

Paden, J. N. 1973. *Religion and Political Culture in Kano.* University of California Press.

Palmer, H. R. 1908. 'The Kano Chronicle'. Translated with an introduction by H. R. Palmer, *Journal of the Royal Anthropological Institute,* XXXVIII.

Perham, Margery. 1960. *Lugard: The Years of Authority, 1898–1945* (being the second part of a life of Lord Lugard). Collins, London.

Perham, Margery (ed.). 1946. *The Native Economies of Nigeria,* 1, Faber, London.

Postan, M. M. 1972. *The Medieval Economy and Society: An Economic History of Britain in the Middle Ages.* Weidenfeld and Nicolson, London.

Pullan, R. A. 1974. 'Farmed parkland in West Africa'. *Savanna* (Ahmadu Bello University, Zaria), III, 2.

Robinson, K. and Madden, F. (eds.). 1963. *Essays in Imperial Government.* Blackwell, Oxford.

Rowling, C. W. 1952. *Report on Land Tenure, Kano Province.* Government Printer, Kaduna.

Ruxton, F. H., 1916. *Maliki Law.* London.

Sanneh, L. O. 1976. 'Slavery, Islam and the Jakhanke people of West Africa'. *Africa,* 46, 1.

Shea, P. J. 1975. 'The development of an export oriented dyed cloth industry in the nineteenth century'. Unpublished Ph.D. thesis, University of Wisconsin.

Skinner, G. W. 1964. 'Marketing and social structure in rural China', Part 1. *The Journal of Asian Studies,* November.

Smith, H. F. C. (Abdullahi). 197. 'Some considerations relating to the formation of states in Hausaland'. *Journal of the Historical Society of Nigeria,* v, 3.

1971. 'The early states of the Central Sudan', in Ajayi, *et al.*

Smith, J. 1968. *Colonial Cadet in Nigeria.* Duke University Press.

Smith, Mary. 1954. *Baba of Karo: A Woman of the Muslim Hausa.* Faber, London.

Smith, M. G. 1955. *The Economy of Hausa Communities of Zaria.* Colonial Research Series No. 16, HMSO, London.

1960. *Government in Zazzau, 1800–1950.* Oxford University Press, London.

1962. 'Exchange and marketing among the Hausa', in Bohannan (ed.) (1962).

Stenning, D. J. 1959. *Savannah Nomads: A Study of the Wodaabe Pastoral Fulani of Western Bornu Province*. Oxford University Press, London.

Temple, C. L. 1918. *Native Races and their Rulers*. Reprinted, Cass, London, 1968.

Usman, Y. B. 1974. 'The transformation of Katsina: c.1796–1903. The overthrow of the sarauta system and the establishment and evolution of the Emirate.' Unpublished Ph.D. thesis, Ahmadu Bello University, Zaria.

Index

Adamu, Mahdi, 12
adashi, contribution club, 173
administration, village, *see* Village
   administration
aerial photographs, 108, 136
age, of married men: age-groups, 110–
   11; wealth, poverty and, 99–100,
   113–15, 157–8, 164–6
Agriculture Department, N. Nigerian,
   29, 30
alhaji, in Dorayi, 149, 160–3
alkali, Muslim judges, 10, 204
   see also courts, Muslim
alms, Muslim, 171
amana, defined, 132
Antrobus, R. L., 23, 24, 29, 202
Arnett, E. J., 47, 53
aro, borrowing of farmland, 98, 131–2,
   172–3, 179
arziki, prosperity and good fortune,
   109, 112, 155–6
   see also poor men, rich men, wealth
Ashanti, household heads in, 182–3, 184
Assessment Reports, 2, 26, 201, 215

Baden-Powell, B. H., 62
bara (pl. *barori*), servants and clients,
   219
Barth, H., 50, 58–9, 60
   on: cotton cloth production, 13;
   Kano population, 3
Batagarawa, xi, xii, 96–104 *passim*, 104–
   5
   age and wealth in, 157
   and *arziki*, 156
   economic inequality in, 106–21
     passim

extreme poverty in, 164–5
farm-holdings, size of, in, 121–2
farm-plots, size of, in, 130
slave-descendants in, 218, 220
Bauchi Province, farm-slavery in, 222
Bebeji, 5, 60
Bell, Sir Hesketh, 27, 28, 30, 31, 62
Benin, pre-colonial kingdom, 17
bicycles, 86
Bida, 32
biki relationships, 173
birane, see birni
birni (pl. *birane*), city, 3, 5, 65
borrowing, of farmland (*aro*), 98, 131–2
boundaries
   farm, henna bushes as, 92
   of Villages and Hamlets in Dorayi,
     76, 77, 78
Bradbury, R. E., 17
British Cotton Growing Association, 31
brothers
   co-residence of, 101, 180
   and inheritance of farmland, 126–7
   migration of, 149
builders, 82, 171
Bull, Mary, 211
Burdon, J. A. (Sir John), 221
bush-farms, 124, 165
butchers, 103, 171

Caldwell, J. C., 19
Caliph, at Sokoto, 40
capital, slaves as agrarian, 208
caravan
   tax, 32–3
   trade, 7
   see also fatauci, long-distance trade

Cargill, F., 26, 36–8, 43, 44, 45–6
cassava, 81
cattle
  in Dorayi, 77, 82
  in KCSZ, 70
  in Kirimbo, 94
  tax (*jangali*), 52
census, *see* population
Chamberlain, Sir Joseph, 24, 200
Chief Blacksmith, Kano, 213, 215
chiefs
  Fulani Emirs as 'native', 22
  Kano *dagatai* as, 48
  in Katagum, 9
  in Katsina, hierarchy of, 1–2
  in N. Nigeria and India, 23
  N. Nigerian and taxation, 35
  in pre-colonial Benin, 17
  town heads (*masu gari*), 5
  in Zaria, 209
  see also dagaci, hakimi, mai gari,
    sarki, stateless societies, Village
    administration
China
  sons' position in, 138–9
  rural periodic markets in, 10
Chiromawa, 45
cholera, 79
Churchill, Sir Winston, 24, 28
city, *see birni*
city state, and Hausa Emirates, 16
Clapperton, H., 57–8, 60, 206, 222
clients, *see bara*
cloth, *see* cotton cloth
coinage, 34, 54
Cole, C. W., 212
Colonial Office, and N. Nigeria
  Agriculture Department, 30–1
  parsimony of, 21–2
  policy in, 23–4
  attitude to slavery in, 200, 202
  see also Lugard, political officers
colonial officers, *see* political officers
cooking-groups, 187
corn, *see* grain
cornstalk beds, 119, 170, 178
cotton, 13, 135
cotton cloth,
  beaters of, 14
  trade and production, 12–15

courts, Muslim, 125
  and slavery, 204, 207, 211
  see also alkali
cowry shells, 34, 50, 53–4
crafts, types of
  in Dorayi, 119, 121
  in KCSZ, 70
  poor men's, 170–1
  see also dyeing, occupations, weaving
credit, granting, 172–3
  see also adashi
creditors, Dorayi, 161, 162
crops
  main, at Dorayi, 81–2
  storage, 82
  see also grain

daddawa, locust bean cakes, 54, 85,
  178–9
dagaci (pl. *dagatai*), Village Head, 5
  in Dawaki ta Kudu, 47–8
    Dorayi, 80–1, 110, 112, 156, 198:
      commission on farm-selling, 134;
      Duma, 220; Madaki, 213–14;
      succession to office, 80; wealth
      of, 112
    Kano Emirate, powerlessness of, 9;
      and re-organisation, 42–8
  see also Village administration,
    Village Head
Dalby, D., 20
Dambare, 84
dan duniya, a type of migrant, 143–5
Dan Isa, *see* Kumbotso District
dattijo, defined, 111
Dawakin Kudu District, 47–8
Dawakin Tofa District, 63, 68–9
Dendi, *dan*, a type of migrant, 143–5
development, rural N. Nigerian to 1912,
  27–34
developmental cycle, 157
dimajo (pl. *dimajai*), slave-descendant,
  206–7, 212
  see also slavery
dispersed settlement
  and creation of towns, 44
  at Dorayi, 73–5
  in Kano Emirate, xii, 4, 7
  in KCSZ, 59, 61–2, 63, 64
  and Pax Britannica, 44–5

and roads, 69
and temporal vagueness, 110
see also ḳaraḳara, Kano Close Settled
    Zone
Districts, administrative
    consolidation of, 22
    Kano, 8–9, 36–42
    reorganisation of, 35
    see also haḳimi
District Head, *see haḳimi*
District Officers, 26
    see also political officers
divorce, 84
donkeys, 67, 82–3
    charges for, 177–8
    hire of, 169
    ownership of, and wealth, 169
    transportation by, 169
    and wife-seclusion, 84
    see also caravans, *fatauci*
Dorayi, 73–86
    amenities, lack of, 85–6
    central places, lack of, 75–6
    community tax, 86
    crop, storage of, 82
    crops, main, 81–2
    'exports' and 'imports' of, 86
    farm-holdings, size of, 121–2
    gandu in, 83–4
    grain purchase at, 82
    Hamlet Heads, 81
    henna boundaries, 92–3
    livestock at, 82–3
    manure at, 78
    map of farmland, 76, 78
    medical treatment, lack, of, 79
    migration from, 146–51
    migration into, 77–9: of Fulani, 64
    Muslim seclusion in, 84–5
    personal possessions in, 86
    ploughs, lack of, 82
    population, 77–80, 88–91, 92, 95–104
    sons, position of, 138–45
    slavery in, 200–20 *passim*
    under-utilisation of labour in, 103–4
    Village and Hamlet Areas, 76
    Village Heads, 80
    wives, origin of, 80
Dudgeon, G. C., 29–30, 33
dyeing, 12–14

dye-pits, 12–13, 52

economic inequality, *see* inequality
Elgin, Lord, 24
Emirs, Fulani
    as 'native chiefs', 22
    not sovereign rulers, 40
    see also Kano, Emirs of
Emirate governments, and economic
    control, 95
Evans-Pritchard, E. E., 16

famine, 28, 31, 110
Fanteland, migration from rural, 151
farke (pl. *fatake*), long-distance traders,
    12, 14–15
farm-buying, in Dorayi,
    by city farmers, 133–5
    commission on, 134
    and high price of land, 218
    by rich men, 128
    see also farmland
farm-holdings, in Dorayi and
        Batagarawa, 121–2
    numbers of plots in, 130
    size of: and inequality, 96–7, 116–17;
        and non-farming occupations, 153–
        4; and polygyny, 157; and slave-
        descent, 217–18
    see also farms
farm-labourers
    no class of, 219
    city-farmers and, 134
    and farm-slavery, 208, 218–19
farm-mapping, in Dorayi, 93, 125–6
farm-selling
    at Dorayi, 83, 127–9: and price of
        farmland, 99; procedure, 134; and
        landlessness, 99
    and N. Nigeria Lands Committee,
        211
    pre-colonial, 211
    restrictions on, 211
farm-tools, 86
farming
    intensification of, 101–2
    irrigated: in Dorayi, 101–2, 135–6;
        in Kumbotso, 88; tax on, 51
    no migration for, 149–51
    profitability of, 154–5

farming – *cont.*
 scale of and wealth, 153–5
 technology, 101–2
farmland
 area: per head of population, 118;
  per working man, 102–3
 attitude to, in Dorayi, 124–36
 and big houses, 188
 borrowing of (*aro*), 98, 131–2
 inheritance of, 124, 125–7
 manured, 58–9
 mapping of, 136–7
 pledging of, 132
 price of, 99, 127–9: and *arziki*, 156–7,
  160–1
 purchase of, by city farmers, 133–5
 shortage of, and economic inequality,
  101
 'on trust', 132
 speculation in, 128
 women's, 13
 see also bush-farms, farms, *riko*
farms (farm-plots), Dorayi,
 division on inheritance, 98–9
 mapping of, 136–7
 size of, 83, 98–9, 129–33; and
  inheritance, 125–6
 see also bush-farms
fatauci, long-distance trading, 14–15, 67,
 71
 see also caravan trade, *farke*, long-
  distance trade
fathers, retirement of, 140–2
fatoma, landlord, 14
feudalism, 7–10
fiefs, 8
Fika, A. M., 2, 7–8, 66
Finley, M. I., 203, 208
firewood, 67, 168–9
Forde, D., 17, 63, 96, 108
Fortes, M., 16, 182, 184
Freedman, M., 138
Fulani
 clans, 7
 as conquerors, 8
 in KCSZ, 64–5
 in Kirimbo, 94
 pastoralists, 11, 64
 slavery systems, 206–7, 222
 in Zaria, 209

galla, rent, 211–12
gandu
 and farm-slavery, 204–5
 fathers and sons in, 83–4, 99, 138–43:
  and fathers' retirement, 140–2; and
  house-sections, 187
 fraternal, 125
gari (pl. *garuruwa*)
 and concept of settlement, 20
 defined, 5
 and subordinate settlements, 6
 see also settlement, towns
Gaya, 45–6, 61
gayauna (pl. *gayauni*), farm-plots for
 sons or slaves, 100, 129, 131, 214,
 215, 217
genealogies, house, in Dorayi, 109, 194–
 8
Gepp, N. M., 53
Girouard, Sir Percy, 17, 25, 28–9, 40,
 201–2
goats, *see* livestock
Goody, Esther N., 181
Goody, J. R., 8, 101
Gowers, W. F. (Sir William), 36, 46, 47,
 52, 54
grain
 Dorayi: borrowing at, 173; crops at,
  81, 82; purchase at, 82; storage at,
  82
 in KCSZ, supplies of, 67
 requirements, 117–18
 retailing of, 11–12
 tax on (*zakka*), 51–2
 yields, 118, 122–3
 see also guinea corn, house trade,
  millet
granaries, 82
grass, 170
Greenberg, J. H., 199
grinding mills, 174
groundnuts, 81, 96, 173–4
groundnut cake (*kulikuli*), 81, 85, 173–
 4, 178
groundnut oil, 81, 85, 173–4, 178
guinea corn (*dawa*), stalk (*kara*), 81
Gutkind, P. C. W., 107

hakimi (pl. *hakimai*)
 and consolidation of Districts, 22

Kano: as aristocratic outsiders, 22, 48–9; function of, 7–10
Katsina, history of, 2
Palmer on, 40–1
and pre-colonial land tenure, 35–6
see also Districts
Hamlet Areas, boundaries of, 76
see also unguwa
Hamlet Heads, in Dorayi, 81, 112
Hastings, A. C. G., 41
Hausaland
farm-slaves' rights in, 204
houses in, 181–2
land tenure in, 124, 211
market places, history of, 10–11
migration within, 65
population of, 17–19
slave population of, 203
urbanisation of, 4
hedges, in KCSZ, 58
henna, 92–3, 177
Hewby, W. P., 50, 51, 52
Hill, Polly, 11–12, 150, 178, 202, 209
honey, 170
Hopkins, A. G., 4, 13, 205, 208
Horton, R., 62–4
house trade
and big houses, 187–8
in clothing in Kano city, 15
and *fatoma* (landlords), 11, 14
and *mai gida* (landlords), 11
and slave purchase, 203
types of, 11–12, 15
women's, 173–4, 177, 178–9
household head (*mai gida*), 182–3
relationship of house-members to, 184–5
houses (*gida*, pl. *gidaje*)
big, in Dorayi, 180–99: economic security and, 101, 189; entrance huts to, 182; genealogies for, 109, 194–8; generational depth of, 191–3; growth of, 190–4; kin-structure of, 184–5; as nodes on economic landscape, 187–8; sections of, 185–7; and slave-descent, 217; stability of, 193
big, geographical distribution of: 198–9; in Kawo, 199; in Kirimbo, 94, 199; Maguzawa, 199

Dorayi: distribution on farmland, 73–5; one-man, 190–1; size of, 83, 181
Hausa, 181–2
see also dispersed settlement
Hyam, R., 28

India
and N. Nigeria, 23, 25
ploughmen from, 30, 33
indigo, 13
indirect rule, as rural non-rule, 21–49
see also Lugard
inequality
economic, in Dorayi, 106–21: and big houses, 189; and farm-slavery, 159; and size of holdings, 96–7; and slave-descent, 218; statistics relating to, 108; study of, 104; and stratification, 100–1; and upward mobility, 156–8
economic: perceptions of, 106–7; pre-colonial, 95; and slavery, 208; and stratification, 107
social, among Yoruba, 106
see also poor men, poverty, rich men, wealth
inflation, and rural communities, xii–xiii
inheritance
and *arziki*, 156
and division of farm-plots, 98–9
and economic inequality, 101
of farmland, 124, 125–7: and un-married sons, 126; by women, 133
of farm-slaves, 207–8
farm-slaves' rights of, 207
and Muslim courts, 63
and slave-descent, 217
and wealth, 152–3, 155, 160
see also arziki, wealth
irrigation, *see* farming, irrigated

jakada (pl. *jakadu*), political agents, tax collectors, etc., 2, 10, 16–17, 37, 39, 43, 46, 47
defined, 9, 48
as 'political officers', 22–3
jangali, cattle tax, 52
Johnson, Marion, 15, 53, 54

kaba, palm fronds, 16, 94, 104
Kaberry, Phyllis, M., 17
Kano, Emirs of
  policy of direct rule and, 10
  Sarki Abbas, 40, 41
  Sarki Abdullahi Bayero, 110
  Sarki Aliyu, 214
  Sarki Bello, 50
  as slave-owners in Dorayi, 78, 213,
    214–15
Kano city
  not a city state, 16
  cloth production in, 12–14
  Dorayi commuters to, 176
  Dorayi manure supplies from, 57
  Dorayi migration to, 147–9
  Dorayi traders in, 119–20
  Dorayi workers in, 85, 119–20
  dye-pits in, 12–13
  farm-buying by men from, 133–5
  Kawo workers in, 85
  market-place, 15–16
  population of, 3–4
  relationship with countryside, 1–19
  relationship with KCSZ, 65, 67, 70
  routes centering on, 59, 60
  see also birni
Kano Close Settled Zone (KCSZ), 4, 7,
    44, 55–72 *passim*
  big houses in, 199
  dispersed settlement in, 59, 61–2, 63
  Fulani in, 64–5
  Kano city and, 65, 67, 70
  inner ring of, 56, 57
  market-places in, 68–9
  migration into, 65–6
  migration out of, 66, 150
  pedological conditions in, 56
  population of, 72
  prosperity, former, of, 66
  roads, lack of, 69
  towns in, 60
  urbanisation, 61–2
  variable conditions in, 69–71
  see also dispersed settlement
Kano Emirate
  archival material, dearth of, xii
  area of, 4
  Cargill's tour of, 37
  not a city state, 16–17

  cloth production in, 12–14
  dagatai in, 6, 47
  dispersed settlement in, 4
  District Heads in 1930, 42
  District reorganisation in, 36–42
  famine in, 31
  farm ownership in, 4
  Girouard's tour of, 29
  population of, 3, 17–19
  relationship between city and country-
    side, 1–19
  roads neglected in, 32
  taxation reform in, 49–54
  towns, rank order of, 2
  Village reorganisation in, 43–8
Kano Native Administration, expenditure by, 28
Kano Province
  farm-slavery in, 221–2
  taxation, native assessment of, 26
  town-size in, 71–2
  understaffing of, 25
Kano State, population of, 19
karakara, densely populated farmland, 7
  see also dispersed settlement
karatu, Koranic learning, 94, 119–20,
    121, 196, 197, 198
  see also malams
Katagum Emirate, 9
Katsina city, 165
Katsina Emirate
  hakimai of, 7
  history of urbanisation of, 1
  settlement patterns of, 1–2
kauye (pl. *kauyuka*), village, 5, 20
Kawo Village Area, 67, 85, 199
Kazaure Emirate, 203, 206, 207
Kirimbo, 93–4, 148, 149
Kirk-Greene, A. H. M., 19, 201, 212
kola-nuts, 11, 15
Koranic study, *see karatu*, malams
Kuczynski, R. R., 18
Kumbotso District
  Assessment Report on, 201
  District Heads, 80, 87, 110
  historical notes on, 87–8
  population of, 19, 26, 91–2
  taxation in, 87–8
  see also Dorayi, Kirimbo
Kura, 60, 70

ƙwarami, 'yan, traders, 12

labour
  farm, not scarce, 134
  female, 173
  male, under-utilisation of, 85, 102–4,
    154–5, 164–76 *passim*
'labourers', commuters to Kano city
  from Dorayi, 85, 176
  from Kawo, 85
  see also farm-labourers
Lamb, P. H., 30
land, availability of, and poverty, 165
  see also farmland, farms
landlessness, in Dorayi, 174–5, 179
landlords, and long-distance trade, 11
  see also house trade
Lands Committee, Northern Nigeria,
  42, 211
land tenure
  and attitude to farmland in Dorayi,
    124
  and Land and Native Rights
    Ordinance, 211
  and Land Registry Proclamation, 36
  and land tax, 50, 53
  Lugard's misconceptions on, 35, 210
  and pre-colonial *haƙimai*, 35
  and ultimate rights in land, 8, 36
  in Zaria Emirate, 211–12
  see also farmland
Last, M., 185, 199
Lawal, Mahamman (Hamlet Head), 77,
  79, 81, 109, 128, 133, 213, 220
Leslie, S. A. S., 88, 91, 215
lineage organised societies
  and dispersed settlement, 63–4
  and poverty, 175
livestock, at Dorayi, 82–3, 102
Lloyd, P. C., 100–1, 106, 107, 111, 166,
  181
local administration, *see* Village
  administration
locust bean, 162
  cakes (*daddawa*), 85, 178–9
long-distance trade, 14–15, 67, 71
  in cotton cloth, 12, 15
  Kano, 14–15
  and landlord system, 11
  see also farƙe

Lovejoy, P. E., 15, 66
Low, V. N., 9
Lugard, F. D. (Lord), 3, 9–10, 60
  and caravan tax, 32
  character of, 21
  on District Heads, 41
  and District reorganisation, 22, 36
  on Emirs as 'native chiefs', 21
  on famine relief, 31
  and Indian craftsmen, 33
  and indirect rule, 21–49 *passim*
  on Kano Districts, 9–10
  land tenure, his misconceptions on,
    35–6, 210
  Memorandum on Taxation by, 35, 43,
    44, 52
  Memorandum on Taxation of Natives
    by, 10, 43
  on population, N. Nigerian, 18
  on slaves, fugitive, 210
  on slavery: and Muslim law, 211;
    and *Political Memoranda*, 200–2,
    203, 206, 209–11, 221–2
  his sympathy for slave-owners, 200,
    209–10
  on taxation, 43: of crafts, 52; of land,
    50; moral attitude of, 34
  on towns and hamlets, 44
  on transition from slavery to freedom,
    209–11
  on Treasury control, 21
  and Village organisation, 44–5

MacBride, D. F. H., 2, 47–8
McLoughlin, P. F. M., 208
McPhee, A., 36
madugu, caravan leader, 14, 199
magidanci, defined, 110
Maguzawa, pagan Hausa, 185, 199
mai gari (pl. *masu garuruwa*), town
  head, 5
mai gida, household head, 182
  see also household head, landlords
mai unguwa (pl. *masu unguwoyi*),
  Hamlet Head, 5
Mai Unguwa Cikin Gari (Ciranci),
  see Lawal, Mahamman
malams (Koranic scholars), 94, 153–4,
  160, 197
  see also ƙaratu

manure
  chemical, 57
  latrine, 102
  organic: from Kano city, 57, 79, 102;
    for onion beds, 135;
    transportation of, 169–70
manured farmland, 58–9
mapping, of farmland, 136–7
market-places
  alternate-day, 68
  in Batagarawa, 105
  big houses as, 187–8
  Dorayi, none near, 75–6
  Hausa, history of, 10–11
  in Kano city, 15–16
  in Kano Emirate, 10–12
  KCSZ, dearth of, in, 15, 68–9
  N. Nigerian, 33
  Rimin Gado, 82
  slave-sections of, 203
  and women's house trade, 177
  Yankatsari, 69
  see also house trade
marriage
  age at, and polygyny, 91
  expenses, 158, 172
  and sale of land, 129
  systems, *auren fita*, 84
  see also divorce, polygyny
matsakanci, defined, 110–11
Meek, C. K., 71
messengers, *see jakada*
migration
  from Batagarawa, 105, 143
  into densely populated zones, 66–7
  and dispersed settlement, 63–4
  from Dorayi, 146–51: destination of
    migrants, 148; for farming, 149–
    51; and farm-selling, 129; of slave-
    descendants, 216, 217; of sons, 99,
    142–5; and 'vanishing', 143–5
  into Dorayi in 19th century, 77–9
  from Fanteland, 151
  Hausa, 150
  within Hausaland, 65
  into KCSZ, 65–6
  from Kirimbo, 94
millet (*gero*), 81
money, *see* coinage, cowries
Morel, E. D., 15, 59

Mortimore, M. J., 55–7, 128
mosques, 76
mules, 33
murgu, and slave-ransoming, 204, 211
Muslim law
  and inheritance of farmland, 125
  and slaves' rights, 204
  and slavery, Lugard on, 211
  and women's inheritance, 133
Muslim seclusion, *see* seclusion
Myrdal, G., 168, 175–6

naming-ceremonies, Muslim, 172
Native Administrations, expenditure by,
    28
natron, 14
Nicolas, G., 199
Niger Company, 33
Nigeria, Northern, *see* Northern Nigeria
Norman, D. W., 123
Northern Nigeria
  Agriculture Department, 28
  Europeans in, 27
  Imperial-Grant-in-Aid to, 27
  improvements and developments in,
    27–34
  indirect rule, 21–49 *passim*
  population, 17–19: censuses, 60–2
  Slavery Proclamations, 200
  tax revenue, 1907–13, 25
  see also Lands Committee, Lugard

occupations, non-farming
  men's, 85: poor men, 167–71; rich
    sons, 141–2; wealth and, 118–21,
    154; and under-utilisation of
    labour, 103–4
  slaves', 204
  women's, 85, 93
Oliver, P., 20
Olofson, H., 145, 150
Omosini, O., 30
onions, irrigated cultivation of, 101–2,
    135–6
Orme, R. F. P., 48
Orr, C. W. J. (Sir Charles), 210, 222

Palmer, H. R. (Sir Richmond), 25, 36,
    40–1, 42–3, 51, 52, 214
Perham, Margery (Dame), 21, 39

pledging (*jingina*) of farmland, 132
ploughs
    none at Dorayi, 82, 102
    Dudgeon and, 30
ploughmen, Indian, 30, 33
political officers
    in Kano Province, 25-6
    in N. Nigeria, 23-7
    and slavery, 200-1
    see also District Officers
polygyny
    and age, 113-5
    and economic inequality, 100, 113-15
    and size of farm-holdings, 157
    and wealth, 158
    see also wives
poor men
    concept of 'too poor to farm', 165
    of Dorayi, 164-79: borrowing by,
        172-3; brothers of, 166; and
        co-residence of kin, 172; means of
        livelihood of, 167-71
    Hausa words for, 166
    see also poverty, wealth
population
    censuses, N. Nigerian, 60-2: and
        children, ratio of, 18; misleading-
        ness of, 60-1; and slavery, 87; and
        under-counting, 18, 90, 91
    of Dawakin Tofa District, 63
    density: in Batagarawa, 96, 104; in
        Dorayi, 77; high density zones and
        immigration, 66-7; in KCSZ, 55,
        70, 77; and poverty, 165
    of Dorayi, 77-80, 88-91: of farm-
        slaves, 201, 203; growth in
        Kumbotso and, 91-2; pressure, and
        big houses, 180-99 *passim*; pressure,
        consequences of persistent, 95-104
    of Hausaland, 17-19
    of Kano city, 3-4
    of Kano Emirate, 17-19
    of Kano State, 19
    of Kano towns, 4, 71-2
    of Kumbotso District, 87-8
    of N. Nigerian towns, 60-2
    and numbers of political officers, 26
    see also migration
Postan, M. M., 16
poverty, xi, 107

concept of 'too poor to farm', 165
    in Dorayi, 164-79: and age, 99-100,
        113-14, 164-6; and big houses, 89;
        and landlessness, 174-5; and mar-
        ried sons, 141-2; and wives, 173-4
    and land-availability, 165
    and lineage-organised societies, 175
    see also inequality, poor men, wealth
prosperity, *see* wealth
Pullan, R. A., 79
purdah, *see* seclusion, Muslim

Qur'an on slavery, 204

railway
    to Kano, 28, 41
    need for, in Kano Districts, 29
ransoming, of slaves, 204, 205, 207, 212
renting, of farmland, *see* aro
revenue survey, *see* taxation, *taki*
rich men
    of Dorayi, 152-63: as sole inheritors,
        152-3
    see also arziki, wealth
riko, defined, 132
rinji (pl. *rumada*), slave villages, 209,
    212
roads
    and bridges, lack of, 32
    and caravan tax, 32
    and dispersed settlement
Rowling, C. W., 211
Ruxton, F. H., 207

Sanneh, L. O., 204
sarauta
    masu, 166
    system, Usman on, 2
Sarina, 58
sarki, defined, 5
    see also chiefs, Emir
saurayi (pl. *samari*), young men, 91
schooling
    at Batagarawa, 105
    at Dorayi, 84
    in Kumbotso District, 88
seclusion
    Muslim wife-, 11, 84-5: and house
        trade, 178-9
    see also wives

settlement
  gari and the concept of, 20
  patterns, Dorayi, 73–6
  see also dispersed settlement, Kano
    Close Settled Zone, towns,
    urbanisation
Shea, P. J., 12–14, 66
sheep, *see* livestock
Skinner, G. W., 10
slavery
  agricultural, function of, 208
  discretion over, 200–1
  farm: in Bauchi, 222; Clapperton on,
    222; in Dorayi, 202–20; and big
    houses, 190; and clientage, 219;
    and *gandu*, 204–5; and transition
    to freedom, 209–12; profitability of,
    219
  Fulani system, 206–7
  Hausa definition of, 203
  and inequality, 159
  in Kano Province, 221–2
  Lugard's *Memoranda* on, 200–2, 203,
    206, 209–11, 221–2
  Proclamations, 21, 200
slaves
  capture of, 203
  extra-market trade, 12
  farm, 9: as agrarian capital, 208;
    female, 205; freeing of, and land
    tenure, 211–12; farm-purchase by,
    221; hours and conditions of work,
    221; inheritance of, 207–8; in
    KCSZ, 65; in Kirimbo, 94; occupa-
    tions of, 204; prices of, 208, 221;
    population of, 87, 201, 203;
    property rights of, 207; purchase of,
    203; ransom of, 202, 204; repro-
    duction of, 205; rights of, 204;
    sale of, 205–7, 222; as strangers,
    203
  fugitive, 210
  ransoming of, 204, 205, 207, 212
slave-descendants
  in Batagarawa, 218, 220
  cucanawa, 206–7
  dimajai, 206–7
  Dorayi, 216–18: and big houses, 193,
    194–6; case studies of, 160–1, 163;
    and inheritance, 153; and landless-
ness, 179; migration of, 216, 217;
    status of, 219–20; wealth of, 218
  in Kirimbo, 94
slave estates, *see rinji*
slave-owners
  Alhaji A'ala, 207
  Dorayi, 213–16: Babali dan Mai
    Kanwa, 216; descendants of, 153,
    160, 161, 163, 197–8; Halilu, 214;
    Kano Chief Blacksmith, 215; from
    Kano city, 215–16; land disposal
    by, 215–16; Madaki, 213–14; Mai
    Beza, 216, 217; numbers of slaves
    owned by, 208–9; Sarki Aliyu, 214;
    women, 198, 213
  duties towards slaves, 204
  Lugard on, 200, 209, 210
  private farmers as, 205
  and sale of slaves, 205–7
  as working farmers, 208
slave-raiding, prohibition of, 200
Smith, H. F. C. (Abdullahi), 4, 65
Smith, J., 26, 87
Smith, M. G., 11, 198, 206, 209, 211–
  12, 219
Sokoto, slavery in, 221
sons
  inheritance of farmland by, 125–7
  married, in Dorayi, 138–45: in *gandu*
    and farm-slaves, 204–5; migration
    of, 142–5; numbers, in relation to
    age and wealth, 115–16; relation-
    ship with fathers, 99, 100; and
    retirement of fathers, 140–2; and
    stratification, 100–1; wealth of,
    compared with fathers, 99, 153,
    158–9; and widowed mothers, 90
  migration from Fanteland of, 151
  unmarried, 90–1, 139
  see also saurayi
sorghum, *see* guinea corn
stateless societies, Horton on, 62–4
states, centralised, 17
  see also Emirate, Kano
status
  age, wealth, religious learning and,
    220
  of slave-descendants, 219–20
Stenning, D. J., 64, 207
storage

of crops, at Dorayi, 82, 162, 179
of henna, 92–3
Strachey, C. S., 24
stratification, economic, 100–1
and slave-descent, 218
and upward mobility, 156–8
see also inequality

Tahir, I., 60
taki, see taxation
talaka, poor man, 166
talakawa, subjects, 166
tax collector, *see jakada*
taxation, 7, 9, 10
in Dorayi, 87–8
in Kano Emirate, 37, 42, 42–7:
compound tax, 45, 52–3; of craftwork, 52; of dyepits, 52; in Gaya,
46; and *hakimai*, 10; *jangali*, 52;
kudin kasa, 50; *kudin rafi*, 51;
kudin shuka, 50–1; native assessment of, 26; reform of, 49–54; and
reform of village administration,
35, 39, 42–8; *taki*, 53; *zakka*, 51–
2
in Kumbotso, 85, 88
N. Nigerian: and caravan tax, 31–2;
and chiefs, appointment of, 35;
Lugard on moral benefit of, 34;
and Native Revenue Proclamation,
35; and population statistics, 18;
revenue, 1907–13, 25
technology, farming, 101–2
Temple, C. L., 17, 36, 51, 52, 53, 59
as Kano Resident, 39–40
on taxation in Kano Emirate, 42–3,
44–5, 50, 51, 52, 53
thatching, grass for, 170
towns
in KCSZ, 60
in Kano Emirate, 4–7, 44
in Kano Province, 71–2
N. Nigerian, population of, 60–2
see also gari
trade
extra-market, 11
in henna, 92–3
see also caravan trade, *fatauci*, house
trade, *kwarami*, long-distance trade,
market-places

trade routes
centering on Kano city, 67–8
traders
in Dorayi: limited scale of, 103; rich,
153–5, 161, 162; small-scale, 171;
wealth of, 119–20; women, 163,
173–4, 177, 178–9
extra-market, types of, 11–12
farmers as, 96
grain, in Kirimbo, 94
from Niger, 94
see also farke, long-distance trade
transportation
by head or donkey, 169: charges for,
177–8; manure, 169–70
trees
crops of, 81
at Dorayi, 79
for firewood, 169
tsoho, defined, 111

Ungogo, 48
unguwa (pl. *unguwoyi*), defined, 5
urban exploitation, xii, 159
urbanisation
in KCSZ, 61–2
in Katsina Emirate, 1–2, 4
N. Nigerian, and misleading censuses,
60–1
see also birni, gari, towns
Usman, Y. B., 1–2, 3, 5, 7, 11, 16, 64

Village administration
in Benin, 17
Kano, 39: and compound tax, 45, 52–
3; reorganisation of, 42–8; weakness of, 2–3
N. Nigerian: hierarchical structure of,
6; and taxation reform, 35; weakness of, 23
see also dagaci
Village Areas, boundaries of, 76
Village Heads
and compound tax, 53
defined, 5, 6
in Kano Emirate, 6, 47
payment of, 46
and taxation reform, 35
see also dagaci, Village administration
Village Unit, *see* Village administration

wages
  farm-labourers', 177
  in Kano city, 176
Wallace, Sir William, 32
water table, 57, 79, 84
wealth
  and acreages per head, 118
  and age, 99–100, 113–15, 157–8
  assessment of, 109
  and big houses, 189
  classification, 112–13
  and dependants, numbers of, 115–16
  dissipation on death, 95
  of fathers and sons, 99, 141–2
  and inheritance, 152–3
  and occupations, non-farming, 118–21
  and trading, 153–4
  types of, in 1900, 159
  see also arziki, inequality, inheritance, poor men, rich men
weaving, 12–14, 70, 159
wells, 86, 171
West African Frontier Force, 27
witchcraft, 144
wives, Dorayi
  and cooking-groups, 187
  food requirements of, 139
  and house-sections, 187
  house trade of, 173–4, 178–9
  household expenses, contributions to, 158

  number, in relation to wealth and age, 113–15
  origin of, 80
  of poor husbands, 173–4
  young, 139
  see also polygyny, seclusion, women
women
  Dorayi, mobility of, 146
  earnings from henna-pounding, 93
  and Fante food-farming, 151
  farm-ownership of, 133
  as farm-slaves, 205
  as house traders, 11, 173–4, 178–9
  interests of, ignored by planners, 174
  and markets, 11
  Muslim seclusion of, 11, 84–5
  occupations of, 85, 104, 173–4
  resident with married sons, 90
  rich traders, 163, 177
  as slave-owners, 198, 209
  see also wives

Yoruba
  compounds, 181
  social inequality among, 106

zakka, see taxation
zango, defined, 14
Zaria Emirate
  farm-slavery in, 206–7, 209
  land tenure in, 211–12
Zaria Province, 33
Zawal, Alhaji, 109